Beyond the Mafia

Wilbur S. Shepperson Series
in History and Humanities

ALAN BALBONI

Beyond the Mafia

Italian Americans and the

Development of Las Vegas

FOREWORD BY JEROME E. EDWARDS

University of Nevada Press   Reno   Las Vegas   London

Wilbur S. Shepperson Series in History
and Humanities No. 37
Series Editor: Jerome E. Edwards
A list of books in the series follows
the index.

University of Nevada Press
Reno, Nevada 89557 USA
Copyright © 1996 by University
of Nevada Press
Jacket design by Erin Kirk New
Manufactured in the United States
of America

The paper used in this book meets the
requirements of American
National Standard for Information
Sciences—Permanence of Paper
for Printed Library Materials, ANSI
Z39.48-1984. Binding materials were
selected for strength and durability.

Library of Congress
Cataloging-in-Publication Data
Balboni, Alan Richard
    Beyond the Mafia : Italian Americans
and the development of Las Vegas / Alan
Balboni ; foreword by Jerome E. Edwards.
    p. cm. — (Wilbur S. Shepperson series
in history and humanities ; no. 37)
    Includes bibliographical references
and index.
    ISBN 0-87417-243-8 (cloth : alk. paper)
    1. Italian Americans—Nevada—Las
Vegas—History. 2. Las Vegas (Nev.)—
History. I. Title. II. Series.
    F849.L35B34 1996   95-51534
    979.3'13500451—dc20
    CIP

05 04 03 02 01 00 99 98 97 96
5 4 3 2

This book is dedicated to the memory

of my maternal grandfather,

John Scanga

Contents

Foreword

Las Vegas is the largest city in the United States founded in the twentieth century. For a quarter century after 1905, it remained a sleepy railroad town. But beginning with the construction of Boulder Dam and continuing with the economic opportunities provided by World War II, and especially by the existence of legalized gambling, its growth was striking—rising from 5,165 people in 1930 to 127,016 in the metropolitan area in 1960, to approximately a million in 1995. At the same time Las Vegas gave a flamboyant new culture to the American scene.

Within this context, Professor Alan Balboni of the Community College of Southern Nevada narrates the story of Italian assimilation. The spectacular, late growth of Las Vegas certainly affected the nature of this assimilation. Since the high tide of Italian immigration to the United States had occurred many years before the gambling mecca's rise, immigrants did not arrive in Las Vegas directly from Italy; they had already gone through some process of assimilation. Then, too, with such instantaneous growth and the new housing splattered all over the landscape, there could not develop any Italian neighborhoods to conserve traditional values. As Balboni reminds us, Las Vegas was an exceptionally open and mobile society, and Italian Americans were important to its growth. Their assimilation was rapid.

Particularly interesting is Balboni's demonstration of the indispensable Italian contribution to the development of gambling in Nevada in the 1950s and 1960s when "The Boys" (his preferred term for the Mafia or Mob) held sway. The Mob provided much-needed construction and investment money for the capital-starved gambling industry and expertise in running its casinos.

The Jews and Italians who made up "The Boys" were able to develop the burgeoning gaming industry to the point where it eventually became a significant influence on the American scene. In turn, gambling rewarded Italian Americans in Las Vegas with quick upward mobility and hastened their assimilation into the wider American culture.

At the heart of the book are Balboni's interviews with well over 150 Italian Americans in the community conducted since 1988. Most of these individuals have had successful careers, and many were important to the history of Las Vegas. Their story is a positive one; their lives were filled with hard work, and they contributed much to their city. Balboni relates their experience with sympathy and understanding. This book therefore recounts Italian assimilation from an Italian-American point of view; it provides a window into the Las Vegas Italian community that can be obtained from no other source.

Jerome E. Edwards
Editor, Wilbur S. Shepperson Series in History and Humanities

Preface: The Interviewing Process

Soon after beginning my research in October 1988, I conferred with colleagues who had studied Las Vegas's history. Eugene Moehring and Ralph Roske of the University of Nevada, Las Vegas History Department, Roosevelt Fitzgerald of the Anthropology Department, and Candace Kant of the Community College of Southern Nevada Social Sciences Department urged me to interview senior Las Vegans who might recall some of the Italian-American pioneers. After reviewing U.S. Census records and early issues of the *Las Vegas Age*, I followed Ralph Roske's specific advice and contacted Richard Ronzone, a longtime resident and retired public official. Ronzone, in considerable pain during the interview, provided me with information about Las Vegas "old-timers" who might shed some light on the Italian-American role in Las Vegas's development. Ronzone's death in January 1989 was a reminder of the importance of proceeding with the interviews, even as I conducted more traditional research.

Many potential interviewees I sought out regarding the pre–World War II history of Las Vegas were not listed in the phone book. Contacting many of them required perseverance and occasionally creativity. It was not unusual for me to contact two or three present or former associates of a potential interviewee before I obtained a mailing address and/or a telephone number. Some were impressed by my persistence; others dismayed by it, feeling, I suspect, that I was a prying journalist. The latter refused the interview opportunity.

Initially, my interviews were rather formal. I had a list of questions and tape-recorded the responses. With experience, I took a less formal approach as I noticed that interviewees provided more information when I initially asked open-ended questions, and then followed their sometimes lengthy responses with more specific questions. Soon, after a few interviewees asked me not to record their responses, I stopped bringing the tape recorder. This was a positive development, as it allowed me to meet interviewees in restaurants. Although I conducted most interviews in homes or offices or occasionally by telephone, I found that several Italian Americans enjoyed talking at length after an Italian meal. It was a worthwhile investment, as I had no hesitation in telephoning these five men and one woman later to gain additional information.

I always asked if the interviewee could tell me how to contact others who might substantiate or perhaps even give me a different perspective on the events described. Rarely was my request refused. Nothing succeeds like success, and with each interview my credibility with potential interviewees improved. Publication of my article on Las Vegas Italian-American pioneers in the *Nevada Historical Society Quarterly* further enhanced my credibility. An article on the colorful Tony Cornero, a convicted felon, which appeared in the Sunday magazine of the *Las Vegas Review-Journal* was not as helpful, as some past and potential interviewees questioned why I wrote about a criminal. They were concerned that, my protestations to the contrary, I was planning to write yet another sensational book about the Mafia in Las Vegas.

Often, an individual whom interviewees identified as a great source of information was not. Sometimes, because his memory was poor, he did not understand the purpose of my questions, or he was suspicious of my intentions and chose not to talk with me. On the other hand, I experienced more than one worthwhile interview with an individual who began the session by saying, "I don't think I'll be able to help you." On the two occasions that spouses attended formal interviews, they were quite helpful in refreshing the memories of their partners.

Some interviewees had both excellent memories and an appreciation for my research. Most notable were Tony Allotta, Al Bossi, Phil Carlino, Angelo Cassaro, Phil Dioguardi, and Guido Testolin, all of whom are mentioned in the text, as well as Dr. Russ Anderson, now deceased, formerly a professor in the Resort and Marketing Department at the Community College of Southern Nevada, and Dr. Herman Van Betten, dean of the Henderson campus of the Community College of Southern Nevada from 1984 to 1995. I met with each at least three times and had numerous telephone conversations with each. Anderson's father, a dice manufacturer in the Midwest, came to Las Vegas in the early 1940s and opened a business, Nevada Club Room Supplies. His avocation was gambling. Van Betten was a member of the Clark County School District Trustees in the 1970s and active in Democratic Party politics while an associate professor in the English Department at the University of Nevada, Las Vegas.

I am particularly grateful to those Italian-American interviewees who worked in gaming in the 1950s and 1960s. As my interview requests of some so employed often met with the response "We don't talk to no one," I recognized that the respondents were overcoming a broadly held distrust of outsiders by consenting to be interviewed. One longtime gaming manager, a man who began his career in the Chicago area, told me during our third meeting that a couple of his contemporaries, one of whom refused my several requests for an interview, advised him that he was making a big mistake by talking to me. Some of the men who came to Las Vegas in the late 1940s or early 1950s, having become casino hosts, were reluctant to give me an outright refusal for an interview, preferring to stress again and again that they were just too busy. One, apparently exasperated by my persistence, said, "The only time I have to talk with you is at 3:00 A.M., during my break." When I responded that I would meet him at the Strip resort where he was employed at 3:00 A.M. the next morning, he paused and then replied, "OK, I don't want to talk to you."

Several Italian-American entertainers who resided in Las Vegas were most informative interviewees; some others either refused to be interviewed or professed extraordinarily poor memories. Not surprisingly, two comedians whose routines included social commentary, Peter Anthony and Pete Barbuti, were not only helpful in identifying Italian-American entertainers who performed in Las Vegas (many of whom had changed their surnames), but also insightful regarding the leading roles played by Italian Americans and Jewish Americans in the entertainment business.

Five of the eight top casino executives whom I sought to interview consented, although in some cases it took more than a dozen phone calls and several months before I could meet with them. In each case I sent in advance an article I had already written, and in one instance the executive directed his lawyer to review both my article and my unpublished manuscripts before he consented to an interview. Each answered all my questions and two offered, off the record, their views on the extent of organized crime influence in the Las Vegas casinos in the 1950s and 1960s. The one executive who explicitly refused my request explained bitterly that every time he had given an interview in the past, the reporter had distorted it to make him look like a mobster. My efforts to explain that I was a professor, not a reporter, were to no avail, even though he had read my article on Italian-American pioneers. Another executive, Al Rapuano of the Riviera Hotel, instructed his secretary to tell me he was too busy to talk with me during the three-month period when I called more than a dozen times. Then he resigned just prior to a Nevada Gaming Commission hearing to consider his suitability for a permanent license as a casino executive. He left me no forwarding address.

Thoughtful perspectives on organized crime in Las Vegas, particularly the Italian American and Jewish American role in such activities, were readily available to me. Interviews with two men who had been associated with organized crime were useful. The opinions of one, who must remain anonymous, appear in the text; the other, Willie Fopiano, recently the author of a book about his experiences, contributed almost all of his considerable ill-gotten gains to the Las Vegas economy on his visits to Las Vegas from Boston in the 1970s and 1980s. Equally illuminating was an off-the-record discussion with two law enforcement agents who had considerable experience investigating organized crime in Las Vegas. They and I agreed on some matters and disagreed on a few others. Ralph Lamb, Clark County Sheriff from 1961 through 1978, was reluctant to give me a firm no to requests for an interview, initially saying he was too busy and then directing his secretary to tell me that he could not take my calls. His predecessor, Wilbur "Butch" Leypoldt, readily answered my questions. John Smith's columns in the *Las Vegas*

Review-Journal were an excellent source of information on the activities of re-puted organized crime figures. He assisted me in contacting Willie Fopiano, shared with me his perspective on the issue of Italian-American predominance in Nevada's Black Book, and commiserated with me regarding our respective fail-ures to contact Al Rapuano.

Particularly as at least eight interviewees had died by December 1994, I have no regrets about having actively sought out interviewees so as to greatly enhance my knowledge of the Italian-American experience in Las Vegas. They shared with me both a wealth of knowledge about particular aspects of the development of Las Vegas and a variety of perspectives on issues such as the Italian-American role in the post–World War II growth of the Strip, the nature and extent of organized crime influence in Las Vegas, relations among Italian Americans and Jewish Ameri-cans in the gaming industry, and the history of Italian-American organizations in Las Vegas. They brought life to what would otherwise be an informative but nar-row study of Italian-American migration and employment patterns.

Acknowledgments

I received encouragement and assistance from many, none more than Donna Shandler Balboni, my wife. She proofed every sentence, usually several times, made numerous valuable suggestions about the integration of material, and urged me to press forward when repeated rebuffs from potential interviewees weakened my resolve. My goal of writing a book about the Italian-American role in the growth and development of Las Vegas would have remained no more than that without her substantial commitment of time and expertise.

I am indebted to University of Nevada, Las Vegas History Professor Eugene Moehring. His many criticisms of my initial writing efforts and his insightful recommendations regarding the organization of material greatly improved the quality of the finished product. In addition, I am one of many students of Las Vegas history who has benefited from Dr. Moehring's well-documented *Resort City in the Sunbelt: Las Vegas, 1930–1970.*

Many colleagues cheerfully offered assistance. Joseph Albini, Thymios Carabas, Ron Farrell, Andrea (Andy) Fontana, Candace Kant, and Jerry Simich were most helpful among the several University of Nevada, Las Vegas and Community College of Southern Nevada faculty members who made useful suggestions about either research techniques or more effective communication. The librarians at these two institutions and the Las Vegas–Clark County Library District were always helpful. Special thanks go to Susan Jarvis and her associates in Special Collections at UNLV. Dave Millman and Letty Meinhold of the Twin Lakes Museum and Historical Society patiently assisted me in my efforts to learn about Las Vegas Italian-American pioneers. Jerome Edwards, Editor of the Wilbur S. Shepperson Series in History and Humanities, and Thomas R. Radko, Director of the University of Nevada Press, often gave me much-needed encouragement during the past three years.

I appreciate the support of the Nevada Humanities Committee for both a 1991 research grant and the opportunity to be part of the 1992–94 Humanities on the Road program.

Finally, I was fortunate to have the services of Shirley Sova, an excellent typist and, more importantly, a keen student of Nevada history.

Introduction

Las Vegas has provided opportunities for economic advancement to hundreds of thousands of immigrants since its establishment in 1905. It has also provided those who have sought fame or power a chance to attain civic leadership positions. Essentially a railroad town until the Nevada legislature re-legalized gambling in 1931, Las Vegas welcomed entrepreneurs regardless of their ethnicity, religion, or previous affiliations. Italian Americans were able to move more rapidly into the upper middle class in Las Vegas than were their counterparts in the Eastern cities of the United States. They were not unique; Las Vegas gave German Americans, Irish Americans, Jewish Americans, and many others opportunities for economic advancement and community leadership.

Italian Americans were among the pioneers who built Las Vegas. Italian Americans owned Las Vegas bars and hotels when the city's only source of fame was being the major railroad stop between Los Angeles and Salt Lake City. Tony Cornero opened the first plush casino with carpets and live entertainment in 1931, immediately after the re-legalization of gambling. An Italian American, Frank Detra, owned and managed the Pair-O-Dice, the first casino on the Los Angeles Highway. Pietro Orlando Silvagni, an Italian-born contractor from Utah, built the Apache Hotel—the most modern and elegant of Las Vegas's many hotels in the 1930s and early 1940s. Another Italian American, Al Corradetti, supported Las Vegas's growth and development while serving on the Las Vegas City Commission from 1938 through 1947.

World War II brought an end to the dusty desert town of Las Vegas with its small hotels and casinos along two major streets. The growth of defense industries in California and the establishment of military bases in both California and Nevada significantly increased the number of potential gamblers. Las Vegas attracted the capital of legitimate and not-so-legitimate businessmen, too. Two investors, owners of hotel and theater chains respectively, opened hotels and casinos in the empty stretch of desert on the Los Angeles Highway, the area that would eventually become the Strip. Even more important, men with extensive experience in running large-scale illegal gambling operations in the East or in California visited Las Vegas and decided to invest in the city's future. Meyer Lansky and Benjamin "Bugsy" Siegel were only the most visible of many individuals with shady pasts who brought their capital and expertise to Las Vegas. For the most part, the newcomers were welcomed. This was the tradition in Las Vegas. Newspaper editors and local law enforcement officers made strong statements about not tolerating the Mob in Las Vegas, but during the 1940s, with rare exception, the notorious but well-heeled men from the East or California easily bought property and became licensed casino operators or found Las Vegans to act as their agents.

Italian Americans were well represented among those with shady pasts who came to Las Vegas during and immediately after World War II. The Mob, Mafia, The Boys—whatever term one uses—were a major presence in the boom years of the late 1940s through the late 1960s and remained so through the corporate era (the 1980s)—a predictable part of an economy based on cash transactions.[1] Italian Americans were overrepresented among The Boys, but so were Jewish Americans. The Mafia, originally strictly a Sicilian organization, was not an equal opportunity employer, but clearly American Mafia leaders, most notably Lucky Luciano and his successor Frank Costello (né Franco Castiglia), cooperated closely with Jewish Americans. Although Meyer Lansky was the best known of the Jewish-American mobsters who worked closely with the Mafia, he was not alone. Moe Dalitz and Phil Kastel, prominent developers of Strip hotels, had close business and social relationships with reputed Mafiosi. Anglo-Saxon, Arab, Greek, Irish, and Scandinavian Americans with shady pasts also invested in Las Vegas. Organized crime has never been the exclusive preserve of any one, or two, ethnic groups.[2]

The national media's focus on the role of Italian Americans with alleged Mob connections in gambling and other illegal activities has too often distorted the diverse and important contributions Italian Americans have made to Las Vegas's growth from a sleepy desert town to a world-renowned resort city. Italian Americans have worked in every casino as dealers, pit bosses, floormen, and shift managers. Although they made up about 6 percent of the United States population in the 1950s and 1960s, Italian Americans constituted more than 25 percent of the singers, musicians, and comedians whose names were featured on Las Vegas hotel marquees. They were headliners such as Tony Bennett, Dean Martin, and Frank Sinatra; lounge-show performers, of whom Louis Prima was the most notable; orchestra conductors and musicians. As developers and construction company owners, Italian Americans built many of the commercial and residential developments that fostered Las Vegas's rapid growth. They managed many of the notable restaurants in post–World War II Las Vegas and were well represented as entrepreneurs, small businessmen, professionals, government managers, and elected officials. Italian Americans who pursued nongaming careers generally found the media's fascination with the Mob annoying but not harmful to their businesses or professions. On the other hand, the focus on underworld connections made it more difficult for Italian Americans to gain high-profile positions in the gaming industry in the 1950s and 1960s, especially when the federal government's threats to intervene reached a peak in 1961, motivating Nevada authorities to increase their regulation of gaming. Yet by the 1980s Italian Americans occupied top positions at such Strip properties as the Desert Inn, Hilton, Riviera, and Tropicana, as well as at the Palace Station and the Showboat. More Italian Americans were appointed chief executive officers of hotels during the corporate era than during the 1950s and 1960s, when The Boys dominated Las Vegas gaming.

Italian Americans in Las Vegas today are a well-assimilated ethnic group. The assimilation process occurred more rapidly in Las Vegas than in the Eastern cities from which the great majority of Southern Nevada immigrants came during the post–World War II years. No doors were closed to the Italian-American immigrants in the West. There were so few Las Vegans of Italian descent before World War II that neither ethnic neighborhoods nor ethnic organizations developed. Houses and apartments were in short supply periodically during the 1950s and 1960s, when the largest number of Italian Americans migrated to Las Vegas, so newcomers could not choose their neighborhoods, but Italian Americans probably would not have gravitated toward ethnic enclaves had they existed. In Las Vegas they did not need the security of ghettoes. No private- or public-sector careers were closed to them and, indeed, most Italian Americans followed the example of the early Italian-American pioneers by marrying non-Italians at a time when Italian immigrants in the East were choosing Italian spouses. Italian Americans were well represented among the early entrepreneurs of Las Vegas.

The nature of the ethnic organizations formed by some Italian Americans, and the extent to which they participated in such groups—initially in the late 1950s and 1960s and then in the 1980s—reflected their rapid assimilation. First, the majority of Italian Americans never joined any of the seven organizations that were eventually established in Las Vegas. Second, the group leaders conducted all meetings in English and rarely had contact with Italian government agencies or cultural groups. Third, American holidays such as Halloween and Valentine's Day were more likely to be celebrated than were traditional Italian holidays. Furthermore, the two largest organizations formed in the 1980s were composed of men and women who had achieved financial success in law, medicine, gaming, or other businesses. Their major focus has been emphasizing the contributions of Italian Americans to Las Vegas and the nation.

Las Vegas and Italian Americans have served each other well. The city has provided unique opportunities to Italian Americans willing to invest energy and expertise. Las Vegas is a bigger and more exciting adult Disneyland because of their accomplishments.

Chapter One

The Early Years:

From Laborers to Successful Entrepreneurs

Immigrants and Their Children

Italians and their descendants have always played a major role in Nevada. Nevada's first Anglo-European settlers did not arrive until 1850, and the first Italian Americans came in the 1860s to work as miners on the Comstock Lode. With the primary goal of farm ownership, these previously landless peasants usually saved most of their meager wages to buy property. Compared with the East Coast, where the majority of Italian immigrants first settled, Nevada offered more opportunities for rapid economic advancement and social acceptance. By the end of the nineteenth century, the Italian born and their children owned substantial land in the Truckee Meadows area surrounding Reno; in Dayton, a farming community near the once mineral rich Virginia City; and in Eureka, a central Nevada town where the first wave of Italian immigrants were mostly low-income charcoal burners for the silver and lead furnaces. Eventually they settled in all sections of the state, and by the last two decades of the nineteenth century Nevada had the nation's highest proportion of foreign born among its population. In 1900 the Italian born, who represented only about .2 percent of the national population, comprised 3 percent of Nevada's population. In 1910 the Italian born constituted 3.5 percent of Nevadans and 16 percent of Nevadans born abroad.[1] By the 1920s Italian Americans were well represented among the ranchers, farmers, businessmen, bankers, and politicians of Nevada.[2] They soon became influential in other areas, including agriculture, construction, and, several decades later, tourism and finance.

Their opportunities had to be great to compensate for the difficult lives these immigrants faced. For instance, in a contentious labor dispute in 1879, a sheriff's posse near Eureka killed five Italian charcoal burners. Italian railroad workers, like members of other immigrant groups, were both the perpetrators and the victims of violence. Like their counterparts in the mines, they often suffered from various disabilities and died young owing to poor health and safety conditions. Persevering nonetheless, the great majority of Italians and their children bought land and participated in the social and political life of Nevada.

1

When compared with their relatively meager numbers, Italian Americans played an impressive role in the economic development of Southern Nevada. Early Italian settlers in Las Vegas and surrounding areas quickly adapted to the fluid social system of a new town. Some even moved into an upper-middle-class lifestyle within the first generation; their fellow immigrants in the Eastern United States often had to wait for the second or third generation to acquire that status.[3] The Las Vegas townsite established in 1905 offered great opportunities for immigrants with an innovative spirit to advance to leadership positions. Among Western towns Las Vegas was not unique in this respect. After studying Italian immigration to the Western United States, historian Andrew Rolle reported the following: "In the Far West what proved to be more important than nationality were such much more tangible matters as how well a man integrated himself into frontier life; how quickly he could put up a house or clear a field; how well he could break the sod. These qualities frequently determined acceptance. In this sense the frontier did not coerce; it emancipated."[4] Rolle and other immigration historians have asserted that too many of the earlier studies of American immigrants—Oscar Handlin's *The Uprooted* is the best example—unduly focus on the hardships of those who settled in urban ghettoes.[5]

The first Italians in the Las Vegas area, like their Greek, Mexican, and Japanese counterparts, came primarily to work on the railroad or in nearby mines.[6] Men and women of Italian background constituted just less than 1 percent of the total Clark County population in 1910, with fewer than 10 of the total of 32 Italian born living in Las Vegas.[7] The 1910 U.S. Manuscript Census reported Italian laborers living in construction cars along the railroad with laborers of Japanese and Mexican descent. One Italian family of four lived nearby in an area mostly inhabited by Mexican families. The census also mentioned Rosa C. Marchetti, age twenty-five, married for the nine years she had lived in the United States, who was a hotel housekeeper. As her marriage a year later to a prominent local businessman, John F. Miller, received front-page coverage in the September 9, 1911, issue of the *Las Vegas Age*, one must assume that she, like her new spouse, had divorced her mate earlier that year.

The tolerance of Las Vegans for the unusual facilitated Rosa Marchetti's move into the upper middle class. John F. Miller, who owned the Nevada Hotel (which was later expanded and renamed the Sal Sagev) and other properties, served as city commissioner in 1918–19, and invested in various other businesses, was mentioned often in Las Vegas newspapers for the next thirty years. No references were made to Rosa, though an elderly Italian-American interviewee who demanded anonymity confirmed both that Rosa had been a maid in the Nevada Hotel and that she and John Miller had had two children, Abe and Helen. Abe later managed the Sal Sagev and then bought the property on which the Golden Gate Hotel is presently located.

No Italians lived in Las Vegas's mainly Mormon precincts of Overton, Bunkerville, and St. Thomas in 1910, but at least six Italian males were among the miners dwelling in the Goodsprings and Potosi precincts. With one exception, they immigrated between 1901 and 1905 and were between twenty-six and thirty-eight years of age. Vincent Matteuci, his family, and eight unmarried Italian laborers lived in the Arden precinct, near the gypsum mill.[8] Vincent and at least one of his sons worked in the mill, and the family also raised fruits and vegetables, some of which they sold in Las Vegas.[9] In the Nelson and Searchlight precincts, also mining areas, there were at least two individuals of Italian background, one of whom was Victor Troici, a Searchlight barkeeper originally from New York.[10]

Newspaper reporters in the early 1900s sometimes discriminated against the Italian born. In any community tempers flare, personalities clash, and violence results, but when Italians were involved, the *Las Vegas Age*—the only newspaper in Southern Nevada until 1909—blamed such incidents on Italians' "volatile nature." Perhaps because virtually all the Italians in these early years were laborers or miners, and thus of lower socioeconomic status, they were more easily denigrated by ethnic stereotypes. In August 1905 an article appearing under the heading RACE WAR described an altercation among railroad workers:

> Three Italians and fifteen Greeks, proteges of the Salt Lake railroad, recently opened hostilities about fifteen miles south of this place. The Italians were worsted in the conflict and to wreck [sic] vengeance had three sons of Greece arrested and brought before the bar of justice. The case was tried before the justice of the peace last Friday. Judge Brennan was engaged as legal sponsor for the Greeks and Dan V. Noland appeared for the banana sellers, and it is only fair to state that between them they conducted a highly entertaining trial. Justice Ralph, not to be outdone, found both the prosecution and defense guilty of assault and battery, and fined each individual warrior the sum of $10.00. The judge evidently desires to discourage foreign hostilities on American soil.[11]

A month later another newspaper story complained that Italian, Greek, and Austrian railroad laborers living in tents near the Armour Icing Plant had created a terrible nuisance with noisy carousals each evening.[12] Even a decade later the critical attitude was evident as the *Las Vegas Age* reported: "Deputy Sheriff Joe Keats arrested an Italian at Moapa on a charge of attempted murder sworn out by the man's partner. One Italian tried to carve another, but the party assailed, although somewhat injured, got a gun, and put his assailant to the bad."[13] Even when violence came to those who had left the ranks of miners and laborers, the newspaper reinforced the stereotype that Italians are volatile. For example, in 1917 Peter Lorenzo, Tony Andrino's partner in the Miners Bar at Goodsprings, was fatally stabbed by Peter Piantoni following what the *Las Vegas Age* described as "a drinking bout in which a number of Italians were celebrating the New Year's holiday."[14]

The First Entrepreneurs

In contrast, *Las Vegas Age* correspondents accorded a good deal of respect to those Italians who achieved financial success. Foremost among the early entrepreneurs of Italian ancestry was Domenic Pecetto, who came to Las Vegas in 1905 and had the foresight to open a liquor store in a building he constructed on First Street between Clark and Lewis Streets.[15] The liquor business was generally a profitable one in Las Vegas, especially because the large number of hardworking and thirsty railroad workers who lived nearby could be counted on as steady customers. Since Mr. Pecetto built a twenty-five-room hotel six years later, one may presume that running a liquor business was a good method for amassing the capital necessary for financing other commercial undertakings.[16] The *Las Vegas Age* positively noted his investments, which included a bar and twenty rental cabins, and emphasized his contribution to Las Vegas's progress toward becoming a major commercial center.[17]

Some Italians made money in the city and later used it to finance a return to the farm. For instance, Manuel Champo, a native of Italy, immigrated to Mercur, Utah, in 1903 to work as a miner, married an Italian woman in Mercur, went back to Italy, and then returned to Mercur before moving to Las Vegas. He stayed there only briefly before moving on to Sparks to work in the railroad yard. Several months later he and his family returned to Las Vegas, and Manuel became a bartender in the Union Hotel, which was owned by Domenic and Josie Pecetto. Manuel's wife cooked for thirty or more boarders there, most of whom were railroad workers. After several years tending bar, Manuel bought a small ranch at Cow Springs, south of the present Green Valley. Like Matteuci, he raised fruits and vegetables and peddled them in Las Vegas in the early mornings. The city residents eagerly bought the grapes, melons, garlic, asparagus, peppers, and onions grown by this enterprising businessman, and Manuel was soon able to buy property in Las Vegas.[18]

A major flood in the summer of 1921 completely destroyed Manuel's fields at Cow Springs, and he never again farmed them commercially. He went on to contribute to the Las Vegas social scene by purchasing the Green Lantern Bar on North First Street, close to Block 16, the red-light district. Despite Prohibition, the Green Lantern quite likely dispensed more than fruit juice and soft drinks. In any event, Manuel Champo was successful and subsequently leased the Green Lantern to new owners who renamed it the Log Cabin. Manuel went on to gain revenue from this investment, as well as from other properties, for several decades.[19]

Joe Graglia tending bar at the Union Hotel, present site of the Union Plaza Hotel. (Courtesy Horden-Graglia Collection, Special Collections, University of Nevada, Las Vegas)

Joe Graglia was another pioneer who responded to the needs of Las Vegas residents and visitors for food, drink, and entertainment and was accorded a position of respect in the community. Certainly being Domenic Pecetto's brother-in-law facilitated his success in Las Vegas. In the 1912 Prosperity Edition of the *Las Vegas Age,* he was identified as a proprietor, along with Domenic Pecetto, of the Union Hotel and Bar. The two men were lavishly praised for their contribution to the community's advancement, especially for their operation of "a family liquor store, where a large stock of bottled goods, domestic and imported wines and liquors was kept for family trade."[20] If the praise seems to have exceeded the accomplishment, one must remember that Pop Squires, the *Las Vegas Age* editor, was the number one booster of Las Vegas in its early years.

These positive comments about Las Vegas's early entrepreneurs of Italian background contrasted markedly with the national hostility to immigrants during and after World War I, especially those from southern and eastern Europe. Persons of Italian descent were among those apprehended in raids against subversives conducted by U.S. Attorney General A. Mitchell Palmer; Nicola Sacco and Bartolomeo Vanzetti were only the most noteworthy among those who were hauled in. Italians were among the major targets of the series of immigration restrictions that Congress passed between 1917 and 1924.[21] The Ku Klux Klan, a growing organization in many parts of the country in the 1920s, included Italian Americans among those it considered unworthy of citizenship.

In contrast to other parts of the country, if a district attorney in Las Vegas accused enterprising members of the Italian-American community of violating the law, they were treated with respect by the press and also by juries. Charges against Joe Graglia for violating gambling laws were dropped in 1916, and one year later a jury exonerated Domenic Pecetto from charges of receiving stolen goods from railroad employees. Neither Graglia nor Pecetto fit the image of poor, confused immigrants unable to defend themselves in court. Indeed, Pecetto retained a Los Angeles lawyer in addition to Las Vegas attorney Thomas Ham.[22] Vincent Matteuci's first and only conflict with the law came during Prohibition, when he continued to dispense liquor at his Las Vegas saloon despite passage of the Volstead Act. During the trial Matteuci demonstrated both a knowledge of court procedure and, by forgetting his fine command of English and lapsing into Italian from time to time, a sense of humor. Sympathetic court watchers considered his trial quite entertaining. In the end the jury found Matteuci guilty, but the judge gave him a light sentence.[23]

Another major figure among the Italian Americans who contributed to Clark County's early development was D. G. Lorenzi, who operated several businesses, sometimes simultaneously, during the two decades he lived in the Las Vegas area.[24] His most lasting contribution followed his discovery of underground water just north of Las Vegas in 1914.[25] Trained as a stonemason, Lorenzi tapped underground water sources to create two artificial lakes, and under his management they became major recreation areas in the 1920s and 1930s. Native Las Vegans recall how popular Twin Lakes was before the age of air-conditioning.[26] Lorenzi's other business endeavors included a confectionery shop he opened soon after arriving in Las Vegas in 1913, a grocery store he established in 1919, a coal and wood yard he started in 1927, and a gold mine he acquired during the same year.[27] He was the first Italian-surnamed Las Vegan to seek a Clark County Commission seat, receiving 154 of the 1,333 votes cast in the 1920 election.[28]

Al Corradetti was more successful in his quest for public office. He came to Las Vegas in 1916 to work in the Troy Steam Laundry and Cleaning Works. A newspaper report described him as "an experienced man in this line of business and thoroughly acquainted with the most modern methods in use in the larger city establishments."[29] Successful in this and other business ventures, Corradetti was often praised by the press. He became a citizen of the United States in 1923, was called to jury duty the next year, entered local politics soon thereafter, and was appointed a city commissioner to fill a vacancy in 1938.[30] Thereafter Corradetti was elected to the city commission twice, serving through 1947, when he was defeated. Unlike most other successful Italian Americans, Corradetti was not directly involved with the liquor, food, or hotel businesses.

Construction of Boulder Dam, beginning in 1931, stimulated the Las Vegas

The Hotel National, built by Joe Graglia in 1923, was one of the earliest Las Vegas hotels. (Courtesy Horden-Graglia Collection, Special Collections, University of Nevada, Las Vegas)

economy and provided Italian Americans, as well as other citizens, with expanded opportunities for jobs and investments. Two changes in Nevada law in 1931 also improved the fortunes of Las Vegans. The first lowered the residency period required for a divorce from three months to six weeks; the second returned legalized gambling to Nevada.[31] Although both developments initially benefited Reno more than Las Vegas, 1931 marked a turning point in Southern Nevada history.

The legal changes and the influx of several thousand dam construction workers brought to Las Vegas new Italian-American entrepreneurs who would succeed Joe Graglia and Domenic Pecetto as leaders in the business community. Joe Graglia, initially a partner with Pecetto in the Union Hotel, had built the Hotel National on Fremont Street in 1923. His son John, a pharmacist, was Las Vegas's first Italian-American professional. When his father became ill, John sold his interest in Boulder Drug Company and took over the management of the Hotel National.[32] When his father died, the front-page obituary in the *Las Vegas Age* acknowledged Joe Graglia's involvement in several fraternal and civic organizations and described him as "a man of fine character and the highest integrity."[33] After Graglia died, Pecetto leased the Union Hotel to his wife's brother, John Vinassa, and moved to California.[34]

Depression and World War II Entrepreneurs

Most prominent among the new entrepreneurs were the Ronzone, Cornero, and Silvagni families. Rapidly declining silver prices and hopes for prosperity from the construction of Boulder Dam brought Attilio Benjamin Ronzone and his wife to Las Vegas in 1929. Leaving their general store in Tonopah, they opened a clothing store, which quickly attracted a large clientele and later became the premier department store in Southern Nevada.[35] Attilio died in 1938, but his son Richard later played a major role not only in the management of the department store, but also in the overall expansion of the Ronzones' Las Vegas business. (The store was sold to the Dayton-Hudson [Diamond's] Corporation in 1969 and then to the Dillard's Corporation.) Richard served first as president of the Las Vegas Chamber of Commerce and later in a variety of elective offices, including the Clark County School Board, the University of Nevada Board of Regents, the Nevada Assembly, and the Clark County Commission.[36]

Richard Ronzone, only partly of Italian background, recalled, as did Manuel Champo's daughter Stella, that there were very few men and women of Italian ancestry in Las Vegas prior to the late 1940s. No Italian organizations existed, and Ronzone did not recall hearing any Italian spoken. He also remembered, as did Stella Champo, that men of Italian ancestry were prominent among the early hotel and casino owners.

Whereas the Ronzones were conventional entrepreneurs, the Cornero brothers—Frank, Louis, and Tony—engendered controversy because of the way they organized and operated their businesses. Having accumulated capital and expertise as bootleggers and gamblers in California, Frank and Louis decided they could make a handsome profit by supplying liquor and prostitutes to the men working on Boulder Dam. When gambling was re-legalized in Nevada in March 1931, they decided to focus their talents in this area.[37] As Tony had just finished a prison term for smuggling liquor into California, Frank and Louis served as the front men for this operation. The Cornero brothers employed a variety of local tradesmen to construct Las Vegas's first legal hotel/casino, thereby greatly boosting the local economy. Local business and civic leaders expressed their appreciation for the new business in a special ten-page supplement of the May 3 *Las Vegas Age*. In promotional fashion, the newspaper described the casino as follows: "Potent in its charm, mysterious in its fascination, the Meadows, America's most luxurious casino, will open its doors tonight and formally embark upon a career which all liberal-minded persons in the West will watch closely."[38]

The Meadows, located near the road from Las Vegas to Boulder City, was a plush casino, a *carpet-joint*, to use the term of that time. Unlike the many small casinos on or near Fremont Street, the Meadows had no sawdust on the floors, and photographs show guests dressed in their Sunday best rather than the more

The movers and shakers of Las Vegas gather at Tony Cornero's Meadows supper club, 1931, Las Vegas's first "carpet joint." Cornero is seated far left; attorney and civic leader Artemus Ham Sr. stands at far right. (Courtesy Betty Ham Dokter Collection, Special Collections, University of Nevada, Las Vegas)

common jeans and boots. A few of the relatively rich and famous of southern California and Nevada visited the Meadows; nevertheless the Depression was not a propitious time to operate a hotel and casino far from Fremont Street. Two months after the Meadows opened, the Cornero brothers sold the twenty-five-room hotel to Alex Richmond, a southern California hotel owner and builder, but they retained the casino and ballroom.[39] In February 1932 the Corneros leased the casino (for $5,000 per year) to three associates, including Guido Marchetti, "better known to his many Las Vegas friends as 'one hand Hogan.'" Marchetti was a candidate for president of the local chapter of the Catering Industry Employees in January 1932 and was mentioned in a newspaper article a month or so later as having been involved with two partners in the operation of the Meadows since its opening.[40] Although for several years the Meadows was the center of Las Vegas social activity, it never fulfilled the promise of becoming a gambling mecca because the country was in the midst of tough economic times. Instead, it eventually became an exclusive house of prostitution.

Tony Cornero was not discouraged by this initial lack of success. In 1944 he tried to invest in Las Vegas some of his substantial profits from "high seas" gambling off the California coast.[41] Then in 1951 he returned to build the Stardust Hotel. (Cornero's later history is discussed in subsequent chapters.)

Less prominent than Richard Ronzone, Tony Cornero, or Pietro Orlando Silvagni was Frank Detra. Little information about Detra exists, although Stella Champo Iaconis recalled that Detra came to Las Vegas with his wife and son in 1931 and

The Pair-O-Dice Club. (Courtesy Horden-Graglia Collection, Special Collections, University of Nevada, Las Vegas)

rented a cabin from Stella's father. Detra worked briefly as a dealer at the Boulder Club on Fremont Street before he opened the Pair-O-Dice Club on the Los Angeles Highway. In the Friday, December 15, 1933, issue of the *Las Vegas Evening Review-Journal,* Detra ran a quarter-page advertisement announcing the grand opening of the Pair-O-Dice on the following day. The club featured Italian dinners, dancing, and entertainment. Apparently the Pair-O-Dice was successful enough to catch the attention of Guy McAfee, a Los Angeles police captain. McAfee supplemented his income by running large-scale gambling enterprises until he quit the force when a reform mayor was elected. In 1938 he bought the Pair-O-Dice and renamed it the 91 Club.[42]

The contribution of the Silvagni family to Clark County's growth was more consistent than that of the Cornero brothers but not as conventional as that of the Ronzones. Before arriving in Las Vegas in 1929, Pietro Orlando "P.O." Silvagni had been a successful contractor in Carbon County, Utah, an area with a substantial Italian population. When the Depression brought a decline in Utah construction, Silvagni came to Las Vegas to pick up some of the initial construction contracts for Boulder Dam. Quickly figuring the profits of serving the drinking, eating, and entertainment needs of the thousands of construction workers pouring into the Las Vegas area, he bought a prime piece of real estate at the corner of Second and Fremont Streets for $40,000 and borrowed heavily to build the Apache, Las Vegas's first hotel with elevators and air-conditioning (swamp coolers).[43] Left without liquid assets, Silvagni leased the hotel to a group of Los Angeles and Yuma, Arizona, investors headed by Bob and Matilda Russell.[44] The press enthusiastically greeted the grand opening of the Apache Hotel in March 1932, giving

P. O. Silvagni receiving the deed for the lot on North Second Street he purchased at auction in the spring of 1948. The lot is the site of the old fire station and jail. Interested spectators include some old-timers who attended the first auction of town lots in 1905. Left to right: Chief of Police George Thompson, Fred Pine, Charles Aplin, C. W. "Pop" Squires, Ed Von Tobel Sr., Silvagni, Walter R. Bracken, and Sheriff Glen Jones. (Courtesy Aplin Collection, Special Collections, University of Nevada, Las Vegas)

particular attention to its several shops, including a drugstore, barbershop, and ladies-wear store.[45] Soon after receiving a gaming license, Silvagni opened the Pache Club Garden in the hotel, which featured casual-style ballroom dancing. The Pache Club Garden, like the hotel casino, bars, and restaurant, attracted both Southern Nevada natives and tourists, particularly many women wishing to take advantage of Nevada's liberal residence rules for divorces.[46] Al Cahlan, a respected journalist for many decades, wrote the following description of the Apache in his February 9, 1966, *Sun* column: "The Apache was headquarters for Boulder Dam big wigs, the many subcontractors on the job, visiting dignitaries from Washington who flocked in to keep track of what was going on down in the Canyon, and Nevada political leaders. You might say without being too far wrong, that the Apache Hotel was the hub of Nevada during construction days and until Tommy Hull built the El Rancho Vegas out on what's now the Strip; was the number one hostelry in the area."

In the Italian tradition, Silvagni, a strong-willed man, always maintained solid family ties. When his daughter Lena married Roberto Testolin, an Italian Ameri-

Fremont Street, the heart of Downtown Las Vegas, in 1948. (Courtesy Manis Collection, Special Collections, University of Nevada, Las Vegas)

can from Wyoming, Silvagni brought his new son-in-law into the management of the Apache Hotel. Testolin had begun his career as a bootlegger during Prohibition and then had bought the Cinnabar and Mission bars near the present location of the Golden Nugget Hotel. Silvagni also encouraged his sister Filomena and her family to leave the depressed economy of New Jersey and relocate in Las Vegas. In 1940 Filomena Mirabelli, her husband Carmine, and several of their children arrived in Las Vegas from Newark.

The Mirabellis had previously resided in Carbon County, Utah, and once settled in Nevada they took full advantage of the opportunities for economic advancement and, eventually, civic leadership that the city offered. Carmine "Pop" Mirabelli worked as a tailor at Gates Cleaners in the center of Las Vegas, and one of his sons, Dante, was initially a custodian at the Apache Hotel and later worked in Fremont Street casinos. Two other sons—Phil, who came with the family in 1940, and Mike, who arrived in Las Vegas after World War II—later held elective office. Phil was a city commissioner in the 1960s, and Mike, who moved to Washoe County after teaching in Las Vegas, served as state treasurer from 1963 through 1978. Proud of his Italian heritage, Pop was an active member of both the Italian American Club and the Sons of Italy in the 1960s and 1970s. He lived forty years in Las Vegas, dying at the age of eighty-eight. His son Phil served as president of the Club from 1973 to 1975.[47]

The Italian-American population of Southern Nevada increased during the 1930s, but not at the same pace as the general population. The increase in the number of voters with Italian surnames between 1924 and 1936, while substantial, was not commensurate with the increase in the number of voters generally. The 1930 U.S. Census recorded 49 Italian-born citizens in Clark County, while the 1940 U.S. Census recorded 60 Italian-born citizens.[48] Italian Americans, both the Italian born and the American born, constituted less than 2 percent of the Las Vegas population of 8,422 in 1940. The Ronzones, the Corneros, and the Silvagnis were the Italian Americans who contributed most significantly to Southern Nevada's pre–World War II growth, but they were not the only ones. During the 1930s and 1940s, Italian Americans opened and operated restaurants, taverns, liquor stores, butcher shops, grocery stores, barbershops, repair shops, gas stations, and plumbing and heating companies. Others continued to work in a variety of occupations for the Union Pacific Railroad.[49]

Two California families, the Barozzis of Los Angeles and the Peccoles of Stockton, helped develop Las Vegas real estate in the 1930s. They came to Las Vegas in 1931 seeking business opportunities, and although they lacked the capital of Attilio Ronzone, the Cornero brothers, and P. O. Silvagni, they established small businesses, bought inexpensive properties, and gradually gained substantial real estate holdings. Anna and Angelo Barozzi had previously operated small businesses in several different states before coming to Las Vegas. They bought a small piece of property on the corner of North Second and Stewart Streets and opened the Roma Café, the first of many Italian restaurants. In 1934 they purchased several nearby apartments when the owner, Joe Santini, another Italian American, died without heirs in this country. Having great faith in the potential of Las Vegas, Anna and Angelo immediately reinvested the profits from the restaurant and income from their rentals in additional property, particularly in the area where many African-American Las Vegans lived in the 1930s and 1940s on the northwest side of Second and Stewart Streets (where the Casino Boulevard freeway off-ramp is currently located), as well as in the areas of the present California Hotel and the Binion's Horseshoe Casino parking garage. Their son Aldo, in addition to assisting with the management of the Barozzi family properties, became a highly regarded public servant, working for nearly thirty years in the city's Water Department in a variety of engineering positions, including acting general manager.[50]

Soon after his arrival from California's San Joaquin Valley, Pete Peccole, a friend of Angelo Barozzi, bought property and opened a bar on South First Street. He, too, invested in property, initially in the bars and brothels of Block 16, the infamous red-light district of Las Vegas. Peccole then reinvested his earnings in more substantial residential dwellings and commercial buildings, and within a decade he had become a major property holder. Peccole was not the first or the last Las Vegan to operate in this manner. Las Vegans were tolerant of those who earned their fortune by serving their fellow man's need for wine, women, and song; they did not question how Pete Peccole or others before and after him amassed the capital they invested in Las Vegas. Perhaps they recognized that if they took a more vigilant attitude, Las Vegas would be doomed to remain just another small town in the Mojave Desert.

Pete Peccole's rather rapid rise to wealth and power would probably prove a most interesting story, but Peccole family members and Italian-American seniors refused to reveal details about his business and personal life. Evidence drawn from newspapers published in the 1930s substantiates the assertion of some interviewees that Peccole used a pseudonym, Pete Pansey, when purchasing some of his Block 16 property holdings.[51]

Peccole's sons, Robert and William, carried on this tradition of financial success, the former as a casino executive and the latter first as the owner of an insurance company and later as a prominent real estate developer. In his second bid for public office, William won a seat on the Las Vegas City Commission in 1949. (Aldo Barozzi's and William Peccole's careers are covered in greater detail in subsequent chapters.)

Andrew Petitti, a friend of both the Barozzis and Pete Peccole, also found Las Vegas to be a city of economic opportunity. He left the depressed economy of Carbon County, Utah, for Clark County in 1932 and began working at several different jobs, including dealing at clubs in Las Vegas and along the road to Boulder Dam. Pete Peccole hired him to tend bar at the Exchange Club. Petitti, like so many other Italian Americans, wanted to establish his own business. He soon leased the Hofbrau Bar, located across the street from the Exchange Club, and later bought the property at a public auction in 1942 after the owner committed suicide.[52] Andrew's son Jack, who had converted to the Mormon faith while in Utah, achieved fame in Las Vegas in the late 1930s as an outstanding high-school and college football player. After World War II Jack, like Dick Ronzone, Phil Mirabelli, and William Peccole, became a successful politician.[53]

Italian Americans continued to play an impressive role in the economic and social development of Las Vegas during World War II. John Vinassa managed the Union Hotel, John Graglia operated the National Hotel, P. O. Silvagni owned Las Vegas's finest hotel and meeting place, the Apache. Anna and Angelo Barozzi and Pete Peccole were major property owners, and Al Corradetti was a senior member of the city commission, having served a term as police commissioner. In contrast to Italian-American politicians in East Coast cities, Corradetti did not represent an Italian neighborhood or district, and when he served as police commissioner no questions were raised about Mafia influence, as probably would have been the case in the East.

John DeLuca's experiences upon settling in Las Vegas during World War II reemphasize the fluidity of Las Vegas society—the willingness of economically and politically successful Las Vegans to accept newcomers, regardless of their ethnicity. DeLuca left his executive position with Acme Brewery in Los Angeles in 1941 and entered into partnership with J. T. Watters, a longtime liquor wholesaler in Las Vegas. Foreseeing Las Vegas's potential as a major entertainment center near increasingly populous southern California, DeLuca soon bought Watters's share of the business and established DeLuca Importing Company in 1944. The next year he leased a fireproof building with 4,000 square feet of floor space located on a railroad spur track to house the importing company.[54]

Subsequently, DeLuca became a partner with Pat Clark, a city commissioner and the owner of Nevada Beverage Company, the other major liquor distributor in Southern Nevada during World War II. In 1951 John DeLuca became the dominant liquor wholesaler in the burgeoning Las Vegas market when he purchased Pat Clark's share of the Nevada Beverage Company. He moved quickly to gain long-term franchise rights from such major liquor producers as Seagrams, Cutty Sark, and Hiram Walker. As the resort industry rapidly expanded following the opening of Ben "Bugsy" Siegel's Flamingo Hotel in 1947, DeLuca prospered.

Like many of his wealthy contemporaries in Las Vegas, John DeLuca became involved in several philanthropic and civic undertakings in the decade preceding his death in 1960. His contributions were most appreciated by Clark County's Jewish-American and Italian-American communities. His daughter said that B'nai B'rith granted him the Man of the Year award several times, and Las Vegas's first permanent organization promoting Italian-American social relationships was named the John DeLuca Italian-American Club.[55]

The good reputations of many Las Vegas Italian Americans did not help Tony Cornero when he returned from Los Angeles during World War II. Cornero's high-seas gambling operations and many disputes with California legal authorities, especially U.S. Attorney General Earl Warren, were well covered by Southern Nevada newspapers during the late 1930s. The city commission did not welcome Cornero's efforts to become Silvagni's not-so-silent partner in 1944 by establishing the S. S. Rex casino (named after Tony's gambling barge off the Santa Monica coast) in the Apache Hotel. At a meeting of the city commission to consider Silvagni's application for a gaming license, Mayor Ernie Cragin charged that there had been "considerable conniving going on among commissioners."[56] Perhaps to rebut the inference that money had changed hands, they voted 3–2 to deny a license to P. O. Silvagni. Al Corradetti explained his stand by saying, "I would like to see P. O. Silvagni clean house. It is our business to see that we know who is going to run this place for Silvagni. I don't want Bugsy Siegel and people of his stripe in here, and, until I know who is going to run Silvagni's place, I'll vote against the license."[57] Two weeks later Silvagni convinced Al Corradetti and two colleagues of his integrity, and he received his gaming license three days before Christmas.[58]

There was profound irony in the continuing story of the city fathers' concern about Tony Cornero. Six months after obtaining his gaming license, Silvagni was again accused of cooperating with Cornero in the operation of the S. S. Rex.[59] Threatened with losing his license, Silvagni completely severed connections with Cornero and leased the club, now known as the Rex Club, to Dr. Marty Bernstein, a Los Angeles physician, in February 1946.[60] Three months later, a quarter-page advertisement in the *Las Vegas Evening Review-Journal* announced that Moe Sedway was manager of the Rex Club.[61] Sedway was widely reputed to be Bugsy Siegel's advance man in Las Vegas. Bernstein may have been the nominal owner, but Sedway and Siegel were in control.[62] Rebuffed by Las Vegas, Tony Cornero bought a bigger ship, the S. S. *Lux,* and in partnership with Wilbur Clark (later a partner with Moe Dalitz at the Desert Inn) he continued to conduct high-seas gambling off the California coast.[63]

The city fathers were more concerned about an Italian-American gambling entrepreneur from California, Tony Cornero, than about his Jewish-American counterpart from New York, Moe Sedway, for two possible reasons. First, Las Vegans were quite familiar with Cornero's legal problems because his illegal gambling operations were only a day's drive from Las Vegas and were often the subject of local newspaper articles. Sedway and Siegel, while more notorious nationally, were not so often the focus of negative local newspaper stories.

Another explanation as to why so many Jewish Americans, despite their possible ties to organized crime, achieved prominence in the gaming industry in the years during which the major Strip hotels were built, was that they actively sought and achieved legitimacy and respectability through acts of philanthropy and participation in civic and religious affairs. They understood better than their Italian-American counterparts that money, prudently spent, could buy a positive reputation in Las Vegas. For example, immediately upon coming to town Sedway became involved in Jewish cultural affairs, serving as chairman of the United Jewish Appeal (UJA) in 1946. Even though the Jewish population of Southern Nevada was small, this was an important position, as evidenced by the attendance of Las Vegas Mayor Ernie Cragin, Judge George Marshall, Clark County Sheriff Glen Jones, and City Commissioner Pat Clark as guests at the May 5 UJA fund-raiser at the Last Frontier Hotel. Nate Mack, Sedway's business partner, was president of the Jewish Community Center at this time. Indeed, Mack, a respected Las Vegas businessman, invested in gaming properties not only with Sedway but also with several other Jewish-American gaming pioneers with alleged organized crime backgrounds—most notably Sanford Adler, Gus Greenbaum, Charley Resnick, and Art Rosen—yet Mack was never publicly criticized for his business associations.[64] In 1954 he was a cofounder of the Bank of Las Vegas (reorganized as Valley Bank in 1964), the first bank to extend credit to the gaming industry.[65]

Summary

The boom-and-bust economy of many Western states, especially Nevada, precluded the development of rigid social structures. In a new desert city in an underpopulated state the immigrants and migrants could assimilate more rapidly than in the well-established cities of the East with their many ethnic ghettoes. For people with entrepreneurial spirit the tolerant, fluid nature of Las Vegas society facilitated economic advancement and movement into positions of civic leadership. The early entrepreneurs of Italian ancestry—most notably Vincent Matteuci, Domenic Pecetto, Manuel Champo, Joe Graglia, D. G. Lorenzi, and Al Corradetti—committed their energies and modest finances in Las Vegas, an area of the Mojave Desert that at first was distinguished only by natural springs and a railroad repair yard and rest stop. These early settlers and those who followed—particularly Attilio Ronzone, the Cornero brothers, P. O. Silvagni, Angelo and Anne Barozzi, Peter Peccole, and John DeLuca—invested in a sparsely populated area the long-term potential of which was evaluated inaccurately by most of their contemporaries. They were well rewarded financially for their contribution to Las Vegas's development. Only the Cornero brothers were unable to achieve social acceptance.

Although the American West was by no means free of ethnic prejudice, its effects were not as deeply felt by Italian Americans as by people of other races and ethnicities. (The Western prejudice against Asians was quite substantial from the 1850s through World War II.) John Pollostro and Olga Silvagni Moe, two Italian Americans who grew up in Carbon County, Utah, remember Ku Klux Klan cross burnings directed primarily against Italian and Greek immigrants in the 1920s, but neither in Utah nor in Southern Nevada did the local power structure cooperate with the Klan. When Klansmen planned to attack Italian-born miners in Pioche, Nevada, the sheriff of Lincoln County (adjoining Clark County) not only warned the Italians but also invited them to retaliate. The Italians ambushed the Klansmen, humiliated them, and were not bothered again.[66] Italians and the foreign born of many nationalities in Nevada were not so affected as were their Eastern counterparts by the post–World War I Red Scare and the growing hostility to immigrants that culminated in the restrictive 1924 Immigration Act. The Nevada legislature did repeal a section of the Nevada Constitution that guaranteed equal property rights for the foreign born, but foreign-born Nevadans were not subjected to the massive roundups that befell immigrants in some Eastern states during the Red Scare.

The rapid assimilation of Las Vegas Italian Americans was facilitated by their relatively small numbers during the first half of the twentieth century. In contrast to many cities in the East, no distinctively Italian neighborhood existed in Las Vegas, and unlike other Western cities such as Reno/Sparks, San Francisco, and Los Angeles, all of which could claim more Italian Americans, there were no

Italian-language newspapers or radio programs and no Italian-American cultural or social organizations.[67] Indeed, Italian Americans were so few that children of the first settlers most often married members of other ethnic groups. Their East Coast counterparts, on the other hand, usually married other Italian Americans. While inner-city Italian neighborhoods provided a secure and familiar environment, too often they also isolated the immigrants, their children, and grandchildren from the customs and values of the larger society, reproducing in miniature the social system of a particular region of rural Italy. Italian Americans in Las Vegas avoided holding on to the ways of their motherland, and members of the second and third generations did not join cultural organizations to reaffirm Italian values.[68] They applied their energies and talents to economic and social advancement rather than to preserving remnants of the past.

Chapter Two

The Rapid Growth Years:

Italian Americans Come to Las Vegas

During the twenty years following the second and successful opening of Bugsy Siegel's Flamingo Hotel in 1947, Italian Americans provided the building blocks for Las Vegas's gambling industry, the foundation upon which the town rapidly grew into a major resort city in the Sunbelt.[1] They were well represented among the dealers, pit bosses, floormen, shift bosses, and casino managers. A rare week passed that Italian-American entertainers were not among the star performers; it was rarer still that Italian Americans were not among the lounge performers. Italian-American contractors helped to build not only the Strip and Downtown hotels, but also the homes, apartment houses, churches, and schools for the city's expanding population. While Italian-American businessmen and public officials contributed to Las Vegas's transformation from a small desert town to a modern city, they were also most certainly overrepresented among "The Boys"—influential Las Vegans with shadowy pasts.

Averaging 6 percent of the U.S. population as a whole, Italian Americans constituted a growing proportion of the Las Vegas population, their numbers increasing from 2 percent in 1940 to almost 10 percent in 1960.[2] In contrast to the earlier Las Vegas settlers, almost all of whom were originally from California, northern Nevada, or mining areas in the West, the overwhelming majority of post–World War II Italian Americans predictably came from the large urban areas east of the Mississippi River, where more than 90 percent of all Italian Americans lived at the time. Interviews with Roman Catholic priests serving Las Vegas parishes as well as Italian Americans who came to Las Vegas during the 1950s and 1960s, and a perusal of the obituaries of Italian Americans that appeared in Las Vegas newspapers, indicate that particularly significant numbers of Italian Americans came from Buffalo, Brooklyn, Pittsburgh, Steubenville and Cleveland, Ohio, Chicago, Detroit, and St. Louis. Many came from Boston, the other boroughs of New York City, Kansas City, New Orleans, Newark, Philadelphia, Providence, Rhode Island, and Newport, Kentucky. Of course, some Italian Americans from northern Nevada and California continued to move to the Las Vegas area; included among these migrants were some who had been raised in the East and who had later moved to California during or after World War II.

Because legal gaming was profitable and expanding, and employment in the industry was based on personal relationships, Las Vegas was particularly attractive for the many Italian Americans with experience in gambling.[3] Ironically, Senator Estes Kefauver contributed to the appeal of Las Vegas through his well-publicized investigations of organized crime in 1950–51, which led the public to demand enforcement of state laws prohibiting everything from numbers rackets to slot machines. This publicity attracted professional gamblers from every ethnic background to the legal gaming in Las Vegas, but it also acted as a magnet, drawing Italian Americans and Jewish Americans whose established success in illegal gambling enterprises had already made them the focus of national and local law enforcement. The testimony of two individuals in particular, Emilio Georgetti and Moe Sedway, revealed how attractive Las Vegas had become to both East Coast and West Coast gambling entrepreneurs. Both Georgetti and Sedway admitted their extensive involvement in illegal gambling and their efforts to gain at least partial ownership of Las Vegas's increasingly lucrative Downtown casinos.[4]

Several Roman Catholic parish priests discerned some basic patterns in the migration of Italian Americans from Eastern cities. Not infrequently, one family member gained employment in the gaming industry and then, upon learning of other job opportunities, informed other family members or friends from the former Italian neighborhood. Sometimes older family members who had relatives and friends in Las Vegas retired there, too.[5] No distinctively Italian neighborhoods existed. Indeed, Las Vegas growth patterns, including periodic housing shortages, precluded the development of white ethnic neighborhoods. New arrivals were often pleased just to find a house or an apartment; they could not worry about moving into an area with an ethnic makeup that mirrored the one they had left in the East or in California.

Italian Americans in the Gaming Business

Contrary to rather widely held beliefs about the extent of Italian-American ownership of Las Vegas casinos, only one major Strip property, the Stardust, was built by an Italian American, Tony Cornero. His pre–Las Vegas career was similar to those of Moe Dalitz, Jake Kozloff, Milton Prell, Jay Sarno (a Jewish American whom some Las Vegans mistakenly thought was of Italian background), and Bugsy Siegel—men associated with the establishment of the Desert Inn, the Last Frontier, the Sahara, Caesars Palace, and the Flamingo, and, in turn, with earlier illegal operations elsewhere. Tony Cornero had an indomitable spirit. Although he encountered hostility from Las Vegas city commissioners in 1944, came under attack by competitors—resulting in a gangland-style attempt on his life at his Beverly Hills home in February 1948—he fought back.

Cornero was accustomed to facing adversity. California officials, most notably U.S. Attorney General Earl Warren, had vowed twice during the 1930s to close down his lucrative gambling barges anchored off Long Beach and Santa Monica, California. Although Warren was only partly successful in this attempt, federal authorities later effectively put Cornero out of business when he tried to return to offshore gambling after World War II. Predictably, he recovered and moved to Las Vegas to build the world's biggest hotel, with a thousand rooms. Originally planning to name it the Starlight, he later settled on calling it the Stardust. He certainly did not comply with Securities and Exchange Commission regulations in raising the capital for the project. Indeed, there is good evidence that he sold more than 100 percent of the ownership shares in the Stardust. Cornero was an effective salesman, and his unorthodox business methods did not deter investors. The Stardust moved forward rapidly in part because Cornero, much to the consternation of other gambling entrepreneurs, paid double wages to skilled tradesmen.

Tony Cornero played as hard as he worked, often gambling well into the early morning at Moe Dalitz's Desert Inn. Shortly after shooting craps on the morning of July 31, 1955, he collapsed from a heart attack and died. The next day Las Vegas newspapers carried front-page stories about his life and death. *Review-Journal* reporter Bob Holdorf best captured the circumstances of his death:

Tony died the way he had lived.

He died at a gambling table.

Probably, the diminutive gambler was happy as hell when he felt the surging heat whip across his chest and blot out the world.

What other way was there for him to go?

In a bed? Never!

In a gun battle? They tried that!

In an ambush? They tried that, too!

Tony went the way any tough gambling hombre wants to get it. Fast and painless!

The pain that hit Tony Cornero Stralla lasted something less than 10 seconds and then it was all over.

He had crapped out.

The whole organization that Tony had formed while he'd been in Las Vegas was in a state of shock.

They amassed their strength in Room 109 at the Desert Inn.

Tony lay dead in Room 107.

The army of "technicians" that Tony kept amassed in 109.

They discussed quietly and then loudly who was going to take over the action at the new hotel.

Farmer Page? Jim Bradley? Louie Stralla?

All of them were discussed as being a new head of the multi-million dollar empire Tony was building when he died.

Tony, meanwhile lay in the next room, his body stiffening under the sheet they had thoughtfully placed over him.

His body lay there for better than three hours while the brains sat next door and pondered the fate of the Stardust Hotel.

Tony Cornero died at fifty-five with the Stardust about 70 percent complete. No Italian American took over his role; rather Moe Dalitz and his top associates, Morris Kleinman and Sam Tucker, together with Jake Factor oversaw the completion of a less lavish Stardust.[6]

Several other Italian Americans owned gaming properties on the Los Angeles and Boulder Highways, in the outlying areas of Clark County, and in Las Vegas's Downtown area. Sam Baker (né Panetri), the son of Sicilian immigrants, had a past no less shadowy than many other Las Vegas entrepreneurs. He came to Las Vegas in 1947 from Chicago after living in New Orleans and Albuquerque. He saw Las Vegas's potential as a gambling center, but not having the capital of men like Bugsy Siegel and Tony Cornero, Baker acquired the Big Hat, a small casino with a bar and grill, located on the old Los Angeles Highway.[7] The club was successful in spite of a temporary interruption of business after Baker shot Arthur Morgan, a former acquaintance from Albuquerque, following a long argument at the bar. Sheriff Glen Jones investigated the incident and eventually concluded that Baker had acted in self-defense.[8]

John Ligouri and his family came to Las Vegas from Des Moines, Iowa, in 1959. Well aware of the area's past growth and potential, Ligouri quickly opened a restaurant in Henderson, on the Boulder Highway (the major route to Arizona). Successful in this initial undertaking, four years later he built the Skyline Casino nearby and operated it through the 1960s. He subsequently sold the Skyline, but he still manages Ligouri's Restaurant and Casino. Unlike Sam Baker, Ligouri was able to maintain a low profile.

Willie Martello, a southern Californian with experience operating Los Angeles–area bars and clubs, recognized the potential for business opportunities in the small town of Searchlight, 40 miles south of Las Vegas.[9] A bustling gold-mining center at the turn of the century, by the time World War II began, Searchlight was only a small town. But Martello believed that servicemen stationed nearby in the Mojave Desert Army Corps and construction workers building dams along the Colorado River would welcome a place to eat, drink, gamble, and buy female companionship. He not only established El Rey Club and a small hotel in Searchlight shortly after the war; he also built an airstrip to attract gamblers from California. Although El Rey Club was destroyed by fire in 1962, Sharon Richardson,

Willie's niece, reported in a 1991 interview that Martello was not discouraged by this turn of events. With some financial assistance from Las Vegas casino owner Warren"Doc" Bayley, Martello bought the Crystal Club, located on the other side of Searchlight's main thoroughfare, and renamed it El Rey Club. Unfortunately his efforts to transform the little town of Searchlight into a resort city were doomed by the rapid growth of Las Vegas. Two years later, Martello, in declining health, sold his interest in the El Rey and returned to California.[10]

Emilio Georgetti is the most prominent among the Italian Americans who contributed to the development of Downtown gaming during the 1950s. He had left Italy for California's Bay Area when he was seventeen, and, like so many other Las Vegas gambling entrepreneurs of this era, he already had experience in managing illegal gambling enterprises when he settled in Las Vegas. Georgetti had been particularly successful in running illegal slots operations in San Mateo County, and, again like many others, he had also invested in legitimate businesses, namely, a packing plant in Oakland and a restaurant in San Francisco.[11] Frank Catania, a San Mateo County native who came to Las Vegas to operate the golf-cart concession at Moe Dalitz's Desert Inn in 1956, remembered Georgetti as "a very powerful man" in the Bay Area who owned two popular nightclubs, Rose's Dine and Dance and Biggio's, both located near Daly City.

Shortly after Georgetti and his wife became Las Vegas residents in 1948, he entered into partnership with Benny Binion, who had previously built a gambling empire in Dallas, Texas. Binion, of Anglo-Saxon heritage, apparently had no qualms about forming a partnership with the Italian-born Georgetti. Since Binion had run his illegal business in Texas without the involvement of Italian Americans, he probably would not have formed a partnership with Georgetti had he perceived that men of Italian background would be unacceptable to Las Vegas's civic and political leaders. Nevertheless, the relationship between the two as owners and operators of the Westerner was characterized by distrust and disagreement. Georgetti testified before the Kefauver Committee that Binion was extremely dissatisfied with the men Georgetti hired to run the Westerner.[12] Binion agreed with this in a 1976 interview. Their attorney, Harry Claiborne, also substantiated the tenor and history of the relationship in a 1991 interview with the author, adding that the decision as to which partner would buy out the other was made by a flip of a coin.[13]

Georgetti won the toss and remained at the Westerner, but his troubles persisted. Rumors were constantly circulating about his Mafia connections, and he was cited for contempt of Congress for his initial failure to testify before the Kefauver Committee. Although Las Vegas authorities did not initiate any effort to revoke Georgetti's gaming license (Nevada state officials did not gain substantial power to regulate gaming until 1955), Georgetti was subjected to negative publicity. Finally his pit boss, Robert Peccole, sued him for breach of contract, claiming that Georgetti had reneged on his agreement to accord Peccole a .0916 percent interest in the Westerner. Judge Frank McNamee decided in favor of Peccole. That Robert Peccole was the brother of a city commissioner and was represented by Attorney George Franklin, a former county commissioner (1948–50), may have contributed to Georgetti's decision to return to the Bay Area, where he had better knowledge of the power structure.[14]

Italo Guelfi, another enterprising Italian American from the San Francisco Bay Area, was among several other investors (mostly Italian Americans) to whom Georgetti later sold the Westerner. Guelfi's business experiences with food and liquor distribution in Oakland prepared him well for casino and hotel management in Las Vegas. In 1954, after selling his share of the Westerner, Guelfi and several other associates of Italian background bought the Golden Gate. He and his partners (most of whom he subsequently bought out by 1970) successfully managed the property, eventually employing another Californian, Syl De Gregorio, as pit boss and later general manager. Not becoming active in any business, civic, or philanthropic organizations, Guelfi, his Italian-American associates, and De Gregorio maintained a low profile.[15]

Whereas Emilio Georgetti and Italo Guelfi were the only major Italian-American owners of Downtown gaming properties in the 1950s, other Italian Americans owned small shares of various Downtown casinos. Andy Fava, who like Georgetti first came to the Bay Area from northern Italy as an adolescent, remained the best remembered of the several Italian Americans who were partial owners of the Westerner. Fava had operated a restaurant and small hotel in the Russian River area of northern California before relocating to Las Vegas. Several Italian-American interviewees, as well as District Court Judge Thomas Foley, who had worked as a lawyer in the 1950s, recalled Fava's outgoing personality and penchant for earthy malapropisms, which reflected his lack of English-language skills prior to arriving in this country. They also recalled that Fava and a partner bought the Villa Venice Restaurant after Fava sold his partial ownership in the Westerner in 1960. They renamed the establishment Anjoe's Café Continental and operated the business until 1962, when Fava returned to California.

Italian Americans were well represented as owners and managers of a specialized type of gaming property—race books, which were located in the Downtown area. Race-book owners catered to tourists and locals who enjoyed betting on horse races (and later, other sporting events) even more than playing the slot machines or shooting craps. The most prominent Italian Americans among the partial or principal owners of the Downtown race books in the 1950s were Frank Sala (Santa Anita Race Book) and Sonny Remolif (Saratoga Race Book). The noteworthy managers, perhaps *associates* is a better term, of the race books were George Ligouri and Gaspare "Jasper" Speciale. Sala came to Las Vegas from Reno, and Remolif—like Georgetti, Guelfi, and Fava—came from the San Francisco Bay Area. Ligouri and Speciale had grown up in the greater New York City area.[16] Italian Americans would later play an important role in the expansion of race and sports books during the 1980s.

George Ligouri, the owner of a Las Vegas recycling company for the past twenty years, provided some insight about the prominent role Italian Americans and Jewish Americans played in horse-race betting. Ligouri's Italian-born father, a successful bookmaker in Hoboken, New Jersey, was pleased when George followed in his footsteps. Arriving in Las Vegas in 1960, George immediately started at the Santa Anita Race Book as an assistant to Sammy Cohen, the principal owner (Frank Sala was the junior partner at the time). Ligouri recalled that Jasper Speciale conducted his operations in the Santa Anita, referring to Speciale's "concession area" at the race book. Because Speciale had come to Las Vegas with a reputation for being an associate of New York City's Gambino crime family, the Nevada Gaming Commission denied him a permanent gaming license, so he was forced to operate on the edge of the law. He was convicted of illegal sports bookmaking in 1965, 1966, and 1973. Speciale invested in legitimate businesses as well, first the Tower of Pizza and then Jasper's Manhattan Florist, but by most accounts, he continued his bookmaking activities. He prospered, buying a home in the Scotch 80's, an exclusive neighborhood only two miles west of the Strip. He served a brief federal prison sentence in the early 1980s for failing to cooperate with organized crime investigations, and in 1989 the Nevada Gaming Commission accepted the recommendation of the Gaming Control Board and put Speciale in the Black Book, the list of ten to fifteen individuals who are not allowed under any circumstances to enter a Nevada casino. Ligouri, in contrast, avoided brushes with the law during the almost ten years that he worked for Cohen. He recalled that Italian Americans and Jewish Americans dominated both legal and illegal sports betting enterprises throughout most of the country. Before entering the recycling business, Ligouri worked as a "right-hand man" for Shecky Greene, a Jewish comedian of national renown.

Like many other interviewees, Ligouri mentioned that neither Jewish nor Italian cultural values were in conflict with gambling; neither Judaism nor Roman Catholicism regard moderate gambling as a serious sin. For many of the millions of Eastern European Jews and Italians who, fleeing persecution and abject poverty, had come to America's cities between 1880 and 1924 (when the federal government passed the restrictive Immigration Act), gambling was a pleasant and profitable way to escape the tedium of urban ghettoes. For some, especially young males, managing bookmaking operations or even illegal casinos provided an opportunity for financial and social mobility. Since during the first half of the twentieth century Anglo-Saxon–dominated banks, brokerage houses, and insurance companies seldom recruited employees from among the Italian and East European Jewish populations concentrated in East Coast cities, illicit gambling enterprises were particularly attractive to aspiring businessmen with energy and organizational skills.

After Tony Cornero's death, the Canino brothers, Frank Schivo, and Vic Silvestri became the most prominent Italian-American owners and operators of gambling establishments on the Strip.[17] From 1956 through the mid-1960s, Joe and Tony Canino served as manager and assistant manager, respectively, of the Silver Slipper, a small Strip casino, formerly located between the Stardust and Frontier hotels, with dimensions more appropriate to a Downtown club. They brought a great deal of experience to the Silver Slipper. Ted Canino, a younger brother from Las Vegas, said that their Italian-born father, Antonio, had been a successful Denver gambler who had eventually owned and operated Canino's Corner, a casino where the Denver elite, business leaders, as well as city officials came to play. Tony Calabro, president of Western Nevada Community College from 1982 through 1995 and formerly a Denver resident, recalled that his father used to speak highly of Antonio Canino and his casino.

Joe Canino worked for Tony Cornero and Wilbur Clark on offshore gambling barges; later he joined Wilbur Clark at the Desert Inn as a shift boss. Both Joe and Tony Canino had great faith in Tony Cornero's genius and invested heavily in the Stardust. As Cornero did not maintain formal written records and sold 1 percent interest in the property to many more than one hundred investors, the Caninos, along with others, lost virtually their entire investment when Cornero died.

Like Georgetti and Guelfi, the Caninos were rumored to have Mafia connections. They weathered the familiar charge, but they lost their club when Gaming Control Board agents discovered five shaved dice and padlocked the Silver Slipper on April 23, 1964—the first time the board had ever taken such action. The Canino brothers and the principal owners, Frank King and Robert Schulze, pleaded ignorance, but the Gaming Commission revoked their licenses five weeks later.[18] Ted Canino continued to work in gaming, but the Canino brothers never again owned any gaming properties.

Frank Schivo and Vincent Silvestri had more long-term success than did the Canino brothers. Schivo had been manager of the Club Bingo, which opened in 1947. Silvestri had developed his expertise in gambling management in western Pennsylvania, his birthplace. They accepted an offer from Milton Prell, a Jewish American who had run a very profitable gambling club in Butte, Montana, during World War II, to invest in the Sahara Hotel, which opened in October 1952. Schivo and Silvestri worked at the Sahara's casino through the 1960s as day-shift boss and slots manager, respectively.[19] They were recognized as effective managers who helped establish the Sahara as a major Strip resort.[20]

Tony Cornero was the only Italian American with a major public role in the construction of any of the ten internationally known Strip hotels—the Aladdin (originally the Tally-ho), Caesars Palace, the Desert Inn, the Dunes, the Riviera, the Sahara, the Sands, the Stardust, and the Tropicana—that were built between 1947 and 1967. Most of the hotel builders were Jewish Americans. Jay Sarno and Nate Jacobson were associated with Caesars Palace; Moe Dalitz, Morris Kleinman, and Sam Tucker with the Desert Inn (and, along with Jake Factor, with the Stardust after Cornero's death); Sidney Wyman, Al Gottesman, and Jake Gottlieb with the early years of the Dunes; Gus Greenbaum, Moe Sedway, and Charlie Resnick with managing the Flamingo after Bugsy Siegal's death; Ben Goffstein, Willie Alderman, and Davie Berman with the building and running of the Riviera; Milton Prell with the establishment of the Sahara and then with the transformation of the Tally-ho into the Aladdin; Hyman Abrams, Carl Cohen, and Jack Entratter with the ownership and operation of the Sands; and Ben Jaffe, Phil Kastel, and J. Kell Houssels (the latter of Anglo-Saxon background) with the construction and operation of the Tropicana. Of course, a few Italian Americans in addition to Frank Schivo and Frank Silvestri, most notably Frank Sinatra and Dean Martin at the Sands, held minor ownership shares in casinos (or "points," to use the term of the 1950s and 1960s).

The relative paucity of Italian-American investors is surprising for two reasons. First, Italian Americans were coming to Las Vegas in great numbers, primarily to work in gaming. Second, Italian Americans were widely reputed to control most major illegal gambling in the East and in California.

One explanation for the apparent dearth of Italian American investors was that official records provided little information about the real owners of the Strip hotels (or for that matter, the smaller Downtown hotels). Sam Giancana, Johnny Rosselli, Jack and Louis Dragna, and Marshall Caifano, though not officially registered owners of any Las Vegas properties, were treated like major investors by the staff and management during their frequent visits to Las Vegas. This is hardly a radical thesis. Virtually everyone who has written about Las Vegas in its formative period (1947–67) has argued that such additional kingpins as Joe Adonis, Vincent Alo, and Frank Costello (né Franco Castiglia), as well as Jewish Americans Meyer Lansky and Doc Stacher, owned very substantial pieces of major Las Vegas hotels and casinos.

A typical example of an "unofficial owner" was Raymond Patriarca, from Providence, Rhode Island, who was widely reported to be the head of Mafia activities in New England. Patriarca was never officially listed as an investor in any Las Vegas gaming property. Yet several Italian Americans interviewed for this book believed that Joe Sullivan, a Rhode Island restaurateur and one of the major investors in the Dunes (which opened in 1955), acted as a front man for Raymond Patriarca.[21] Obfuscating ownership was a relatively common practice during the 1950s.

Another explanation for the apparent dearth of Italian-American investors was that the public's association of Italian names with organized crime—as well as the fact that a few Italian Americans were organized crime figures—virtually prevented Italian Americans from taking official leadership in gaming properties. A third explanation is that men of Italian ancestry may have been more inclined than their Jewish-American counterparts to operate from behind the scenes. Jimmy Fratianno, a Mob hit man and later a government informer, thought the latter assertion best explained the phenomenon. Ed Becker, coauthor with Charles Rappleye of *All American Mafioso* and an internationally recognized expert on organized crime, attributed the reluctance of Italian Americans to take high-profile positions in the gaming industry to the traditional Italian, particularly southern Italian, distrust of government and every entity beyond the extended family.

Others, including attorneys and gaming managers of Italian background, took the position that the stereotyping of Italian Americans discouraged them from seeking leadership positions in gambling enterprises. One of the most convincing arguments came from a seventy-seven-year-old gentleman who contacted me in the summer of 1990. He had visited Las Vegas regularly for more than four decades to, in his words, "represent various business interests." He strongly believed that Italian Americans with gaming management experience understood well that philanthropy and civic involvement brought legitimacy, but that they faced more scrutiny by both politicians and law enforcement officials than did Jewish Americans or members of any other ethnic group. He asserted that as the myth grew during the 1950s and 1960s and all organized crime was coordinated by Mafia leaders, it became increasingly difficult for Italian Americans with illegal pasts to buy legitimacy in Las Vegas. He and several others suggested that organized crime leaders, very definitely including Italian Americans, recognizing that individuals with Italian names invited scrutiny, often used Jewish Americans as front men. Certainly, the fact remained that Marshall Caifano, Sam Giancana, and Johnny Rosselli were treated deferentially by such Jewish-American owners as Maurice Friedman (the Frontier), Moe Dalitz and Morris Kleinman (the Desert Inn), and Bernie Rothkopf (MGM).[22] Most Italian Americans associated with the gaming industry in its formative years believe all the explanations have validity.

Although Italian Americans were not the chief executive officers of any major Strip or Downtown hotels or casinos in the 1950s and 1960s, they were very well represented at every other level in the gaming industry. The lure of Las Vegas was irresistible for thousands of young men of Italian background, most of whom had experience in gambling or entertainment. Phil Dioguardi, for example, is now an executive casino host at the Stardust Hotel. The circumstances surrounding his coming to Las Vegas and his experiences in the 1950s and 1960s were rather typical of those of most Italian Americans who pursued careers in gaming. The son of Sicilian immigrants, he grew up in an Italian neighborhood of Chicago. As an adolescent he worked as a dealer in one of the many gambling establishments in Cicero, a suburb of Chicago where Al Capone and later his Jewish-American associate Jake "Greasy Thumb" Guzik exercised great influence. When Dioguardi returned to Chicago after serving in World War II, he recalled that "the heat was on."

He sought opportunities in the West, first in Palm Springs, California, and then in Las Vegas in 1949. Initially, he was skeptical about settling in a place that he, and many others who arrived in the late 1940s and early 1950s, regarded as a hick town. Acquaintances who had come to Las Vegas earlier, mostly Italian Americans and Jewish Americans from Chicago, advised him that Las Vegas had the potential to become an international center of gaming. In Palm Springs Dioguardi had become friends with Carl Cohen, who achieved brief national fame many years later when, as an executive at the Sands Hotel, he slugged a particularly obnoxious Frank Sinatra. Cohen, who many Italian Americans remembered spoke a nearly perfect Sicilian dialect, helped Dioguardi get a job as a dealer at El Rancho Vegas on the Strip.

Within a few weeks Dioguardi developed a more positive attitude about Las Vegas. The tips (*tokes* is the term used in Nevada) were good ($40 to $50 per shift), and since he had recently divorced his first wife, he enjoyed the opportunity to meet and sometimes date the beautiful women from southern California who frequented El Rancho Vegas. Dioguardi was not alone in recalling the joys of bachelorhood; many of the men the author spoke with enjoyed reminiscing about the availability of so many lovely ladies. Dioguardi formed a close friendship with Pete Brady (né Genchi), who, like Carl Cohen, had learned gambling management in Cleveland. He and Brady enjoyed gambling, good Italian food, and the company of attractive women. This friendship, too, was rather typical, as most Italian-American men kept company with other Italian Americans, though not exclusively.

Dioguardi worked at many different casinos during his first nine years in Las Vegas, a time of frequent staff turnover. Gaming expanded rapidly during this period, and experienced dealers and managers were always in demand. In addition, casino employees, from dealers to top managers, had no job security because there were no unions for the men and women who worked in the casinos as there were for the hotel and kitchen workers. It was not unusual for casino workers to be fired without advance notice. Until very recently, most dealers accepted this situation without public complaint.

Dioguardi was fired from El Rancho Vegas because Beldon Katleman, the owner, did not appreciate the attention one of his girlfriends showed Dioguardi. Dioguardi then dealt at Eldorado Casino for almost a year, moving to the Sahara Hotel when it opened in 1952. He dealt 21 and roulette there until, disappointed that he could not gain a promotion, he moved to the New Frontier Hotel to work as a pit boss. He stayed at the New Frontier until bankruptcy forced it to close temporarily in 1958.

Such temporary closings were not unusual during the boom period of the 1950s and 1960s. Even the Dunes Hotel, located at the busy intersection of Las Vegas Boulevard and Flamingo Road, had to close its casino in 1956, one year after it opened. The Royal Nevada, a Strip casino adjacent to the New Frontier Hotel, was another property that went bankrupt in the mid-1950s. Dioguardi lost the money he had invested there. Properties failed for a variety of reasons, including expansion during recessionary times, poor marketing, mismanagement, and grand-scale employee theft. Phil Dioguardi recalled that all of these factors contributed to the demise of the New Frontier and the Royal Nevada.

In finding yet another job, Dioguardi, rather typically, was assisted by the network of Jewish Americans and Italian Americans who held so many of the casino management positions. While it would be an overstatement to characterize the social and business relationships among Italian Americans, and often Jewish Americans, as a surrogate employment agency, the ethnic networking that took place in the gaming business was much like what went on in churches and unions in other cities. First, the Canino brothers hired Dioguardi to deal at the Silver Slipper. Then, he was hired by Syl Petricciani, the Stardust's casino manager, when it opened in July 1958. Petricciani, a highly regarded manager who had learned gaming in his family's casino in Reno, had been hired by Moe Dalitz on the recommendation of Carl Cohen, a former Cleveland gambling associate. Dioguardi was soon working as a floorman, and he has continued to serve in casino management positions for more than three decades.

Dioguardi's first two decades in Las Vegas provided him with an excellent overview of the gaming industry, particularly the relationships between Italian Americans and Jewish Americans. In a 1991 interview he emphatically stated that Italian-American gaming expertise was a vital ingredient in Las Vegas's emergence as an internationally renowned center of legal gambling. While acknowledging that Italian Americans were not as visible in ownership or chief executive officer positions as were Jewish Americans, he asserted that Italian Americans provided a good deal of the capital for both Strip and Downtown gaming establishments. Like many others, he attributed the relative absence of Italian Americans at the highest levels in the gaming industry to their reluctance to undergo scrutiny from gaming regulators.

Dioguardi also emphasized that Italian Americans and Jewish Americans generally cooperated at all levels in the gaming industry. He and other interviewees suggested several factors that account for this cooperation. First, rarely did a member of either group consider gambling to be immoral. Second, both Jewish Americans, particularly those of East European background, and Italian Americans, particularly those of southern Italian ancestry, had faced discrimination. Most opportunities for climbing the traditional corporate ladder were closed to them through the 1950s. Finally, men of both backgrounds had cooperated in business, often of an illegal nature, in Eastern and West Coast cities.

A review of the careers of Pete Bommarito, Pete Brady, and Jerry Filipelli provides further evidence of the significant role Italian Americans played in Las Vegas gaming during the 1950s and 1960s. Their careers also serve to further highlight the social and business relationships that Italian Americans developed among themselves and also with Jewish Americans. Bommarito was, like Dioguardi, a second-generation Italian American whose parents had been born in Sicily. He and other members of his family had been involved in the management of gambling enterprises in Michigan and Ohio. Coming to Las Vegas with his second wife, Joan, in 1949, Bommarito worked at Moe Dalitz's Desert Inn as a supervisor at the craps tables. Joan recalled that Pete and Moe Dalitz had been friends for many years. In 1951 Pete left Las Vegas to take a casino management position at the Golden Hotel in Reno. Joan observed that when the people in power asked an employee to accept a new assignment, he did so knowing that if he performed well he would be rewarded. After less than two years in Reno, Pete returned to Las Vegas, and for the next sixteen years he worked as a floorman, a pit boss, and a shift boss at the Sands, the Dunes, and the Silver Slipper (where he had a modest financial interest), and, finally, when Howard Hughes bought the Silver Slipper in 1968, Pete moved on to the Riviera. Bommarito was more widely known than Dioguardi outside of gaming circles. He was the second president of the Italian American Club of Southern Nevada (discussed in Chapter 4) and was acquainted with local elected officials as well as with Frank Sinatra and Dean Martin.

Both Joan Bommarito and Al Bossi, the first president of the Club and an astute observer of local affairs, felt strongly that the cloud of Mafia association prevented Pete Bommarito from achieving greater success in the gaming industry. Neither denied that some members of Pete's family were involved in organized crime and that Pete had managed gambling operations in states where such activities were illegal. They stressed, quite correctly, that everyone else who came to Nevada to build or manage casinos had the same background. Yet at the same time they believed that Italian Americans were more suspect because of the widespread public belief, also shared by the Nevada gaming regulators, that the Mafia was an especially powerful and nefarious force in vice.

Even Italian-American casino supervisors enjoyed great mobility in an industry where shifting job conditions and personal loyalties shaped careers. Pete Brady's career was somewhat similar to Pete Bommarito's. He, too, had managed illegal gambling enterprises in the East before coming to Las Vegas after World War II. A Cleveland native, he had known Moe Dalitz, so it is not surprising that when the Desert Inn opened, Brady left his job as manager of a small Downtown casino and began working as a floorman in the Desert Inn's 21 and roulette areas. In 1954 Dalitz and his associates, along with local casino owners William Moore and

J. Kell Houssels, built the Desert Showboat Motor Inn on Boulder Highway, several miles east of the Strip. When the Showboat opened, Brady took a job there as shift boss. The Showboat experienced several difficult years, so Brady returned to his position at the Desert Inn. Soon he took a similar position at the Cal Neva Lodge at Lake Tahoe. Phil Dioguardi and Joan Bommarito, who married Pete Brady after Bommarito's death, recalled that Brady later worked at the Hacienda, finishing his gaming career as a floorman at the Stardust.

Although Jerry Filipelli was a generation younger than Dioguardi, Bommarito, or Brady, his background and experiences were broadly similar. Like them he is of southern Italian ancestry. His family, too, was substantially involved in gambling enterprises in the East—in his case in Utica, New York. He recalled that while he was still an adolescent in the 1950s, his family and friends would discuss crackdowns on illegal gambling in New York and moving to Las Vegas for its legalized gaming and tremendous growth potential. Coming to Las Vegas in 1962 at the age of twenty-one with significant gaming experience, he dealt at Eldorado in Henderson, an industrial suburb of Las Vegas. In less than two years, he was promoted to shift manager. By the early 1990s he was casino manager at the Fremont Hotel. Experience in eastern gambling establishments served him, as it had many others, quite well.

Frank Modica and Frank Fertitta are two of the most successful Italian American gambling executives who started as dealers and worked their way up through the ranks. More than once, each left relatively secure positions in order to advance his career. Frank Modica, the recently retired chief executive officer of the Showboat, now a profitable hotel/casino on the Boulder Highway, had come to Las Vegas with his parents from Jamestown, New York, in 1947. He began his atypical career in rather standard fashion as a dealer at the Eldorado Club in the Downtown area. He then moved to the Showboat as a 21 dealer and later worked as a supervisor at the craps tables. Promoted to assistant to the president in 1967, he then served in executive positions first at the Landmark and later at the Desert Inn in the early 1970s, before eventually returning to the Showboat. Modica's career was atypical because he rose quickly to a chief executive position; however, his moves from gaming property to gaming property were quite typical.

Frank Fertitta's career illustrates the ease with which ambitious men could move from one casino game to another, from one major position to another, and from one hotel to another. Few, if any, businesses provided as much opportunity for rapid upward mobility as did Las Vegas gaming. At the suggestion of his uncle, a floorman at the Stardust, Fertitta came to Las Vegas in 1960 from Galveston, Texas, at the age of twenty-one, with his wife and first child. Frank worked at the Stardust as a 21 dealer through 1963, when he moved to the Tropicana to work in the same capacity. He recalled that the tokes were much better at the Tropicana because the players were wealthier. In 1966 he was promoted to floorman, and eventually to shift manager, before moving to the recently opened Circus Circus as baccarat manager. When Bill Bennett bought Circus Circus in 1974, Fertitta took a similar position at the Sahara.

Fertitta recalled that it was at this point in his career that he began to consider seriously owning a gaming property. He pursued this goal as a partner of Carl Thomas during the period that he was general manager of the Fremont (1976–77), a major Downtown property. They and another partner negotiated the first of several loans from Valley Bank and opened the Bingo Palace about half a mile west of the Strip in the latter part of 1977. Fertitta affirmed in a 1990 interview that he could not have been so successful without the strong support of Valley Bank executives. This bank, founded by Nate Mack and Mormon banker Parry Thomas, was the first lending institution to make loans to gaming properties, and it also facilitated loans from the Central States pension fund of the Teamsters Union to Las Vegas resorts during the late 1950s and 1960s. Without the infusion of Teamsters' capital, Las Vegas would have grown more slowly. When Carl Thomas was recorded in a wiretap explaining to Nick Civella and other Kansas City Mob bosses how to skim at Strip casinos, Fertitta bought Thomas's and the other partner's shares. He then oversaw the development of this property, now called the Palace Station.

Union Officials

Many Italian Americans held managerial positions in the casinos, but only two held managerial positions in the Las Vegas labor unions that represented private-sector employees. This should not be surprising considering that Italian Americans, when not employed in management roles, gravitated toward nonunion casino positions. They were well represented among the ranks of both dealers and proprietors of shops located in the hotels; in contrast, their representation among construction trade workers or service providers in hotels was much lower. Mike Pisanello, who came with his family to Las Vegas from Pennsylvania in 1955, was one of two Italian Americans to attain a labor union leadership position during the 1950s and 1960s. After working as a waiter in the Dunes showroom, in 1959 he became a business agent for the largest labor organization in Southern Nevada, the Culinary Union. Subsequently he was promoted to assistant to the president, and much later, in 1978, he was elected vice president.[23]

Mark Massagli, the other post–World War II private-sector union leader of Italian ancestry, was born in New Jersey and raised in southern California. A bass player, he joined a small band that played at the Golden Nugget in 1957. He and the other band members decided that Las Vegas was "their kind of town." Massagli, then a bachelor, recalled that he found everything—the sounds, sights, lights, and especially the many attractive women—to be fascinating. While continuing to play at Strip and Downtown lounges, he also became active in the musicians' union and was elected to its executive board in 1966. With his election to the post of secretary-treasurer in 1968 he stopped playing professionally. Ten years later he was elected president and served through July 1991, when he left for New York City to become president of the American Federation of Musicians.

Entertainers and Maitre d's

Italian Americans from Eastern cities or who had recently arrived from Italy were well represented among the more widely known gourmet room and showroom captains and maitre d's. Nick Kelly (né Fiore), Bruno Mandini, Mario Marino, Johnny Morelli, Ray Pistelli, Pietro Museto, Emilio Muscelli, Arturo Trapletti, and Marty Antonucci were among the most prominent. Nick Kelly was certainly the best remembered. Before coming to Las Vegas to serve as maitre d' at the Sands in the 1960s, Nick had worked at the Copacabana in New York City, where he had become acquainted with Jack Entratter and other Jewish Americans who later became major investors in the Sands. A bachelor, he devoted virtually all of his leisure time to developing the Italian American Club. Whether in an official leadership position or not, Mike was the guiding force of the Italian-American organization whose membership in the 1960s was dominated by resort industry employees.[24]

Among the Italian-American performers who were drawn to Las Vegas, Frank Sinatra and Dean Martin were only the most prominent. There were many others, ranging from headliners to afternoon lounge singers, but Italian Americans were also well represented among both the onstage performers and the club employees who planned and carried off the numerous stage extravaganzas on the Strip. Many particularly noteworthy musicians were of Italian heritage. Singer Lorraine Hunt (née Perri) asserted that no ethnic group was better represented among the performers of the 1950s and 1960s than Italian Americans.

It was a rare week that Tony Bennett, Vic Damone, Dean Martin, or Frank Sinatra was not featured on a Strip marquee. It was equally rare that a single performer or a group of Italian Americans was not onstage on the Strip—whether it was a comedy group like the Characters, comprising four Italian Americans from South Philadelphia and Blackie Hunt, or the Mary Kay Trio, another group of Italian Americans. Often Lorraine Hunt and other Strip entertainers, mostly Italian Americans, would visit Jasper Speciale's Tower of Pizza after their performances. Lorraine, like other entertainers and gaming employees, affirmed that Italian Americans often socialized with one another, though never to the exclusion of others.

Lorraine Hunt began her fifteen-year singing career with Jerry Colonna at the Riviera in 1957, worked with Roland DiIorio, a prominent member of Louie Prima's band, as well as Peter Anthony (né Laurino) and Pete Barbuti, two longtime Las Vegas comedians who began their entertainment careers as musicians. Her career was novel. Virtually all the other Italian-American entertainers had launched their careers in the East, yet Lorraine had come to Las Vegas with her parents from the Niagara Falls area in 1943. She resided for several years in the closest thing to an Italian neighborhood—four or five Italian-American families lived in homes built by Tony Toleno near the intersection of Sahara Boulevard and Beverly Street. In traditional fashion, several of them raised and exchanged vegetables with their neighbors, along with a few Italian expressions. "I certainly did not suffer because of my Italian heritage. There were so many entertainers of Italian background," Lorraine Hunt reflected in an October 1990 interview at her Bootlegger Ristorante.

Roland DiIorio's career was more typical of Italian-American entertainers. Rollie D, as he was more commonly known, grew up in Providence, Rhode Island, and moved to Trenton, New Jersey, after World War II. He played bass in the Chuck Leonard (né Angelline) Quartet, which won an Arthur Godfrey talent show competition in the early 1950s and as a result got a booking at the New Frontier. Successful engagements at other Las Vegas, Lake Tahoe, and Reno hotels followed. Subsequently DiIorio received an offer to join Louie Prima's band. Unsure about leaving the quartet (two of the other three members were Italian Americans), he sought advice. Sam Butera, another Italian American who has figured prominently in Las Vegas entertainment for almost forty years, urged his friend to accept. Roland DiIorio spent the next twenty-three years with Louie Prima, Keely Smith, and Sam Butera. DiIorio agreed that it was quite comfortable to be of Italian background in Las Vegas, especially because so many of the performers and entertainment directors were Italian Americans.

Joe Delaney, *Las Vegas Sun* entertainment columnist for several decades, credited Louie Prima and Freddie Bell, another Italian-American band leader, with creating a renaissance of Strip lounge shows in the mid-1950s, and recalled that particularly during the late 1950s and early 1960s lounge acts had very great appeal, attracting large crowds to the casinos where they played. Delaney also lauded Frank and Ted Asunto's Dukes of Dixieland for popularizing Dixieland music in Las Vegas.

DiIorio recalled quite a number of Italian-American entertainers. Tony Bennett, Vic Damone, Sergio Franchi, Al Martino, and, of course, Frank Sinatra were the most prominent headliners. He also mentioned Frankie Avalon, Fabian, and Bobby Rydell as among the better known of the many entertainers who grew up in South Philadelphia, an almost exclusively Italian section. Most notable among the female vocalists of Italian ancestry who often performed in Las Vegas were Joni

Lauri Perry (Lorraine Perri Hunt) entertains at the Landmark Hotel in 1969.
(Courtesy Lorraine Perri Hunt)

James (née Joan Cannello Bobbo) and Kaye Ballard. DiIorio's memory of Italian-American singing and comedy groups in Strip lounges included the Gaylords, Sonny King's Trio, the Vagabonds, the Goofers, the Novelites, and the Happy Jesters. Las Vegas held a great lure for young Italian Americans, many of whom would begin their careers in small clubs in the East and graduate to a more national audience on the Strip and Downtown. DiIorio estimated that 25 to 30 percent of the entertainers, musicians, and house conductors in the 1950s and 1960s were of Italian background. Five house conductors of note were Ted Fiorito (Ted Fio Rito was his stage name) at the El Rancho, Antonio Morelli at the Sands, Louis Basil at the Sahara, Dick Palumbi at the Riviera, Al Johns at the Fremont, and Ray Sinatra at the Tropicana. Joe Delaney recalled that Antonio Morelli was a classical conductor who did not adapt well to Frank Sinatra's impromptu approach to music. Eventually the entertainment director at the Sands decided that Morelli would initially conduct the orchestra, but then someone whose approach to music was more like Sinatra's would take over when Sinatra performed.

Frank Gagliardi, director of both the jazz studies program and the nationally renowned jazz ensemble at the University of Nevada, Las Vegas, came to Las Vegas in 1964 to play the drums in Morelli's orchestra. He termed his twelve-year tenure at the Sands a dream job. The premier Strip hotel at that time, the Sands drew one star after another through the early 1970s. Gagliardi estimated that about 30 percent of the Strip headliners were Italian Americans. In addition to the entertainers already mentioned, he remembered several others. Jerry Vale, a Las Vegas resident who had grown up in South Philadelphia, played in the late 1960s and 1970s at the Frontier to packed houses composed overwhelmingly of Italian Americans from across the country. Gagliardi, who was then playing in an orchestra that would fill in for hotel orchestras on their nights off, said that Jerry Vale pleased the crowd by singing, speaking, and joking in Italian. Like Roland DiIorio and Joe Delaney, Gagliardi identified Vido Musso and Gus Bivona as exceptional musicians. Musso, a tenor sax player in Stan Kenton's band, and Bivona, a clarinetist who traveled the world with his own band, were among the many Italian American entertainers who moved to Las Vegas in the 1960s. Until the end of the 1970s both Musso and Bivona often performed at Strip and Downtown hotels as soloists or as part of an ensemble.

The list of major Italian-American entertainers, men and women who helped to draw millions of visitors to Las Vegas during the 1950s and 1960s, seems endless. Pete Barbuti, after reviewing DiIorio's list of Italian-American entertainers (most of whom had modified their family names), also mentioned Bobby Darin, a South Philadelphia native, and Johnny Desmond as Las Vegas headliners in the 1950s and 1960s. Connie Stevens's name often appeared on hotel marquees during the same decades, and Gia Maione sang with Louie Prima's band. Pat Cooper (né Pasquale Caputo), Jimmy Durante, and Pat Henry played in almost all the major showrooms; Pat Henry often opened shows for Frank Sinatra. Pete Barbuti reserved his greatest praise for Guy Marks, another South Philadelphian. Marks was an impressionist and a comedian's comedian. He was well admired for his willingness to innovate. Barbuti was particularly impressed by Marks's impersonations of various crustaceans, which he admitted were often too avant-garde for Las Vegas audiences. Joe Delaney enthusiastically agreed with Barbuti's assessment. He said that Shecky Greene, who headlined in Las Vegas for many years, would literally fall off his seat, convulsed with laughter, during many of Guy Marks's impromptu routines. Marks had a major influence on the routines of the younger comedians.

Delaney also emphasized that Italian Americans were well represented among entertainment directors. This, in turn, undoubtedly promoted the booking of new Italian-American talent in Las Vegas. Hank Saricola and Bill DeAngelis served as entertainment directors at the Sands and the Bonanza Club (located where Bally's now stands), respectively. Frank Sennes had the longest tenure and was arguably the most creative of all the entertainment directors. A friend of Moe Dalitz, Sennes left his position as manager of a Hollywood nightclub to become entertainment director at the Desert Inn. He returned to Hollywood in 1953 to open the Moulin Rouge, which during the 1950s became the largest nightclub and showroom in the United States, seating 1,150 patrons. When Moe Dalitz, Jake Factor, and other Las Vegans with shadowy pasts took over the Stardust following Tony Cornero's death, Dalitz called Sennes back to Las Vegas. In 1958 as entertainment director at the Stardust, Sennes developed the Lido de Paris, the longest running of Las Vegas's many stage spectaculars. Sennes was not bound by tradition; he was always willing to try novel acts. Among his firsts were shows featuring bare-bosomed showgirls, ice shows, Latin and Asian reviews, and the first revolving stage. He also served as entertainment director at the Frontier and the Holiday Inn.

Delaney believed that Frank's brother, Rocky Sennes, who produced many Las Vegas stage spectaculars, would be willing to share additional information about Italian Americans who had been prominent in developing the lavish stage shows for which Las Vegas is famous. Unfortunately, after two months of indecision and delay, Rocky Sennes, then entertainment director at Harrah's Las Vegas (formerly the Holiday Inn), refused an interview. It is the author's belief that Rocky's refusal was at least partly influenced by the fact that his older brother Frank had admitted in a court deposition (*Maheu* v. *Hughes*) to loaning Johnny Rosselli, the Chicago Mob's alleged representative in the entertainment industry, $150,000 to defray his legal expenses in 1970.[25]

Rocky Sennes was one of about a dozen Italian Americans who refused to be interviewed. The others were casino executives who, like Sennes, had begun their Las Vegas careers when The Boys were in town. A few asked me to leave them in peace, emphasizing their advanced years; others asserted that because the media were anti-Italian, they had decided never to grant interviews; many were haunted by the fear that past associations would lead to investigations by gaming regulators. These men, all in responsible positions, had never been able to relax and enjoy their success. They knew that merely a suggestion of an unsavory past could be grounds for inclusion in the Black Book. Whereas Las Vegans were generally willing to forgive past indiscretions, image-conscious Nevada gaming regulators were often not so generous. Since the Mafia was perceived nationally as the most pervasive, the most evil of criminal enterprises, men of Italian ancestry often feared that if they revealed past business and personal associations, even those long past, such information might be the basis for legal action being taken against them.

Peter Anthony's career was typical of that of many musicians. Tired of short engagements in cities where everything except the Greyhound Bus terminal's cafeteria closed after midnight, he decided to pursue his career in Las Vegas, The Place for Live Entertainment, arriving in Las Vegas from New Jersey in 1962. Mark Massagli, not yet an official of the musicians' union, initially helped Anthony, a trumpet player, find employment. He played in a group at the Bourbon Street Lounge in the Downtown area and then went to the Castaways, one of the smaller casinos on the Strip. By 1964 Anthony was first trumpet at the Sahara in a band led by Louis Basil, but soon thereafter he decided to become a comedian. With no regrets, he recalled that it was tough to get started. Indeed, before he finally started to succeed in his career in the early 1970s, he had to earn money several times by going back to playing trumpet at the Bourbon Street Lounge. Like Lorraine Perri Hunt, Roland DiIorio, and Pete Barbuti, Peter Anthony recalled that Italian Americans were overrepresented in all aspects of Las Vegas entertainment, a fact substantiated by a review of the entertainment sections of local newspapers.

Italian-American entertainers came to Las Vegas in the 1950s and 1960s for some of the same reasons that Italian-American gamblers did. Italians accepted gambling as a normal activity, but they regarded music and entertainment as one of life's necessities. Second-generation Italian Americans received strong family encouragement to develop their musical and creative talents. Frank Gagliardi's father, barely literate, knew all the characters and stories of Italian opera. He was very pleased when one of his sons became an accordion player and another, Frank, joined the Denver symphony orchestra as a percussionist shortly after high-school graduation. Parents had good reasons for encouraging such careers. Being a musician, singer, or comedian brought Italian Americans not only prestige but also more financial success than their fathers had known working in blue-collar occupations, and there were opportunities for travel and possibly national recognition.

Young Italian Americans with musical talent also had many successful role models in both Italy and the United States. As successful Italian-American gamblers sought out Las Vegas, the heart of the action, Italian-American entertainers wanted to perform in the city widely billed as the Entertainment Capital of the World. When they arrived, they were well received. Many Italian Americans held important positions in the hotels, and others, some perhaps from the same home-towns or even the same neighborhoods (common for South Philadelphians), were already performing in Las Vegas. Every Italian-American entertainer interviewed for this book agreed that being an Italian American probably helped one's career, that is, unless one was seeking a casino license. Several acknowledged that, in contrast, African-American entertainers faced significant disadvantages. Not un-til the mid-1960s did the hotels hire African Americans in other than the most menial positions. Black men and women were not admitted to the showrooms, and prominent black entertainers had to stay at the Moulin Rouge, a hotel lo-cated in the Westside, the city's black ghetto.

Italian Americans also entertained Las Vegans on local radio and television. Gus Giuffre was the best known of the three Italian Americans who had Las Vegas radio or television shows during the twenty years following the opening of the Flamingo. Refusing to assume an entertainment name out of respect for his Sicilian immigrant parents, Giuffre began his career as a disc jockey, worked as a newsman, and spent many years as the host of afternoon or graveyard movies. With his well-modulated, sincere voice, he became quite popular among Las Vegans. Listeners had faith in Giuffre; if he endorsed a product it had to be good. His independent spirit also appealed to Las Vegans. If he felt that an old movie was particularly terrible, he stopped it, apologized, and started a new film. Occa-sionally he repeated movie scenes that he enjoyed. Giuffre's popularity with Las Vegans was reflected in the success of a Giuffre Appreciation Day in 1969, which was designed to raise funds to pay his and his wife's medical bills.

Izzy Marion had less impact on Las Vegas than Gus Giuffre did, but he, like Giuffre, had an independent spirit, and at least some viewers appreciated him. Marion, whose Las Vegas careers have included beauty-salon owner, singer, ex-ecutive casino host, and restaurateur, had a television show on KSHO (Channel 13) with his first wife, Sandi, from 1962 through 1966. They would discuss enter-tainment and community affairs between replays of what Marion called the great fights of the century. Marion, a Runyonesque, controversial character, has been described in numerous newspaper articles during the past twenty years as a re-puted Mob associate. His education and diction may have been limited, but his self-confidence was not. One college-educated Italian American who came to Las Vegas in 1965 recounted that he was shocked to tune in the television and hear Marion mangling the English language. He then called KSHO to complain, only to be told that since Marion paid for the time, as TV host he could do what he wanted. Las Vegans tended to tolerate, indeed to enjoy, behavior that probably would have dismayed listeners or viewers in more socially conservative cities. (Izzy Marion's role in Italian-American matters is discussed later, in Chapter 4.)

Restaurateurs and Food and Beverage Managers

Scores of Italian Americans owned or managed Strip and Downtown restaurants, many of which were among the finest eating establishments in Las Vegas. Italian Americans with experience in the restaurant business began coming to Las Vegas soon after the opening of the Flamingo in 1947. By the mid-1950s, 30 to 40 percent of Las Vegas's dining establishments, located both in the casino centers and the suburbs, were owned by Americans of Italian background. Throughout the latter part of that decade and into the 1960s, more than half of the most renowned restaurants were owned or managed by Italian Americans.[26] None was more prestigious than Louigi's, located on the Strip between the Desert Inn and the Sands. The restaurant was started in 1951 by two partners. Louis Coniglio, the Italian-American partner, had come to Las Vegas from Los Angeles in 1946.[27] "Louigi's was the flagship Italian restaurant." "Everyone—politicians, entertainers—went there." These are typical of the comments the author heard about Louigi's from men who worked in Las Vegas in the 1950s and 1960s.[28] Frank Sala, part owner of a race book and later a real estate business, recalled that patrons at Louigi's would be four- or five-deep at the bar, waiting for an opportunity to dine.

Some Italian restaurants had the added charm of being reputed hangouts for organized crime figures. The Villa Venice, located near Louigi's and owned and operated by former Chicagoan Sam Baker and his wife, was another one of the better restaurants in the 1950s and early 1960s. Probably more than coincidentally, there was a Villa Venice restaurant in Northbrook, Illinois, just northwest of Chicago, and Sam Giancana and his associates often met there in the late 1950s and early 1960s. The Las Vegas Villa Venice was particularly popular with Strip casino and hotel workers. Some Las Vegans recalled that Italian Americans reputedly involved with organized crime dined there on visits to Las Vegas.

By the early 1960s Joe Pignatello's Villa d'Este, located just east of the Strip, was both a contender for "best Italian restaurant in Las Vegas" and a reputed meeting place for Mafiosi, according to many Italian Americans the author spoke with. During the 1970s and 1980s the alleged Chicago mob enforcer Tony Spilotro dined there often. Several interviewees recalled that Joe Pignatello, also a Chicago native, was Chicago Mob boss Sam Giancana's favorite chef in Las Vegas during the 1950s and 1960s. Some recalled that Cioppino's, located several miles east of the Strip, offered not only fine food but also the excitement of dining in a Mafia-owned establishment. Peter Zavatarro, who often dined there on his many business trips to Las Vegas for EG&G Energy Measurements in the early 1970s, recalled seeing patrons who fit the Mafioso stereotype. Waiters would present bills to customers and then lower them commensurate with the amount of protest that followed. Zavatarro and his associates, like many other Las Vegas visitors, found that sort of atmosphere quite attractive.[29]

Frank Musso's Italian Restaurant and Tony Mazzucca's Antonio's were well-regarded Strip restaurants. Tony Mazzucca had come to Las Vegas from the East Coast in 1947 to enjoy the dry climate. He worked as a chef at El Rancho, a Western-style hotel and casino built in 1941 on what is now the Strip, and later for Frank Musso before opening his first restaurant, La Vista, and, later, Antonio's in the mid-1960s. Mazzucca remained the owner of Antonio's for almost twenty years and later contributed much of his leisure time to establishing the Italian American Club as a setting for fine Italian dining.

In a 1990 interview, Frank Musso explained that he closed the Italian Restaurant to pursue business interests in southern California, but some Italian Americans suggested that financial irregularities at his establishment led to his quick departure. Musso was never charged with any crime, and he returned to Las Vegas in the mid-1980s to work at the Golden Steer, a popular steakhouse located only a block west of the Sahara Hotel and frequented by tourists.

Italian Americans also established popular restaurants in Downtown Las Vegas. Tom Vannozzi recalled that after working many years for the Ronzoni Spaghetti Company in New Jersey, his Sicilian-born grandfather, Anthony Messina, opened an Italian grocery store in Los Angeles and then in the late 1950s moved to Las Vegas, where he opened an Italian restaurant, Tony's, on Fremont Street. "Their pasta was renowned throughout the valley," Vannozzi said. "They were kings of pasta. It was wonderful stuff. Casino managers and businessmen frequented my grandfather's place."

Two sisters from the Niagara Falls area also greatly contributed to satisfying the appetites of both locals and tourists for fine Italian food. Maria Perri, Angie Ruvo, and their husbands, Albert and Louis, opened the Venetian Pizzeria near the Downtown area in the mid-1950s. The pizzeria quickly became recognized for its pizza and spaghetti, and the Perris and the Ruvos soon added other Italian specialties to the menu. After almost ten years of success, they built the Venetian Restaurant about one mile west of the Strip. Lorraine Hunt, Maria and Albert's daughter, recalled that her parents and the Ruvos retired around 1971, selling their popular restaurant to several Italian Americans who had recently come from Chicago. The Ruvos had hoped to travel and enjoy a leisurely existence, but temptations to return to the restaurant business proved too strong. In the mid-1970s Angie and Louis bought back the Venetian and soon reestablished its reputation for providing fine Italian food.[30]

In beverage and food distribution four Italian Americans were prominent: John DeLuca, Frank Longo, Mike Maini, and Tony Messina. John DeLuca has already been mentioned. His company, Nevada Beverage, dominated liquor distribution in the Las Vegas area throughout the 1950s. Although DeLuca Wine and Liquor, Ltd., exists to this day, John DeLuca's children sold their interest in the company several years after his death.

Frank Longo was the operating manager of New York Meats. He had lived in New York before moving to Las Vegas and was widely reputed to be an associate of Italian-American and Jewish-American East Coast crime figures. The meat company, owned by Irving Devine—a dark-complexioned Jewish American known to all as "Nigger," a well-known gambler and reputed Mob associate—enjoyed a near monopoly on the distribution of meats to the major Las Vegas hotels in the 1950s and 1960s. Las Vegans generally accepted individuals with shadowy pasts, and rumors of Longo's and Devine's past associations interfered with neither their gaining business licenses nor their becoming members of the prestigious Las Vegas Country Club in the late 1960s.

Less controversial during this period were Mike Maini and Tony Messina (not to be confused with the restaurant owner). Whereas Longo had resided in New York prior to relocating to Las Vegas; Maini, born in Providence, Rhode Island, had grown up and pursued his early business career in Los Angeles before moving to Las Vegas and becoming a produce distributor.[31] He led the Las Vegas Junior Chamber of Commerce and the Food Service Executive Association and was also a member of the board of directors of the Club in the mid-1960s.

Arriving in Las Vegas from Chicago after World War II, Messina opened a market a couple of blocks south of Fremont Street in 1948 in partnership with long-time Las Vegas resident Mike Hixenbaugh. Mike's Market flourished in the 1950s, but competition from supermarkets in the next decade left Messina and Hixenbaugh with a declining clientele of mostly senior citizens. Tony Messina married a woman of German and Dutch background and didn't participate in any Italian-American organizations. Messina's son Anthony recalled that Hixenbaugh and his father had closed the business by 1970.

Waste Disposal and Construction

Aside from the gaming, entertainment, and restaurant fields, Italian Americans also pursued other lucrative business ventures in Las Vegas. A lot of Italian Americans settling in East and West Coast cities gravitated toward waste disposal and construction businesses. Success more often came to those who were both hardworking and knowledgeable about local politics than to those who had formal education. Not surprisingly, Italian Americans with experience in waste disposal and construction were well represented among the several thousand Italian Americans who migrated to Las Vegas after the opening of the Flamingo in 1947. In fact, two families related by marriage, whose ancestors had lived in the same region of northern Italy and who also had the same surname, have provided garbage-disposal services to greater Las Vegas for more than thirty-five years.

Before coming to Las Vegas, Al Isola and his brother-in-law John "Red" Isola had operated a major garbage-disposal business in Oakland, California. When Al visited Las Vegas in 1954, he saw the potential of this small but growing desert city and persuaded John to join him in buying 45 percent of Max Chason's waste-disposal business; Chason remained a partner until illness forced him to retire in 1965. Their company, Silver State Disposal, or one of its subsidiaries, has held contracts for waste disposal with Las Vegas and Clark County from the mid-1950s through the present; in 1965 the company gained Henderson's contract. The Isolas never experienced any serious competition, in part because they and other top managers of Silver State, most of whom were of Italian background, were committed to containing costs by using the latest waste-disposal technologies.

Of course, the Isolas' substantial involvement in civic affairs contributed to the success of their business. Al Isola's son Tom, the company's chief operating officer in recent years, mentioned in a 1990 interview that he had been serving on so many boards of directors that he had too little time to manage the growing company effectively. He has reduced his involvement in such activities, but he and other Isola family members have continued to maintain good relations with Las Vegas and Clark County business and political leaders. They and their wives were also active in the establishment and development of the Italian American Club.[32]

Serious charges of dishonesty or even mismanagement have never been leveled at the Isolas, but their Italian ancestry and the nature of their business has occasionally led to vague rumors of organized crime connections. When Ed Reid, a Las Vegas reporter, and Ovid Demaris were doing research for their book *The Green Felt Jungle*, Reid contacted Oakland residents who knew the Isola families to determine whether there were organized crime links. Reid later told Al Isola at a social event, much to the embarrassment of Al's wife, that Al should feel pleased that no such links had been uncovered.[33]

Not surprisingly, a number of young Italian Americans with experience in construction moved to Las Vegas in the years after World War II, hoping to take part in the building boom that accompanied the rapid expansion of gaming. Several prospered and developed construction companies that were significant to Southern Nevada's growth for several decades; others succeeded moderately and found a niche in some aspect of commercial or residential construction; and, of course, a few failed. Italian Americans were well represented among both general contractors and tradesmen specializing in masonry, painting, and plumbing.[34]

The careers of two early contractors, Bernard Provenzano and Mike Terlizzi, illustrate the opportunities that Las Vegas presented at different stages of its growth. Provenzano established a plumbing business in Las Vegas during World War II. He was moderately successful and became active in civic affairs, but a series of what Provenzano's attorney described as "commercial legal difficulties" culminated in his being convicted in federal court. He spent several months at a mini-

mum security facility.[35] After serving his time, the strong-willed Provenzano returned to Las Vegas, re-entered the construction business, and eventually built
many homes, including a major development of half-acre estates on Vegas Drive,
west of the Strip. His election as president of the Italian American Club in the
early 1970s was one more example of Las Vegans'—in this case Italian Americans'—willingness to forgive successful citizens for past transgressions.[36]

Mike Terlizzi grew up in New York City and in Italy and came to Las Vegas from
southern California in the late 1940s. He recalled being impressed by the opportunities in Las Vegas. In 1953 he built a successful commercial development, the
Mike Terlizzi Shopping Center, at the intersection of West Charleston Boulevard
and Hinson Street. After spending a number of years back in fast-growing southern California to take advantage of better opportunities, he returned to Las Vegas
construction in the mid-1960s and began building primarily apartments and
motels.

Dominic Bianchi and Tony Marnell did masonry work on most of the major Las
Vegas construction projects not only in the 1950s and 1960s, but also through the
1970s. Bianchi, born in Italy and raised in Indiana, and Marnell, born in Pennsylvania of Italian parents, both came to Las Vegas from southern California. They
worked first on the final phases of the Sands Hotel construction and then spent
several years working primarily for Pardee Construction, the area's major home
builder in the early 1950s. In 1956 they formed a masonry contracting partnership of their own, which lasted for two decades, expanding with Las Vegas. Thanks
to the opportunities available in a growing city, they acted as subcontractors in
home construction, business developments, hotel construction on the Strip, and
casino renovations in the Downtown area. The success of their firm's work drew
the attention of city and county officials who contracted with the pair in the late
1950s and 1960s to do much of the original masonry work for the convention
center.[37]

Dominic Bianchi felt that one of the Marnell and Bianchi Masonry Contractors'
most significant achievements was getting paid in full for its extensive masonry
work in 1966 at the Landmark Hotel, located across from the convention center
and a block east of the Strip. (Until it finally closed in 1991, the Landmark was
often in debt, so quite a few creditors were pleased to get even partial payment.)
Frank Carroll (né Carrachiola), who built the Landmark, did not enjoy the good
reputation of most other Italian-American contractors. Indeed, one interviewee
who had served as an executive at the Landmark asserted, "Carroll cut so many
corners in the construction that it is a wonder that tower did not collapse years
ago." Carroll never operated the Landmark because allegations of his having associations with criminals led the state to deny him a gaming license.

As subcontractors, Bianchi and Marnell worked closely with other major Italian-
American builders such as Frank and Louis Miranti, Ray Paglia, and Gus Rapone.

Having previously worked in southern California, the Miranti brothers, executive officers of the company American Homes, built several large single-family home developments in the Las Vegas area during the late 1950s and early 1960s. Ray Paglia came to Las Vegas from Cleveland in 1960 and began building homes. He then expanded to large-scale apartment construction, and finally in the late 1970s he played a major role in the construction of the Continental, about a mile east of the Strip. The U.S. Army Air Force sent Gus Rapone to the Las Vegas Gunnery School during World War II. Following the war he decided to launch his career in Las Vegas. By the early 1960s he had become a principal officer of Sierra Construction, a company that specialized in federal government projects in the 1950s and later successfully competed for gaming property construction.[38]

J. A. Tiberti, the premier Italian-American general contractor in Southern Nevada, employed Marnell and Bianchi for extensive subcontracting. Like Rapone, Tiberti had come to Las Vegas during World War II, when he served as a surveyor for the Army Corps of Engineers and was assigned to work at the Gunnery School. After the war the Colorado native decided to stay on in Las Vegas. Tiberti was one of many military personnel once stationed near Las Vegas, who, upon finishing their army service, decided to stay on and help build the city. Tiberti and two associates formed Waale, Camplan and Tiberti Construction. Among other accomplishments, they built homes in the Bonanza Village area near Downtown.[39] In 1950 Tiberti and his Italian-American wife established their own company, which over the next twenty years undertook many successful projects, including the following: Boulder Dam renovation, Downtown hotel remodeling, Strip hotel construction and remodeling; construction of the First Interstate Bank Building, two Roman Catholic churches, and numerous public buildings including schools and fire stations. In addition, the Tibertis won many contracts from the federal government for construction or renovation projects at the Nevada Test Site and the Indian Springs and Nellis Air Force bases. In short, during the postwar years they built everything but homes.[40]

John DeBiase, a successful painting contractor for more than four decades, was, like Tony Marnell, born in an Italian neighborhood in the East and raised in southern California. Arriving in Las Vegas in 1940, DeBiase got a job as a painter at Basic Magnesium, where he worked until he was drafted. Impressed by the potential of Las Vegas, he returned after military service and started his own business in 1949. He recalled, "They were putting a one-hundred-room addition on the Flamingo, and we did it." DeBiase gained the contract to paint the Riviera, Las Vegas's first high-rise, and later, the Tropicana. "I liked working for gaming people. Their word was good. They were honorable men," recounted DeBiase. Not limited to working on the Strip, he painted the expansions for several Downtown hotels and casinos. He expanded his business, offering dry wall installation, plastering, and fireproofing, and explored the use of new materials to reduce external building cracks caused by Las Vegas's sunny, dry climate. Once while visiting Germany, he discovered a material he later successfully used on the Barbary Coast, a smaller Strip gaming property. Unlike Gus Rapone and J. A. Tiberti, DeBiase did not actively seek many federal government contracts. "Too many hassles, too much paperwork," he recounted when asked about his relative lack of such contracts. Instead he confined his work to the expanding private sector.

Italian-American contractors clearly played a significant role in Las Vegas's development during the twenty years between the opening of the Flamingo in 1947 and Howard Hughes's purchase of the Desert Inn in 1966. And Las Vegas, a boomtown in the Mojave Desert, gave contractors opportunities for success, if not beyond their imaginations, then at least greater than they could expect in the East or in California.

Banking, Real Estate, and Insurance

Italian Americans were not as well represented in banking as in construction, yet several Italian-American bankers contributed greatly to the area's development. Harry Manente, who grew up in Reno, managed the main Las Vegas office of the First National Bank of Nevada (FNBN). During the 1950s he was known as "Mr. Banking of Southern Nevada," and to this day he is warmly remembered as a generous man whose word was his bond. Manente's superiors in Reno were skeptical about Las Vegas's long-term growth, believing throughout the 1950s that Southern Nevada's boom would soon end. Struggling against this narrow viewpoint, Manente advanced credit to many Las Vegans beginning or expanding their businesses.[41] Of course, no credit could be advanced to entrepreneurs in the gaming business, because Manente and his superiors in Reno regarded such investments as too risky. Italian-American bankers in Reno and the San Francisco Bay Area lacked the foresight of Nate Mack and other local and Salt Lake City businessmen who founded the Bank of Las Vegas in 1954 and extended loans to gambling businesses.

When the FNBN opened a second office in Las Vegas in 1953, Italian American Reno Fruzza, originally from the Reno area, was appointed assistant to the manager, Reed Whipple. In 1962 Fruzza was promoted to manager of the new FNBN branch on the Tonopah Highway (now Rancho Drive). A third Italian American, Ollie Raggio, came to Las Vegas from California in the mid-1950s to manage the installment loan department of FNBN. After a promotion Raggio worked as Harry Manente's assistant until a stroke incapacitated Manente in 1961; Raggio then took over as manager.[42]

Italian Americans also held leadership positions in the banking community. Despite the notorious image of the Mafia, men (and eventually women) of Italian ancestry were trusted to run banks. Guido Testolin, who served as assistant vice president of the Bank of Nevada and managed its Strip office in the 1960s, originally came to Las Vegas in 1938 from Wyoming at the urging of his uncle, Berto Testolin. The elder Testolin ran a successful bootlegging operation from an area due north of Las Vegas where a nature preserve now stands.[43] His son Guido returned from military service after World War II to work for John DeLuca. Not enjoying his assignment in a liquor distribution warehouse, he soon thereafter became a clerk at the Bank of Nevada and advanced into management positions, first serving as manager of the West Charleston branch and then in 1962 as manager of the Strip branch. Guido Testolin also served as treasurer of an Italian-American organization, a precursor to the Italian American Club, which William Peccole, then a city commissioner, founded in 1951.[44]

Six Italian Americans achieved prominence in real estate or insurance. Their careers, while varied, exemplify the great opportunities the rapidly growing city of Las Vegas provided businessmen in the 1950s and 1960s. Like most Las Vegans, these businessmen were not natives of the city. William Peccole and Al Aniello came from California. After beginning his insurance career in Rhode Island, Aniello arrived in Nevada in 1961. Lou La Porta, who grew up in Westchester County, New York, was assigned to the U.S. Army's Gunnery School at roughly the same time as Gus Rapone. Seeing the potential of the Las Vegas area and recognizing that the dry climate would reduce his wife's sinus problems, he stayed.[45] Angelo Manzi and Frank Sala were raised in northern Nevada. Manzi came to Las Vegas from Yerington in 1942; Sala came to Las Vegas in 1958 from the Reno/Sparks area. Sam Iacovetto was raised in Steamboat Springs, Colorado, and operated a restaurant in nearby Dinosaur before moving to Las Vegas in 1953.

William Peccole was the most successful among these businessmen. He had become well known before World War II for organizing youth sports competitions in the Las Vegas area. After attending the University of Nevada in Reno and serving in the Army, he returned to Las Vegas and entered the real estate and insurance businesses. By the early 1960s he was a leading landowner and developer. Peccole, a most reluctant interviewee, identified Builders Square and Charleston Plaza as two of his most successful malls during the late 1950s and 1960s. Perhaps the wisest of his many real estate purchases was the area west of Rainbow Boulevard and north of Sahara Boulevard, an area now known as the Peccole Ranch. Peccole bought this land in the early 1950s and retained it for thirty years, even though there was no development occurring west of Rainbow Boulevard. To demonstrate his attachment to his Italian heritage, when he sold the land, Peccole stipulated that he would give Italian names to all streets in the proposed large single-family-home development.

Sent to Las Vegas on special assignment by his employer, Al Aniello saw the business potential of the area, so once his job had ended he established his own insurance agency in 1964. He enjoyed living and working in Las Vegas, particularly because he felt he had opportunities to do creative work. He recalled with pride providing insurance coverage for striking taxi drivers in the late 1960s so that they might use their private vehicles to transport passengers. Subsequently Aniello started both the first self-insured health policies for some of the larger Strip hotels and the first self-insured liability coverage for several of Las Vegas's car rental agencies.

Although Lou La Porta owned and operated his own insurance agency, whereas Angelo Manzi was associated with New York Life, the two were alike in many respects. Both had the energetic outgoing personalities of successful insurance agents. Rev. John McVeigh remembered Lou La Porta's agency as one of two (Cragin and Pike was the other) often used by the growing Roman Catholic population in Southern Nevada. Harry Claiborne, an attorney in the 1950s, remembered Angelo Manzi as "the best salesman I ever saw." Both Manzi and La Porta were active in a great variety of civic organizations and charities, and both sought elective public office, though only La Porta was successful.

The career changes that Frank Sala and Sam Iacovetto made illustrate once again the variety of business opportunities in this desert boomtown and the openness of Las Vegas society. Sala, whose diverse business interests had included real estate and advertising, as well as gambling, was keenly aware of the tremendous post–World War II growth of Las Vegas. He invested in several gaming properties and served as manager of the Santa Anita Racebook during the late 1950s. After becoming active in Las Vegas's booming real estate market, he sold his interests in casinos and race books in 1961 to concentrate on real estate. He and Chuck Ruthe entered a very successful real estate partnership, which lasted until 1975. (Ruthe, of German background, went on to become one of Las Vegas's major real estate developers and, more recently, a principal owner of the Boyd Group gaming properties, which include two Downtown hotels, a suburban hotel, and a hotel in Laughlin, 70 miles south of Las Vegas.) Initially they focused on residential property, but soon they expanded into commercial ventures.

Sala was a leader in the organizations and regulatory agencies of his profession, serving as president of the Las Vegas Board of Realtors in 1967, the State Real Estate Board in 1970, and the Nevada Real Estate Advisory Commission still later. He was one of thirty-four prominent Nevadans Governor Grant Sawyer chose in 1964 to accompany him on a three-week tour of Europe to increase the appeal of the Silver State as a tourist destination. The group, which included several Italian Americans, was composed of casino operators, bankers, government officials, and businessmen, many of whom, like Sala, had achieved financial success by investing their energy and expertise in Nevada's booming economy of the 1950s and 1960s.[46] Sala maintained business or social relationships with many of the Italian-American contractors and real estate and insurance men previously mentioned.

Sam Iacovetto used the casino industry to provide himself with the money and business expertise to enter Las Vegas real estate. He had come to Las Vegas in 1953 to join a friend and then began dealing 21 at the Boulder Club, a small Downtown casino. He then moved to larger and more lucrative Strip properties, the Last Frontier, Stardust, Tropicana, and Sands, during the next six years. Eventually he was appointed graveyard shift boss at the Thunderbird (later renamed the Silverbird and then El Rancho). The ambitious Iacovetto also made a modest investment in the Castaways.

In spite of his achievements, Iacovetto did not seek a long-term career in gaming. He knew well that casino executives had no job security, that they came and went with great rapidity. After passing the real estate broker's exam in 1959, he worked in Nevada State Senator Helen Herr's real estate business. In 1965 he left the gaming industry to found Landmark Realty. He was pleased to devote full attention to real estate, since he believed it was more profitable and stable than gaming. Specializing in the purchase and sale of unimproved land and speculative land ventures, Iacovetto prospered as homes, apartment houses, and commercial developments were built in the once-empty desert. He never missed the always harried and often insecure life of a casino manager. Active in his profession, he eventually succeeded Sala as president of the Las Vegas Board of Realtors.

The Professionals

Italian Americans were found less in the Las Vegas professions than in business ownership and management. Their representation among Las Vegas–area attorneys, physicians, dentists, educators, and journalists was limited in the 1950s, and only in the late 1960s did the number of Italian Americans in these fields approximate their representation in the general population.[47] This should not be surprising, since during the 1950s many Italian Americans from the cities east of the Mississippi River, from which so many originally migrated, were not entering these professions in great numbers.[48]

The first lawyer of Italian background to settle permanently in Las Vegas was John Manzonie. Raised in northeastern Nevada, he passed the bar in 1954, established his practice in Las Vegas in 1955, and soon formed a partnership with Harry Claiborne. Manzonie helped form the Sons of Columbus, a short-lived Italian-American fraternal society that had as members some of the people who went on to found the Italian American Club. Manzonie's association with Harry Claiborne, then a prominent attorney and later a federal district court judge, led to his appointment as Henderson city attorney in 1959, when Claiborne resigned this post.[49] In the mid-1960s Manzonie returned to private practice.

In 1956 and 1961 Gene and Albert Matteuci, grandsons of Las Vegas pioneer Vincent Matteuci, joined Manzonie as the only other lawyers in Las Vegas with an Italian surname. After gaining trial experience as chief deputy district attorney of Clark County, Gene Matteuci was appointed city attorney of Boulder City in 1962 and served until 1965. He then entered private practice in partnership with Mahlon Brown, a prominent Democrat. Remaining active in local politics, Gene served as chairman of the Democratic Committee of Clark County from 1966 to 1967. Albert Matteuci spent most of the 1960s working in the law firm of Milton Keefer, who served as chairman of the Gaming Control Commission in the early part of that decade. The Matteucis were, like their mother, Mormons. They joined the Italian American Club in the late 1960s but did not participate actively in it or in any other Italian-American organizations.

George Graziadei proved the most prominent of the four other Italian American attorneys practicing in Southern Nevada in the late 1960s.[50] He finally relocated to Las Vegas in 1965 after having traveled there frequently to represent various Chicago business interests since 1955. Probably his most notable client was Jake Gottlieb, an alleged Mob associate and the owner of the West Transportation Company. Gottlieb had gained a Teamsters Union loan to build both Las Vegas's first high-rise hotel and the Sultan's Table Restaurant at the Dunes, where he was the major owner. Naming many individual shift bosses, casino managers, junket coordinators, and showroom hosts, Graziadei recalled that men of Italian ancestry were very active in every aspect of gaming in the 1950s and 1960s, and he felt that Italian Americans were well represented among the many hidden owners of gaming properties. Graziadei asserted that gaming regulators, then and now, are harder on Italian Americans and reject their license applications if they so much as merely associate socially with alleged members of organized crime. Like Dioguardi and most other interviewees, he acknowledged that, in general, men of Italian and Jewish backgrounds cooperated in gaming matters. Graziadei was a most informative interviewee, but both attorney-client privilege and discretion precluded his discussing his perception of the full extent of cooperation between Italian Americans and Jewish Americans.

Union Pacific Railroad surgeon John Demman was the first Italian-American physician in Las Vegas. A West Virginia native who graduated from Creighton University Medical School, Demman was appointed the Union Pacific's district surgeon in Caliente, Nevada, in 1935 and continued in that capacity until he was transferred to Las Vegas in 1948. Both his wife, Mary, and Dr. Joseph La Mancusa, who came to Las Vegas in 1961, described Demman as an energetic man who had an extensive private practice as well as the district surgeon responsibilities for the Union Pacific. He was appointed chief of staff at St. Rose de Lima Hospital in Henderson in the mid-1950s, and Sister Roberta Joseph, a longtime administrator at the hospital, reported that he continued in that capacity through the mid-

1960s. He served for several years as physician for the Las Vegas High School sports teams and was, his wife reported, an avid sports fan.

Two other Italian-American physicians from California preceded La Mancusa to Las Vegas. Both came at the request of colleagues who convinced them (and their more reluctant spouses) that Las Vegas offered both professional opportunities and a relaxed lifestyle. Dr. Emil Cava, a San Jose native, had first visited Las Vegas as a member of a band playing at the Last Frontier in 1943. After military service he played with another band at the Last Frontier, in 1947 still only one of three gaming establishments along what was to become the Las Vegas Strip. In 1955, at the urging of a friend who was an orthopedic physician, he returned to begin a practice as an obstetrician/gynecologist.

Similarly, Dr. Donald Romeo left his practice in La Jolla, California, in 1960 and moved to Las Vegas after a colleague he met at a medical convention convinced him that Las Vegas would be an excellent city for continuing his work as a general practitioner. Romeo never regretted leaving the seaside community. As avid a sports fan as Demman, Romeo served as Nevada's ringside physician for more than twenty-five years. In the early 1960s several other physicians of Italian background began practicing in Las Vegas. By the end of that decade Italian-American representation among physicians was similar to the group's representation in the Las Vegas population as a whole.[51]

The teaching profession also attracted Italian Americans. Four who began teaching in Las Vegas in the late 1950s or early 1960s achieved prominence in the following decades. Frank Brusa continues as principal of Las Vegas High School. The Silvestri brothers, Charles and Louis, both had long careers in education. Charles served as deputy superintendent of the Clark County School District, and Louis was principal of a high school and then a junior high school. Both retired in 1989. Mario Monaco was appointed to his first school principalship in the mid-1960s and continued in administration for more than twenty years, retiring from his principalship at the Southern Nevada Vocational Technical Center in 1988. Though Brusa and the Silvestri brothers came from the East, Mario Monaco grew up in Montana. Unlike some of their counterparts in gaming, these Italian-American educational administrators did not find that their careers were hindered by their ethnicity.[52]

Two Italian-American journalists achieved influential positions during the twenty years following the opening of the Flamingo in 1947. One, Adam Yacenda, was a newspaper editor and owner; the other, Gabe Vogliotti, worked as a lobbyist. Yacenda was born and raised in Brooklyn and settled in southern California after World War II. Active in politics, he served as press officer for Richard Nixon's successful senatorial campaign against Helen Gahagan Douglas in 1947. Soon thereafter, his brother Rudy recalled, Adam worked on Charles Russell's successful 1950 gubernatorial campaign. Adam Yacenda then returned to California, where he owned and managed the *Beverly Hills Bulletin,* a local newspaper. He continued to consult with Nevada hotels and politicians. In the mid-1950s he left California to become managing editor at Greenspun's *Las Vegas Sun.* Conflict between Yacenda and Greenspun led to Yacenda's departure from the *Sun* in 1959 to found his own newspaper, the *North Las Vegas Valley Times.* (Rudy had worked in the *Sun*'s bookkeeping department until Greenspun hired relatives from New York to do this work.) Rudy did not forget Adam's difficulties establishing the Las Vegas area's third newspaper. Adam worked long hours to keep his newspaper in business, and he enjoyed writing the "Adam's Atoms" column, where he expressed his opinions about national, state, and particularly local issues. North Las Vegas citizens had felt neglected by Las Vegas's two major dailies, so they welcomed the attention their area was given by Yacenda and his staff. Adam owned and managed the *North Las Vegas Valley Times* until 1975, when he became ill and sold the paper to Bob Brown.

Another Italian-American journalist parlayed his political savvy into an influential position within the gaming industry. Gabe Vogliotti, the only child of Reno hotel owners, worked as a Washington, D.C., journalist and a U.S. Senate staffer before returning to Nevada in 1963 to become second director of the new Nevada Resort Association, the lobbying organization of the major Strip hotels. Vogliotti's experience, education—he held a graduate degree from the University of Rome as well as a degree from the University of Nevada, Reno—and association with Washington power brokers made him a logical candidate for this position. Desert Inn owner Moe Dalitz and the other mostly Jewish-American Strip hotel owners who dominated the association selected Vogliotti even though eight of the eleven names in the Gaming Control Board's Black Book were Italian. Robbins Cahill, Vogliotti's successor, spoke positively of Vogliotti's work on behalf of the gaming industry, although Jean Harris, one of Vogliotti's two secretaries, recalled that Vogliotti's penchant for overspending his budget led to his dismissal in 1968.[53]

Public Service

Italian-American representation among City of Las Vegas and Clark County employees during the 1950s and 1960s was relatively meager, more closely reflecting the proportion of Italian Americans in the Southern Nevada population before 1947 than in the following twenty years. This was not surprising, because the overwhelming majority of people who moved to Las Vegas were drawn by private-sector jobs. Since even dealers at Strip properties realized better incomes than most public-sector employees, few Italian Americans sought positions in government.

Nonetheless, a few Italian Americans achieved responsible positions in Las Vegas–area governmental agencies. The most notable were Al Bossi, Aldo Barozzi,

Julius Conigliaro, Charles Perri, John Pisciotta, and Arthur Sartini. Bossi and Barozzi played important roles in the expansion of Las Vegas's infrastructure.

Al Bossi grew up in West Virginia, earned a degree in civil engineering, and settled in the San Francisco Bay Area after military service. He served as traffic engineer for Alameda County in the early 1950s and at the request of city officials moved on to Las Vegas to serve in the same capacity in 1956. He was a one-man department for the next ten years, working to develop a traffic management system during a time when the number of vehicles on the roadways was growing faster than the street system. He persistently lobbied city commissioners to hire additional employees, and by the mid-1970s he had a staff of ten. Al Bossi was a prime mover in the establishment of the Italian American Club in 1960, and he served as its first president.

Aldo Barozzi was an executive with the Las Vegas Water District for more than a quarter of a century. Mary Jean, Aldo's Irish-American wife, and secretary to the board of directors of the Las Vegas Valley Water District in the late 1950s and throughout the 1960s, remembered that her husband worked for the City of Las Vegas, then Clark County, and finally for the J. M. Montgomery Construction Company, which built water lines linking Lake Mead with Las Vegas and Henderson. Once the lines were completed in 1955, Barozzi was recruited by the Water District, where he served briefly as acting general manager and for many years as chief of operations and maintenance.[54]

Italian Americans held leadership positions in public employee unions. Julius Conigliaro joined the Las Vegas Fire Department in 1953, less than a year after he and his wife had left Brooklyn. He became a Las Vegas Fire Department captain in 1960. After playing a major role in organizing a local chapter of the AFL-CIO–affiliated International Firefighters, he served on its board of directors for five years before being elected secretary-treasurer in 1963. He helped not only to win public support for substantial pay increases, but also to gain collective bargaining rights for members. To achieve the latter, Conigliaro had to spend many days lobbying the Nevada legislature during its biennial sessions. He enjoyed these efforts and felt a sense of accomplishment at the end of each session. William Bunker, Clark County Fire Department Chief, the son of a former Nevada state senator and for several years the department's lobbyist in the state capital, recounted that Conigliaro earned a reputation as an intelligent, well-informed, and honest lobbyist owing to his efforts to win support for the Dodge Bill (which gave public-safety employees the right of collective bargaining) in 1969 and, later, to lower the retirement age for firefighters.

The career of Charles Perri, who came to Las Vegas in 1949 from Larchmont, New York, resembled Conigliaro's. Perri served as secretary-treasurer of the local chapter of the International Firefighters union when Conigliaro was president, and Perri later won election to the top office. He, too, was active in politics, once unsuccessfully seeking a seat on the city commission and later in the Nevada assembly. Both he and Conigliaro were prime movers in creating the Las Vegas firefighters' tradition of carrying large boots to major street intersections for motorists' donations to the Muscular Dystrophy Association.[55]

Among the Italian Americans who began their public-service careers in the 1960s, John Pisciotta and Arthur Sartini were the most controversial. Pisciotta was hired by the Clark County Building Department as a structural engineer in 1967 and was promoted to director in 1972. In 1977 he was forced to resign for allegedly favoring two hotels in which he held ownership. Later he came under considerable criticism in the wake of the tragic 1980 MGM Grand Hotel fire because he had overruled state and local fire marshalls on the question of the need to install a sprinkling system.

Arthur Sartini, yet another migrant from the San Francisco Bay Area, began his lengthy career with the Las Vegas Housing Authority in 1964. Appointed executive director in 1969, he remained in that well-paid position until he resigned under fire twenty years later. After maintaining a low profile for eighteen years, in September 1987 Sartini was investigated by federal authorities on suspicion that he had a long history of overcharging tenants. Soon local authorities charged him with extensive nepotism in hiring at the Authority. During the next twenty-seven months he was the subject of more than fifty news stories.[56] Both Pisciotta's daughter and Sartini's son said their fathers disagreed with the newspapers' evaluations of their performance and would probably welcome talking with me. Yet neither responded to my many requests for an interview. Sartini's son, Blake, married Frank Fertitta's daughter and is now a vice president at Palace Station, as well as chief operating officer of the Loose Caboose saloons, which were found in an increasing number of Las Vegas locations in the early 1990s.

In Nevada, Italian Americans serving at all levels of government faced no discrimination and, indeed, no unusual scrutiny because of their ancestry. Bossi and Conigliaro knew that many Las Vegans linked Italian Americans and organized crime all too readily, but both agreed that this bias did not adversely affect the careers of city or county officials. Nor did Italian ancestry adversely affect the careers of state and federal law enforcement officials. Ray Abbatichio, a former FBI agent, succeeded Robbins Cahill as head of the Gaming Control Board in 1959. George Togliatti served as an FBI special agent with responsibilities in organized crime from the mid-1980s until his retirement in 1996, and Joseph Saitta was the Secret Service agent-in-charge for Las Vegas in 1992. Italian ancestry also did not adversely affect the careers of Nick Aquilina or Peter Zavatarro, men who have held key positions at the Nevada Test Site for the past fifteen years. Aquilina, the Department of Energy's manager in Southern Nevada, and Zavatarro, president of EG&G Energy Measurement, both agreed that their Italian background has never negatively affected their careers.

Italian Americans were well represented among elected officials. Al Corradetti served on the city commission from 1938 through 1947. Corradetti had been criticized as being subservient to Mayor Cragin and the Downtown club owners. He had supported Cragin's efforts to manage the city in a more businesslike manner and had fought for a new municipal airport south of Las Vegas, but he had also made some enemies.[57] After losing his bid for the city commissioner post, Corradetti retired from public life.

In 1949 William Peccole decisively defeated the long-term city commissioner and Nevada Beverage Company owner Pat Clark. William Peccole was not enthusiastic about speaking with this author, but he finally consented to do so only at the urging of his wife (who is a member of the politically powerful Lamb family). Even then, he was very cautious until Hank Greenspun's name was mentioned. After serving on the commission for four years, Peccole lost the 1953 race to Harris Sharp after Hank Greenspun, owner and editor of the *Las Vegas Sun,* charged Peccole with blatant dishonesty: using his office to get a license for a Downtown gaming property in which he had a hidden interest.[58] Peccole was subsequently indicted for soliciting a bribe but was later acquitted. For the rest of his life he blamed Hank Greenspun for the loss of the city commission post. Peccole felt that after running as a reform candidate in 1949 and winning the commission seat, he and Mayor Ernie Cragin had worked quietly to correct misuse of trust fund accounts and to put the city on a solid financial footing, only to have his efforts besmirched by the unwarranted attacks from Greenspun. Peccole's voice became quite animated when he offered his opinions on Hank Greenspun's controversial background and lack of ethics. He mentioned that Greenspun "just a few years [before the 1953 election] had been Bugsy Siegel's publicity director."

William Peccole did not seek public office again, though he must have been pleased when one of his insurance and real estate business employees, Philip Mirabelli, beat out Harrison Sharp in a city commission contest in 1961. Mirabelli served until he was defeated in 1969 by Dr. Alexander Coblentz.[59]

Other Italian Americans also wielded political power locally. While William Peccole was serving on the city commission, two other Italian Americans, who like Peccole had come to Las Vegas as teenagers, entered politics: Jack Pettiti and Dick Ronzone. Jack Pettiti, whose political career spanned thirty years, was elected to the Clark County Board of Education in 1950. He then served twelve years (1959–71) on the North Las Vegas City Council and a decade more on the Clark County Commission. When he was younger Pettiti had gained some fame as a football player and, like William Peccole, became involved in youth sports.[60] Pettiti considered the expansion of recreational opportunities, particularly for young people, to be his most significant achievement while in office.

Dick Ronzone joined the Clark County Board of Education in 1952, a year after becoming president of the Las Vegas Chamber of Commerce and two years after failing to gain election to the state senate. Ronzone, like Pettiti, sought other elective offices after serving one term on the school board. Before winning a seat on the Clark County Commission in 1972, he had been elected to the University of Nevada Board of Regents and later to the Nevada assembly. In an interview only a few weeks before his death in January 1989, Ronzone was reluctant to discuss his personal achievements, stressing only that he was pleased to have participated in the development of Las Vegas. One of his most notable achievements was helping to secure plentiful and inexpensive water resources for the desert community. Appointed to the board of directors of the Las Vegas Valley Water District in 1948, Ronzone served for a total of sixteen years, holding the presidency from 1978 through 1984.[61]

Lou La Porta, whose New York origins were mentioned earlier, began his fifteen-year political career in 1953 when he gained 58 percent of the votes in a five-man contest for the Ward 3 seat (which carried a four-year term of office) on the city council of Henderson. He decisively won reelection in 1957 to a two-year term but lost to Frank Morrell in 1959. The next year two seats were added to the county commission, and La Porta, a Democrat and then president of the Henderson Chamber of Commerce, easily prevailed over his Republican opponent. He won a second four-year term in 1964. In 1968 he decided to concentrate on his insurance business and did not seek reelection. Like Ronzone, he was pleased to have participated in government at a time when both the geographic area he represented and Clark County as a whole were experiencing rapid growth and development. Also, like Ronzone, he felt that he was only a contributor, never the prime mover in the major water and land development projects of the 1950s and 1960s.

Ethnicity was not a significant factor in Southern Nevada elections. Phil Mirabelli, Lou La Porta, Jack Pettiti, and Dick Ronzone agreed that an Italian surname may have gained them a few votes and cost them an equally small number. They agreed that although some of the electorate associated an Italian surname with the Mafia, the great majority of voters were willing to judge Italian-American candidates on their records and campaign promises. The majority of politicians with Italian surnames were, like most Las Vegans, not deeply concerned about their ethnic origins.[62]

Summary

Italian-American gaming executives and workers, entertainers, business entrepreneurs, union leaders, professionals, and elected officials all contributed significantly to the rapid growth of Las Vegas during the twenty years following the opening of the Flamingo in 1947. But Las Vegas was then as much a state of mind, an image, and perhaps even a myth, as it was a physical presence. In Las Vegas dreams could come true. The tired factory worker could hit the jackpot. The bored bookkeeper could think that her companions at the craps table might include a famous entertainer, a high-rolling millionaire, or, most exciting, a Mafioso. Middle-class tourists could sample the trappings of upper-class luxury and privilege, particularly if they stayed at such Strip resorts as the Desert Inn or the Sands, and, later, the MGM or Caesars Palace. Part of the city's lure to millions was the idea that in Vegas the usual rules did not apply. Anything was possible.[63]

What could possibly be more intriguing, more evocative of the mystery of Las Vegas, than the word *Mafia*? The word conjured up images of swarthy men in silk suits, occasionally speaking a strange language in hushed tones and living by standards unfathomable to millions of ordinary people. Reinforcing these images was the fact that criminals of Italian heritage, like criminals of other ethnic backgrounds, invested their capital and expertise in Las Vegas.[64] Hundreds of thousands, perhaps millions, read *The Green Felt Jungle* in the mid-1960s. Some, no doubt, were outraged by the stories of the pervasive corruption of public officials; many others were intrigued by the authors' tales of gangsters, mostly of either Italian or Jewish background, using money from illegal enterprises to build the most lavish hotels in Las Vegas and then skimming the proceeds from the casinos.

In addition, the typical tourist read in the Las Vegas papers about reputed Mafia figures such as Sam Giancana of Chicago or the Civella brothers of Kansas City, men so notorious that their names appeared in the Black Book. The predominance of Italian-American names in the Black Book and the presence of so many dealers, floormen, pit bosses, and shift bosses in the casinos seemed to substantiate the Mafia's presence. In talking with some of these workers, the visitor might well have heard that certain Italian-American pit bosses and shift managers actually ran the Strip property, or even that the leader of the Chicago, Kansas City, or Milwaukee Mob had recently visited the Italian American Club.

The relationship between Italian Americans and Las Vegas was, in general, mutually beneficial. Perhaps Italian Americans, merely by a combination of their image and their major presence in Las Vegas, enhanced the lure of Las Vegas as a unique destination—an adult Disneyland where fantasies came true. In any case, Italian Americans significantly contributed to the transformation of Las Vegas from a small western city to an international center of gambling. At the same time, Las Vegas presented thousands of Italian Americans, the vast majority of whom had no connection, real or imagined, with the Mafia or any other aspect of organized crime, many and diverse opportunities for economic advancement and civic leadership.

The only exceptions were those Italian Americans with experience in illegal gambling enterprises, and, in some cases, a broader and deeper connection with organized crime, who tried to shed their pasts but were unable to do so because Nevada's political leaders, largely in response to pressure from U.S. Attorney General Robert Kennedy, embarked on stricter regulation of gaming. Beginning in 1960, Nevada regulators not only made it more difficult for individuals with an organized crime background to gain a license to run or manage a casino; they also tried to make it clear to the general public that Nevada had gotten tough with organized crime figures. The latter goal was achieved largely through the "List of Excluded Persons," more commonly referred to as the Black Book—a method of excluding individuals of notorious reputation from any business establishment that was involved in gambling. From 1960 Italian names predominated in the Black Book; indeed, frequently 70 to 80 percent of the notorious individuals listed there were of Italian background. While Las Vegas remained essentially a city whose inhabitants were willing to forget past transgressions of the law or social mores, Nevada gaming regulators were not so inclined, and the burden fell heavily on Italian Americans. Italian Americans had played a significant role in illegal gambling, and the regulators felt the need to respond to the widespread perception that the Mafia controlled virtually all of organized crime.

Chapter Three

The Corporate Era:

Italian Americans Prosper

Howard Hughes Arrives

Italian Americans contributed to both the reality and the myth of Las Vegas during the corporate era that began when Howard Hughes purchased the Desert Inn in 1966. Italian Americans, particularly those with expertise in gaming, continued to migrate to Las Vegas from the cities of California, the Midwest, and the East Coast through the early 1990s. In addition, the children of Italian Americans who had come to Las Vegas earlier exerted a positive influence on the city's development. Italian Americans designed, built, and managed hotels and casinos, entertained millions of visitors in the showrooms and lounges, and ran the leading restaurants. They, as well as the Italian-American wiseguys who often captured the attention of the press, contributed to the emergence of Las Vegas as a resort city in the Sunbelt.

To say that Hughes's arrival in Las Vegas signaled an abrupt departure from traditional ways of doing business would be an oversimplification for three reasons. First, The Boys—Hank Greenspun (who, by 1966, had become respectable despite his early association with Bugsy Siegel and his felony conviction for supplying arms to Zionist Jews in Palestine), Moe Dalitz, and Johnny Rosselli, the Mob's chief representative in both Las Vegas and Los Angeles—were very much involved in Hughes's entry into Las Vegas and his subsequent purchase of Strip gaming properties.[1] Second, Hughes Tool Company was not the first corporation to invest in Nevada gaming (later Hughes's Nevada Operations and then Summa Corporation were created to manage Hughes's Nevada investments). The Del Webb Corporation had been active in Las Vegas gaming for many years, initially owning shares of the Flamingo and the Sahara and later, in 1963, the principal shares of both the Sahara and a Downtown property, the Mint.[2] The Golden Nugget, a major Downtown property, had been corporate owned since the mid-1950s, and the Parvin-Dohrmann Company had begun investing in gaming properties.

Third, the management style of Hughes and his executives differed markedly from the impersonal decision making so often associated with corporations because Hughes was an eccentric character. The bizarre behavior of Howard Hughes and his first chief aide, Robert Maheu, has been the subject of many articles. After being whisked into Las Vegas in the middle of the night, Hughes seldom if ever left his suite at the top of the Desert Inn. His aversion to contact with anyone except one or two of his closest aides was so widely known that Nevada gaming regulators suspended the usual rules to grant him a license even though he refused to supply the required information about his many businesses—a previously unknown occurrence. (Later, after Hughes left Nevada, Governor Mike O'Callaghan and other top gaming regulators traveled to London to meet with Hughes—once again, a unique occurrence.)

Robert Maheu ran Hughes's Nevada empire as if it were the Central Intelligence Agency (one of his former employers): no employee knew another's duties. Spending money lavishly, he gave *Las Vegas Sun* publisher Hank Greenspun $500,000 for advertising space that was never used and distributed tens of thousands of dollars to candidates for public office in Nevada.[3] In late 1970 Hughes's Mormon advisers secretly carried him out of the Desert Inn, away from Robert Maheu. Two years later, at one of his rare news conferences, Hughes accused Maheu of theft on a grand scale.[4]

In the broadest sense, though, Hughes's arrival marked the beginning of a new era. He arrived when the Las Vegas economy was in a slump, with too many vacant hotel rooms. Developers, their spirits buoyed by the population growth in Las Vegas, had overbuilt, so recently constructed apartment houses and commercial developments had few tenants, and Las Vegas had lost some of its glitter. Tourists passed partially constructed and vacant buildings as they visited the casinos along Las Vegas Boulevard and Fremont Street.[5] Initially Hughes, who purchased six Strip properties in fewer than three years, was even more welcome than the East Coast gangsters who had built the Strip. The Nevada power structure had accommodated Bugsy and The Boys, and it now accommodated Howard Hughes. New laws passed by the Nevada legislature in 1967 and 1969 to make gaming more attractive to large corporations succeeded admirably.[6] Within a decade, such corporations as Hilton, Holiday Inn, MGM, and Ramada had purchased property.

Men with backgrounds in organized crime—Italian Americans and others, Jewish Americans in particular—adapted well to corporate enterprise and changes in gaming regulations. A look into the goings-on at the Parvin-Dohrmann Company illustrates how The Boys operated. When Albert Parvin, Parvin-Dohrmann's major stockholder, who had operated the Flamingo from 1955 to 1960, decided to sell the club, he paid a $200,000 finder's fee to Meyer Lansky. Parvin then sold the club to several Jewish Americans with alleged links to organized crime, who, like Lansky, were Miami residents. In 1969 the Parvin-Dohrmann Company purchased the Stardust from Moe Dalitz and his associates, after the U.S. Justice

Department had announced it would file an antitrust action to stop Howard Hughes's purchase of the Strip property. Yale Cohen, often identified as a Chicago Mob associate, stayed on as president of the Stardust; another reputed Mob associate, Nicholas "Peanuts" Danolfo, left an executive position at the Desert Inn to become vice president at the Stardust. Two other alleged Mob associates, Al Sachs and Phil Ponti, continued to hold the top positions in the Stardust casino. Nevada may have improved its image by facilitating corporate investment in casinos, but the reality was that The Boys, usually Jewish Americans or Italian Americans, changed their methods; they did not immediately leave town.

Nevada gaming regulators were more stringent about granting licenses to men with connections to organized crime during the 1960s and 1970s than they had been in the 1950s, yet some of The Boys retained their licenses as casino executives. When necessary, The Boys recruited executives with no apparent connection to organized crime. The best example is Allen Glick, who was the ostensible owner of the Stardust from August 1974 until the Nevada Gaming Commission ordered him to put the club on the market five years later. Lefty Rosenthal, a Chicago gambler with alleged ties to the Chicago Mob, then ran the casino until Nevada gaming regulators finally revoked his license to work in a casino in any capacity in 1978.[7] Glick, chief executive officer of Argent Corporation, sold the Stardust to the Trans-Sterling Corporation, whose chief executive officer was Al Sachs. The skimming—that is, the illegal pocketing of casino revenue before it is reported to government agencies and stockholders—continued.

The unorthodox management of Howard Hughes's gambling enterprises also afforded The Boys opportunities for skimming. Howard Hughes's chief aide Robert Maheu valued personal loyalty as much as Hughes did. Soon after becoming de facto chief operating officer of Hughes's Nevada Operations, Maheu asked his old friend General Ed Nigro to serve as president of the Sands, the most famous Las Vegas hotel. Maheu and Nigro had become friends in the early 1940s as classmates at Holy Cross College in Worcester, Massachusetts; they renewed their friendship in the mid-1950s in Washington, D.C., when Nigro served as assistant to the Air Force Chief of Staff in the Pentagon and Maheu was working as a private investigator. Nigro had been a decorated Korean War fighter pilot and later the vice commander of a large Air Force base, but he had no experience managing gaming enterprises. Of course, Maheu, in hiring top executives for personal reasons rather than for their experience acted no differently than his boss.

Ed Nigro, General Nigro's son, and now a Las Vegas home builder, recalled that after taking over the Sands his father immediately sought out men with successful gaming experience. Then and later, when he worked as deputy chief of Hughes's Nevada Operations supervising five gaming property managers, Nigro worked well with those who had come to Las Vegas when Bugsy Siegel invested in casinos.[8] "These guys in gambling for twenty years have a sixth sense," Nigro once said. "We haven't got enough time in our lives to learn what they know."[9]

Nigro, despite his reputation for hard work and integrity, failed to stop the skimming from Hughes's casinos.[10] By 1969 Las Vegas had recovered from its recession and business was good, but Hughes's money was still disappearing. Another Italian American, Andy Baruffi, then the Internal Revenue Service intelligence chief in Las Vegas, admitted that although federal law enforcers knew the total amount of money being stolen, they could not determine who—Maheu, The Boys, or many, many casino workers—was stealing or how much.[11]

Less than three years after he was hired, General Nigro had an argument with Maheu which, as Ed Nigro remembers, ended with Maheu vowing, "You'll never work again in Nevada." Ed Nigro did not say what the argument had been about, but theft and Maheu's failure to adopt appropriate controls were probably major factors setting the two men against one another.

Maheu was wrong about Nigro's job prospects. General Nigro was hired as executive vice president of Del Webb's Sahara Nevada Corporation shortly after Maheu fired him, and soon he was selected by gaming executives to serve as president of the Nevada Resort Association. Subsequently Nigro moved into a top position in the Del Webb Hotel International Corporation's Phoenix headquarters. Like previous jobs, this one proved extremely demanding; it probably contributed to his sudden death from a massive heart attack on July 1, 1973. Friends and associates were shocked by his death, particularly because Nigro, a man who exercised vigorously, appeared to be in superb health. The day after his death, the obituary headline in Hank Greenspun's *Las Vegas Sun* proclaimed "Del Webb Hotel Chief Ed Nigro Dead at 54," and the accompanying text made note of not only his military and gaming careers, but also his contributions to Southern Nevada civic and charitable organizations.

Steve Savoldelli, the other top Italian-American executive in Hughes's Nevada empire, also came to the corporation with no managerial experience in gaming. In his early forties, the widely traveled Savoldelli, formerly president of Pepsi Cola Mexico, a subsidiary of Rheingold, had first become acquainted with Hughes in 1969 when he represented several companies seeking contracts with one or more of Hughes's companies. He said that he could think of no prior experience in U.S. or foreign corporations that could have prepared him for the personal management style of Hughes's corporate empire. Hired by Bill Gay, whom Hughes selected to replace Maheu as his chief of staff in late 1970, Savoldelli was given the official title vice president and director of the Summa Corporation Recreation Group. Like other Summa executives, he never saw Hughes while he managed Hughes's Nevada Operations, though he occasionally heard his voice from an adjoining room. The chief executive officers of the Sands, Desert Inn, Frontier, Castaways, Landmark, and Silver Slipper in Las Vegas and Harold's Club in Reno reported to Savoldelli, who was also responsible for overseeing Hughes's mining claims.

Savoldelli was a clean-living man. He never drank or gambled, and he had refused to move his family to Las Vegas from southern California because he did not believe Las Vegas was a good place to raise his daughters. Savoldelli's aversion to such common vices probably accounts for the fact that he was the only Italian American appointed to a top position by Mormon Bill Gay.

Frank Modica and Al Casarotto, Italian-American gaming executives, reported that Savoldelli, like Nigro, made few major changes to the corporation, and, until he left to take a position with Italian-American Jerrold Perenchio, a southern California entertainment entrepreneur, Savoldelli worked well with the traditional gaming managers. Like most who rose through the corporate hierarchy, he was reluctant in a 1991 interview to speak negatively about Summa Corporation (which he claimed to have named), but he did admit that he had often been frustrated about having to communicate with Hughes through nurses.

Most interviewees reported that Hughes's purchase of Strip properties had little impact on local Italian Americans, whether dealers, entertainers, or managers. Frank Modica, then the top-ranking Italian-American casino executive of Hughes's properties, recalled that Maheu favored former military and law enforcement officials, and his successor, Bill Gay, favored Mormons, but that Italian Americans faced no ethnic discrimination from either Hughes's Nevada Operations or Summa Corporation.

Gaming Career Patterns

Italian Americans with gaming expertise continued to migrate to Las Vegas while Hughes built his gaming empire. The Bommarito family of Detroit is a good case in point. While these newcomers were not directly related to Pete Bommarito, the two Bommarito families had come from the same area of Sicily. Ted Bommarito, a Las Vegas dealer at the time he was interviewed, recounted that his father had considered moving to Las Vegas from Detroit in the early fifties but was dissuaded by older, more cautious relatives. The elders were unsure whether Las Vegas's growth would continue, and they feared that the rapid pace of development might end abruptly. Yet in 1967, during one of the periodic antigambling campaigns in Michigan, Ted's father, who had a history of arrests, moved to Las Vegas, where he passed up management opportunities, preferring instead the fairly substantial tip income he earned dealing.

Ted, who also chose to deal rather than to climb the management ladder, affirmed that many of the dealers, floormen, and pit bosses at the El Cortez—where he took his first dealing job—and other Downtown casinos were of Italian ancestry. He also said that a high proportion of mid-level managers and executives were Jewish and worked well with the Italian Americans. An Italian surname was helpful because hiring was influenced by "juice" (the Las Vegas term for "personal influence"). After twenty-one months at El Cortez, Ted Bommarito moved to the Riviera, a major Strip property, to deal blackjack. Rather typically, the Riviera's owner, Ed Torres, was a Jewish American, and the casino manager, Frank Falba, was an Italian American. After dealing there for about a year, Ted was fired, along with many others. Once again, he quickly found a new position, this time at the Flamingo, because he knew key executives, both of whom were mid-level managers. One of his connections was a Jewish American; the other was a Greek American. Fired after eighteen months at the Flamingo, Ted found employment again thanks to "juice." He joined many other former Detroiters at the Aladdin, the principal owner of which was Arab American Sorkis Webbe and Tony Pisula the casino manager. Finally, when Ed Torres bought the Aladdin, Bommarito left that club for a dealer's job at the Tropicana in 1980. Ted Bommarito's candor concerning the means he used to advance his career was refreshing, and his frequent changes of employer were not unusual.

Vic Taucer's career provides yet another example of the typically high rate of job turnover in the gaming industry. The son of an Italian-American mother and an Italian sailor (who, along with the officers and crew of his ship, surrendered to the United States Navy in New York Harbor in 1943), Vic Taucer grew up in Niagara Falls. His maternal grandfather had been one of the numerous Americans and Canadians, many of whom were of Italian or Jewish background, who had made a living smuggling liquor across the Great Lakes during Prohibition. The Taucer family, like most of their Italian-American neighbors, were as tolerant of gambling as they were of enjoying wine with a meal. In 1975, at the age of twenty-two, Taucer joined several former boyhood friends in Las Vegas. After dealer's school, he took a "break-in" job at the Hotel Nevada for a few months, moved to the larger Mint for two years, then joined the Castaways on the Strip as a dealer. After quickly ascending the management ladder at the Castaways, he then dealt at the MGM (now Bally's) before becoming floorman at Caesars Palace.

Like Ted Bommarito, Taucer was often hired by Italian Americans: Joe Soprano at the Mint; Don Ruggiero at the Castaways; Mokey Faccinto at Caesars Palace. (Soprano and Ruggiero were also from Niagara Falls.) Taucer also corroborated the significant representation of Jewish Americans in casino management positions. But he stressed that being of Italian or Jewish background did not guarantee anyone a job as a dealer, much less a casino management position. Loyalty and performance, not ethnicity, were the key determinants of who was hired and promoted. Indeed, as Taucer is not an obviously Italian name (his father came from an area northeast of Venice that had been ruled by Austria through World War I), Vic was not taken for an Italian American, so he heard many criticisms in the casinos and the community of Italian Americans and their alleged ties to organized crime. He agreed that Italian ancestry was probably a disadvantage for anyone seeking to be licensed as an owner or top executive of a casino in the 1970s and 1980s.

Taucer's career took a different twist after he began coordinating casino marketing at Caesars Palace in 1987. Dr. Russ Anderson, resort programs department chair at the Community College of Southern Nevada (CCSN), convinced him to teach a course. Anderson was impressed by Taucer's performance, and Taucer enjoyed the experience. Three years later he was hired as a full-time casino games instructor at CCSN.

Unlike Taucer and the others, some Italian Americans chose to advance their careers by spending long periods of time at one gambling establishment. After a year in a Pueblo, Colorado, steel mill, Joe Spinuzzi decided to explore job opportunities in Las Vegas. Initially employed as a busboy at El Rancho in 1954, he soon became a break-in dealer at the Pioneer Club in downtown Las Vegas. Thanks to Carl Cohen, in 1958 Spinuzzi began a twenty-two-year career at the Sands. Like many other Italian Americans, he praised Cohen for his intelligence and integrity. Spinuzzi moved up through the ranks—from pit boss to floorman to shift boss. "The Sands was the greatest place in a wonderful town. What an experience," Spinuzzi said in a late 1991 interview. He too recalled the high proportion of Italian Americans and Jewish Americans in gaming, and the generally good relations between members of these groups. Spinuzzi left the Sands in 1980 to work for Burton Cohen at the Desert Inn before moving to two other Strip hotels and then returning Downtown to the Golden Nugget, where he is now an executive casino host.

Al Casarotto's career demonstrates that a manager's tenure was no more secure than a dealer's during the corporate era. Unlike Ted Bommarito, Casarotto chose to move steadily up through the corporate hierarchy. As a fighter pilot, he was assigned to Nellis Air Force Base in 1954. While living off-base in an apartment across from the Sahara, he enjoyed the bright lights and excitement of Las Vegas. Following his discharge from the Air Force, he returned to his native Albany, New York, to open a nightclub, but he often thought of Las Vegas. After a divorce he returned to Las Vegas with his second wife in 1961. In typical fashion, he attended gaming school before securing his first job at a Downtown hotel, Milton Prell's Mint. In 1963 he moved to the Sahara as a dealer, and soon he was promoted to boxman. He then began a rapid climb in management, serving as a floorman, pit boss, shift boss, and finally assistant casino manager. He did not notice any significant differences between the management style at the Sahara, owned by Del Webb Corporation, and the privately owned gambling properties. He too recalled that Italian Americans and Jewish Americans dominated the ranks of casino managers.

In 1975 Steve Savoldelli, Summa's executive vice president for recreation, offered Casarotto a job as casino manager at the Landmark, an off-Strip property that had been unprofitable since its opening. Well aware that several other casino managers had failed to turn the club around, Casarotto nevertheless accepted the position and began working long hours, seven days a week. He was proud that by 1976 the casino was profitable, at least until a Culinary Union strike "virtually closed down" Las Vegas for almost three months. Following major disagreements with the newly appointed Landmark general manager, Casarotto resigned.

His next executive appointment put Casarotto in an unusual work environment, even by Las Vegas standards. Tony Torcasio contacted Casarotto about running the Tropicana casino. Torcasio, a Steubenville, Ohio, native and an Italian American, was a well-known gaming figure who had held executive positions in several Las Vegas hotels, including the Aladdin and MGM Grand. Casarotto and other interviewees described Torcasio as an old-fashioned cigar-smoking Italian who had been acquainted with many of The Boys when he operated gambling enterprises in the East and in Havana, Cuba. He had a very strong sense of loyalty and took care of his friends. Mitzi Stauffer Briggs, the eccentric owner of the Tropicana, had chosen Torcasio to run the casino in December of 1976. Casarotto recounted that Briggs, heiress to the Stauffer Chemical Company fortune and a total novice in gaming, had a most unorthodox management style, although he decided not to discuss specifics. Casarotto managed the Tropicana's casino for about a year.

Casarotto was probably not disappointed when Steve Savoldelli contacted him. Once again, Savoldelli wanted Casarotto to take over the management of an unprofitable Summa Corporation casino, this time the Frontier. Because the casino had lost money for several years, Casarotto hesitated to accept the job until Savoldelli increased the initial compensation package and offered him the title of casino manager and senior vice president. Casarotto claims that he had the Frontier operating in the black within six months. He attributed part of his success to his emphasis on marketing, most notably his recruitment of Nick Gullo to run a casino marketing department. Gullo, also an Italian American, had learned about gambling operations in New Orleans.[12]

Only the opportunity to greatly enhance his income could have made Casarotto leave the Frontier. That opportunity came, or so it seemed, when Deil Gustafson, a Minnesota banker and junior partner with Mitzi Stauffer Briggs in the Tropicana, offered him very generous compensation. Even more important, Torcasio had left the Tropicana to take an executive position in Atlantic City,[13] and Gustafson promised Casarotto full authority to run the club. Upon accepting the offer, Casarotto brought Nick Gullo and several other Frontier casino executives with him. Again all went well initially, although Casarotto later found some of Gustafson's financial procedures irregular and asked him to stop cashing large personal checks in the casino.

Casarotto's diverse experiences in gaming did not prepare him for the bomb-shell that exploded in July 1978 when the U.S. Department of Justice made public tapes purportedly revealing that Joe Agosto, the Sicilian-born entertainment director at the Tropicana, had been running the resort for the benefit of Kansas City mobsters.[14] Nevada gaming regulators investigated and quickly decided that the Tropicana's majority stockholders, Mitzi Stauffer Briggs and Deil Gustafson, would have to leave the property immediately, as soon as they had sold their shares of the Tropicana to Ramada Inn Corporation. (Another hotel chain, Hyatt, had also been negotiating with Briggs and Gustafson but dropped out when the allegations of massive theft became public.)

After the initial shock, Casarotto was optimistic that Nevada gaming regulators would put him in charge of all operations since he had not been implicated in the scandal. He was not alone in believing this, for as Tim Dahlberg, *Review-Journal* reporter, wrote in a front-page article on July 18, "Following the removal of Briggs and Gustafson, it is expected that Tropicana General Manager Casarotto will be named by the State to run the hotel during the interim period." In the same article, Casarotto is quoted as saying that he had been assured by Ramada officials that he and his management team would be kept in their positions.

But the negotiations between the Tropicana's present and prospective owners did not proceed smoothly, and, as the weeks passed, Nevada gaming authorities grew more anxious. On November 4, 1978, Casarotto and more than twenty members of his management team were fired. According to Casarotto, Gustafson (who later served a federal prison sentence for bank fraud) was concerned that Casarotto would learn even more about his dubious financial transactions, so he convinced nervous Nevada gaming authorities that the sale of the property to Ramada could not be completed until he "cleaned out" the present managers.[15] Casarotto emphasized that neither he nor his associates were ever accused of any wrongdoing. Indeed, he and Nick Gullo were subsequently licensed as owners of Big Al's Speakeasy, and in 1980 Casarotto gained approval from local and state authorities, as well as the Federal Bankruptcy Court, to run the Nevada Palace, a financially troubled hotel on Boulder Highway, for a group of Canadian investors.[16]

Nevertheless, Casarotto's dismissal harmed his career in the corporate era of Las Vegas. After Big Al's Speakeasy failed, depleting both his and Nick Gullo's savings, Casarotto worked through 1986 for George McLaughlin, an investor who unsuccessfully tried to raise funds, mainly from wealthy Europeans, to build a major resort in Las Vegas. More recently Casarotto has worked at University Medical Center as director of food service and clinical nutrition. In a 1991 interview Casarotto expressed interest in returning to the gaming industry, although he acknowledged that his prospects were dim.

Neither Ted Bommarito's nor Al Casarotto's experiences were atypical. Casino employees, from dealers to executives, often moved from one property to another. Like Bommarito and Casarotto, they always worked with many other Italian Americans. Without doubt, Italian ancestry was helpful to those seeking casino employment, although Italian heritage never helped anyone get licensed. A review of the careers of many Italian Americans in the gaming industry also affirms that neither the arrival of Howard Hughes nor the entry of major corporations produced striking changes in the ways casinos were managed. The changes—the treatment of food and beverage operations and entertainment as profit-making centers, the training programs for security officers, and the recruitment of college graduates—evolved slowly, giving Italian Americans and others time to adjust.

The corporate era brought about the entry into gaming of executives from lateral positions in other industries. This was quite a departure from past practice. Ed Nigro was the first of several Italian Americans to move from nongaming careers to top jobs in major Strip gaming properties. Nigro hired John Chiero in 1972 as a West Coast representative for the Del Webb Corporation. This was a convenient move for Chiero, who had spent over a decade in the Los Angeles area as an executive of the Bank of America. Less than two years later, Nigro's successor, Jess Hinkle, offered Chiero an opportunity to learn the gaming business. First he was assigned to Del Webb's Sahara Tahoe; then by early 1975 he was appointed vice president in charge of credit and collections. Chiero found the gaming business quite fascinating, but twice he was lured back to southern California by higher paying positions in other fields of business—first with the Bank of America and then with a nationwide auto leasing firm—before he accepted an invitation from the Ramada Corporation to join its planning/management team to work on a noted property in Atlantic City. He rose rapidly in the corporate hierarchy at Ramada, even though he was shifted between the Las Vegas Tropicana and the Atlantic City Trop World. In 1984 Chiero became president of the Tropicana, and soon thereafter he oversaw the growth and development of the property that now bills itself as "The Island of Las Vegas."

John Giovenco spent fifteen years at Pannel Kerr Forster, Certified Public Accountants, before he joined Hilton Hotels Corporation in 1972 as treasurer of the Las Vegas Hilton and the Flamingo Hilton. Like Chiero, the Chicago native quickly climbed Hilton's corporate ladder, serving as chief financial officer and then executive vice president of finance before the board of directors elected him president of Hilton's Gaming Division.

Dan Cassella, too, began his career working for one of the "big eight" accounting firms, Haskins and Sells. In 1972 Cassella, originally from Newcastle, Pennsylvania, welcomed the opportunity to relocate to Las Vegas. Three of his uncles who were musicians had lived in Las Vegas for twenty years. After doing many audits for Summa Corporation, Cassella accepted a position as account manager for Summa in 1975. Although he moved up through the corporate hierarchy, he did not feel professionally challenged. He described the atmosphere at Summa as relaxed, but he observed that little effort was directed toward managing the gaming properties with optimal efficiency.

In early 1980 Cassella gave up his pleasant weekends with his family and joined Caesars Palace as controller. He never regretted the move. He was impressed by the dedication and creativity of the Caesars Palace management team. Initially brothers Cliff and Stuart Perlman and Harry Wald, Jewish Americans, held the top positions. The next rung of management was dominated by Anglo-Saxons. Italian Americans, many of whom were hired by casino manager Mokey Faccinto, were supervising the casino games.

The rapid turnover in top management at Caesars Palace was typical of the gaming industry as a whole during the corporate era. The frequent shake-ups gave Cassella opportunities for rapid advancement. The Perlmans were never able to escape the adverse publicity stemming from their financial connections with Miami attorney Alvin Malnik, an alleged associate of Meyer Lansky. In October 1980 they were judged unsuitable to hold gaming licenses in Atlantic City, and later they were forced to resign their positions at Caesars Palace. Their successor, veteran gamer Harry Wald, was replaced as president of Caesars Palace in September 1984 by hotel executive Donald Allison, whose tenure was also limited. Each change of leadership brought Cassella closer to the top position. He served as treasurer, senior vice president, executive vice president, and finally became acting president in 1988.

Like Frank Modica, Al Casarotto, and John Chiero, Dan Cassella did not hesitate to take on new challenges, especially when they were accompanied by generous compensation packages. In January 1989 Steve Wynn recruited Cassella. Wynn, a Jewish American, owned the Golden Nugget in downtown Las Vegas and was building the biggest hotel on the Strip, the Mirage. He needed the financial acumen and international marketing expertise that Cassella had gained in his nine years at Caesars Palace, so he authorized Bobby Baldwin, Mirage president, to offer Cassella a three-year contract as executive vice president of the Mirage. Cassella worked for the Mirage until September 1992, when he accepted an offer to become chief executive officer of the Desert Inn, a relatively small Strip hotel that catered to a wealthy clientele.

Unlike Italian Americans who had learned the gaming business largely through participating in illegal gambling operations in the cities of the East Coast and Midwest, Chiero, Giovenco, and Cassella experienced no problems when they sought Nevada gaming licenses. Even though they came to Las Vegas at a time when the newspapers were full of stories about the Chicago Mob, these Italian Americans did not have to confront rumor or innuendo about associations with alleged organized crime figures. Whereas most corporate doors had been closed to Italian Americans when men like Pete Bommarito, Phil Dioguardi, and Joe Canino were beginning their careers, entry to top positions was to be had in the

1960s. This new level of mobility hastened the assimilation of many Italian Americans in Las Vegas.

Mafia Rumors

Several Italian Americans opened small casinos in Las Vegas in the 1970s and 1980s, but, as the experiences of Mario Marino and Anthony Robone illustrate, having an Italian surname was not an asset for those seeking gaming licenses. Mario Marino sought a gaming operator's license after working for twenty-six years at the Sands, first as restaurant captain and then as catering manager. Marino was well known when The Boys were in town, and, like so many others prominent in the hotel business, he formed personal and professional relationships with men alleged to be leaders of organized crime. When he applied for a license in 1978 to own and operate the Winner's Circle, a small casino in Henderson, the Gaming Commission initially denied his application. Gaming Control Board members were troubled by reports that Marino, of Sicilian origins, was an associate of Carlos Marcello, the widely reputed head of the New Orleans Mafia. Fighting the allegations, Marino explained that he knew Marcello because their families lived in the same small town in Louisiana. He vehemently denied any business relationship with Marcello. The Nevada Gaming Commissioners were impressed by his arguments, and, contrary to the recommendations of the Gaming Control Board, they approved his license request.[17]

The Winner's Circle casino failed within six months, and Marino had to attend another licensing hearing when he tried to reopen with a new partner. Once again gaming authorities expressed concern about Marino's connections with Marcello and "undesirable types" in the New Orleans area. They were particularly troubled by outstanding loans made to Marino by an alleged crime associate of Marcello.[18] In January 1981 Marino's efforts to be relicensed were threatened by the publication of *The Last Mafioso,* in which former Mafia hitman Jimmy Fratianno claimed that Marino was a *caporegime* (a captain, a manager of several lower-level criminals) with Carlos Marcello's New Orleans crime family. Indignant, Marino promised to sue Ovid Demaris, the author. Once again the Gaming Control Board recommended against licensing Marino as 42 percent owner of the Winner's Circle. Marino retained the widely respected Frank Schreck as his attorney, and, once again, the Nevada Gaming Commission ignored the recommendations of the Control Board and granted Marino a license.[19] Marino's experience was not unique. He was neither the first nor the last individual seeking a license to convince the commission to disregard the recommendations of the board. The Winner's Circle fared no better than previously, so Marino sold his interest to a group of investors headed by Robert Levy.[20]

The Robone family had its own problems stemming from alleged Mob associations. Anthony Robone, currently a clerk in the Los Angeles office of the FBI, came to Las Vegas from southern California with his parents in 1978. Previously property managers, his parents initially pursued this business in Las Vegas. They soon invested in the Granada Inn, a small hotel and casino close to the Strip. The Robones and several Jewish-American partners then, in a bold move, entered into an agreement with contractor Ray Paglia to build the Continental on the corner of Flamingo Road and Paradise Road, almost two miles east of the Strip. After the construction was completed, the Robones formed a separate corporation to operate the casino. Anthony Robone, only twenty-five, was appointed to the challenging position of general manager of the casino in 1981. The Continental was one of many gaming properties trying to lure southern Californians, and the national recession that year made the competition even keener. Indeed, the Continental advertised rooms at only $20–$25 per night to guarantee business for the casino. By 1983 the economy had improved, and the Continental started operating in the black.

According to Anthony Robone, the Robone family and their partners came to "a parting of the ways" in 1985. Anthony's father sold his share in the Continental and contracted with the owners of the Ambassador Inn, a small hotel less than a block away, to operate that hotel and to lease and operate the casino. The ill will that accompanied the end of the Continental partnership caused some problems for the family. Anthony Robone recalled that allegations—he did not choose to speculate about the origins—regarding a connection between his family and organized crime figures delayed their gaining a license to operate the Ambassador Inn's casino. The allegations troubled his parents and him; the Robones were well aware that their Sicilian origins might have added to the rumors. Eventually, the Gaming Control Board determined that the allegations of Mob connections had no basis in fact, and the Robones received their licenses to operate the casino. Robone thought that the thorough background investigation the FBI conducted prior to hiring him as a clerk may have helped to resolve the charges.

Most Italian Americans interviewed for this book felt an Italian surname was at least a minor liability for a gaming license applicant even in the 1970s and 1980s. A few mentioned that they or their close associates had experienced unfair treatment from state or local licensing authorities; others said that the steady stream of newspaper articles and movies linking Italians with the Mafia must have negatively affected state gaming regulators.

Thirty years of skimming, hidden ownerships, and embarrassing revelations made Nevada officials sensitive about the state's image. This concern led state officials to overcompensate, resulting in the victimization of many innocent Italian Americans. The case of John Perazzo demonstrates the harm that could come to Italian Americans as a result of the widespread Mafia stereotype. In the early

1970s Perazzo opened a computerized credit-checking company, Royal Data, which, despite both Perazzo's skill and the rapid growth of gaming, failed because he could not get contracts with major hotels. Perazzo sued his competitors, Las Vegas IBM managers, charging that they tried to eliminate him as a competitor by deliberately spreading rumors that his company was financed by the Mafia. An IBM manager admitted that he and other employees regularly and loudly discussed John Perazzo's ties to the Mafia, even though they knew that their assertions had absolutely no basis in fact.[21] Many Italian Americans believe this kind of character assassination happened too often. The rumors, innuendos, and maladroit attempts at humor were not, and still are not, appreciated by most Italian Americans, especially those who are applying for gaming licenses.

Race and Sports Books

Many Italian Americans in Las Vegas have held prominent positions in race and sports betting, a specialized area of gaming. Although two Jewish Americans, Sammy Cohen, the owner of the Santa Anita, and Harry Gordon, the owner of Churchill Downs, were the premier figures in the race-book business in the 1960s and 1970s, men of Italian ancestry were well represented among the owners and managers of the smaller race books. Frank Sala's and Sonny Remolif's partial ownership of such establishments was mentioned in the previous chapter. Al and Millie Mangarelli owned the Rose Bowl, the first race book on the Strip. Another Italian American, John Buonantony, managed the Rose Bowl for many years, leaving eventually to manage the Santa Anita race book.

Italian Americans figured prominently in the rapid expansion of race- and sports-book business in the 1980s and 1990s. Vic Salerno, owner of Leroy's Horse and Sports Place, located across from the Golden Nugget on First Street, and two of his assistants (neither of Italian background) estimated that about a third of race- and sports-book managers and workers during the past two decades have been Italian Americans. Among the best known were Lou D'Amico, Lennie DelGenio, Vince Di Mare, Joe Lupo, Tony Paonessa, Tom Rinaldi, and Jimmy Vaccaro. They served respectively as director, or assistant director, of the race and sports books at Caesars Palace, Bally's, Excalibur, Sam's Town Gold River (in Laughlin), Sam's Town, the Santa Fe, and the Mirage. Other Italian Americans long prominent in the race- and sports-book industry were Jimmy Graciano, manager of the race book at Palace Station; Vinnie Magliulo, sports book manager at Caesars Palace; Dom Debaco, assistant race- and sports-book manager at the Tropicana: Ray Lenzi, who managed race and sports books at the Fremont, Sundance, and Stardust; and Gino Cappelletti, former manager of the Fremont's race and sports book and now simulcast coordinator for Nevada Disseminator Service. Salerno was quick to add that Italian Americans were equally well represented among the illegal Las Vegas bookmakers in recent decades.

Salerno has been the most innovative of the race- and sports-book owners or managers. He practiced dentistry in Marina del Rey, California, for several years before his love of sports and gambling lured him to Las Vegas. Salerno opened Leroy's in October 1978 with his father-in-law, and six months later became sole owner. Four years later he collaborated with two other Italian Americans—Andy Jerry, an energetic retiree who had been active in New York horse racing and political circles, and Ray Lenzi—to create a race- and sports-book operators' association. They and several other race- and sports-book operators established the Nevada Association of Race and Sportsbook Operators (NARASO) on December 8, 1982. Salerno was elected president at the initial meeting, which was attended by more than fifty representatives of twenty-three race and sports books. Andy Jerry was elected executive director, and Ray Lenzi became one of eight board members.[22]

The three were responsible for major contributions within NARASO, which lasted for more than four years. First, regular communications were established among race- and sports-book operators. Prior to the advent of NARASO, divisive rumors rather than direct communications were the norm. Second, standardized rules concerning such matters as the impact of electrical system failures during a basketball game or rain at a racetrack were put into effect. Finally, through cooperation and the standardization of rules, the association reduced the workload and frustration of gaming regulators, who had complained that, although race and sports books generated only 2 percent of state gaming revenue, they were consuming 40 percent of the regulators' time. Salerno also mentioned that the increased professionalism of the industry probably helped persuade Clark County Community College (now Community College of Southern Nevada) to offer courses on race- and sports-book management in its resort program.

A variety of internal disputes, including strong differences of opinion between Vic Salerno and Andy Jerry about NARASO's goals, as well as the unwillingness of other members to accept the presidency, led to the dissolution of NARASO early in 1987. Salerno expressed no disappointment about NARASO's demise, for in addition to seeing the association accomplish the aims mentioned above, he had become well acquainted with everybody of importance in the industry.

These connections were enormously advantageous to Salerno when he began a computerized statewide race- and sports-book franchise business. Initially, seventeen small casinos—mostly in Nevada border towns and rural areas—did business with him, and then larger properties, such as the Dunes and the Frontier, contracted with Salerno to operate their race and sports books through telephone and computer hookups. By the summer of 1991 Salerno was operating thirty race and sports books with an average monthly gross income of $1 million—equal to the average of Las Vegas's largest race and sports books.[23]

Any discussion of race and sports books must include mention of the businesses that provide information to the books and bettors. Here, too, Italian Americans, notably Chuck DiRocco and Jim Feist, have figured prominently. As a racetrack marketing executive who visited Las Vegas on business several times, DiRocco was always amazed at the lack of publications dealing exclusively with gambling. A journalism major in college, DiRocco considered starting such a publication. A long-term goal became an immediate necessity when DiRocco was fired from his marketing job following a well-publicized shoving match between him and the owner of a Buffalo racetrack. After moving to Las Vegas, DiRocco started *Sports Form* in 1975, a publication addressing all forms of sports betting. Circulation expanded, additional employees were hired, and DiRocco considered expanding readership to the ten major cities from which visiting gamblers originated.

In 1980 DiRocco's plans were interrupted by the challenge of bringing live racing (termed *dissemination* in Nevada) to the race and sports books. "It was," DiRocco later recalled, "a challenge I sometimes wished I had not taken." His first battle was getting licensed. Nevada's one licensed disseminator, Ken Swanson, disliked competition, having enjoyed a monopoly for almost twenty-five years. DiRocco overcame both Swanson's opposition and the skeptical gaming regulators, who, DiRocco remembers well, asked if he knew a long list of Italian-surnamed felons and alleged Mafiosi. DiRocco got his license, but his troubles continued. Three years later, with his disseminator business expanding, Caesars Palace, a corporate giant, also decided to broadcast live horse racing. DiRocco challenged Caesars, and a complex legal struggle ensued, ending later in 1983 with Caesars and DiRocco cooperating to provide live racing throughout Nevada. DiRocco prospered until Michael Gaughan charged him in a Nevada court with overbilling and double-billing hotel owners for his services. DiRocco filed an antitrust suit against Gaughan in federal court. Finally, after a long and costly legal battle, DiRocco agreed to close his dissemination service.[24]

Jim Feist began as a sports handicapper, but he had an entrepreneurial spirit, so he developed businesses dealing with all aspects of sports betting. He established a sports handicapping service when he arrived in Las Vegas from Florida in 1976. Sixteen years later he owned seven companies and employed more than two hundred people. Feist's operations include the Nevada Sports Schedule, the official schedule used by Nevada race and sports books; the Sports 'N Gaming newswire; and a telephone service bureau that provides sports information for clients on 1-800 or 1-900 numbers.[25] Feist, like Salerno, adapted well to the corporate culture, which has affected even sports betting, once the preserve of the corner bookie.

Entertainers

During the corporate era, Italian Americans continued to be in the forefront in Las Vegas entertainment as singers, comics, and musicians. They were as numerous among the ranks of showroom maitre d's as they had been in the 1950s. A review of the entertainment section of the two Las Vegas dailies in the 1970s and 1980s indicated that about 55 percent of the maitre d's were of Italian background. Prior to the advent of reserved showroom seating (first instituted when the Mirage opened its showroom in 1990), the maitre d's position was powerful and extremely lucrative because patrons commonly paid $5 to $25, or more, for choice showroom seats. The ability of Italian Americans to gain so many lucrative positions reflected their substantial involvement in the nightclub and illegal gambling houses of Eastern cities. The owners of the East Coast enterprises, usually of either Italian or Jewish background, were well represented among the early Strip investors. When they came to Las Vegas they relied on experienced and trustworthy men they had brought from the East to run the showrooms.

Las Vegas Sun columnist Joe Delaney recalled that virtually all the outstanding Italian-American entertainers of the 1960s continued to perform in Las Vegas in the 1970s and later. They were joined by, among others, Liberace, Liza Minnelli, and Frankie Valle. One week Tony Bennett headlined at the Sahara; another week Frank Sinatra drew capacity crowds at Circus Maximus in Caesars Palace; Liza Minnelli "took the Riviera Room by storm"; perhaps Louie Prima, undisputed king of the lounge performers, was in his thirteenth week at the Tropicana's Blue Room; and the next week Connie Stevens appeared at the Flamingo's main showroom. During the mid-1970s Dondino joined fellow Italian Americans Freddie Bell and Sonny King as a major lounge attraction.[26]

Delaney remembered some other remarkably talented conductors and musicians who contributed to Las Vegas's reputation as the Entertainment Capital of the World during the corporate era. Joe Guercio conducted the Hilton's orchestra during Elvis Presley's many engagements during the 1970s. Frank Leone conducted for Paul Anka and other headliners at the Flamingo. Russ Martino conducted at several Strip hotels, most recently the Riviera. Vince Falcone played piano at Caesars Palace, led bands for some of Frank Sinatra's many Las Vegas appearances, and then served as music director for Pia Zadora (who is not of Italian background). Delaney also mentioned that Ennio Volognini, a truly fine cellist, always played when Tony Bennett performed. Gus Mancuso, whom Delaney regarded as the best all-around musician (he once played all the instruments for a special Christmas album), continued to play at Strip hotels throughout the 1970s and 1980s. Delaney agreed with Pete Barbuti that Carl Fontana, the world's best trumpet player, and Phil Raffaele, a great jazz pianist, also added to the splendor of the entertainment scene in Las Vegas. Frank Gagliardi emphasized that Las

Vegas continues to attract talented conductors and musicians. He provided as an example Don Menza, a world-famous saxophonist who often performed in Las Vegas. Menza moved to Las Vegas from southern California in 1988, played at the Four Queens (a Downtown hotel noted for its jazz performances), and also began teaching at the University of Nevada, Las Vegas (UNLV).

Italian-American performers recognized that they owed something to the Las Vegas community and often contributed their time and talents to civic fund-raising. Several recent and current officers of the Italian American Club identified Frank Sinatra as a major contributor to its campaigns for providing Christmas gifts to needy children. Sinatra sought no publicity for his contributions. Eugene Moehring, a UNLV history professor, informed the author that Sinatra did two shows in 1978 and 1979 at the Aladdin Hotel's Theater for the Performing Arts to raise money for Southern Nevada's only university. Joe Delaney mentioned that Sinatra and other Italian-American entertainers performed at benefits for St. Jude's Ranch for Children. As an example of Sinatra's support for the cultural development of Las Vegas, Delaney noted that one year in the 1970s Sinatra donated $17,000 to help Channel 10, Southern Nevada's Public Broadcasting Service affiliate, reach its $100,000 goal. Delaney felt strongly, though, that Sinatra's charitable instincts were too often overshadowed by his well-publicized physical altercations with Sands and Caesars gaming executives and his penchant for conflict with Nevada gaming regulators in the early 1960s.

Peter Anthony and Pete Barbuti affirmed that the majority of Italian-American performers in Las Vegas were very generous. Anthony said that he has been known as "the king of the benefits," a title that helped him gain a 1986 B'nai B'rith Man of the Year award. Barbuti recalled that he participated in several fund-raisers for parishes with which Fr. Benjamin Franzirelli was associated, but he, too, has lost track of the many charities to which he has contributed his talent. Only a week before my August 1991 interview with him, he and Carl Fontana had performed at a fund-raiser for music scholarships at CCSN.

Of course, to many male visitors, Las Vegas entertainment means more than performances by well-known singers and comedians, stage spectaculars, or lounge shows. They would prefer to get closer to the city's beautiful women than a front-row seat at a Strip showroom. Often unaware that Clark County is one of several Nevada counties where prostitution is illegal, many male tourists find their sexual appetites stimulated by the "entertainment guides" found on every Downtown and Strip corner. These guides provide information on the particular talents of "entertainers" (the usual term) who are available on call; topless and totally nude bars; adults-only bookstores and theaters; as well as the increasingly controversial sex tease clubs, where a typical patron spending $500 to $600 can get a bottle of grape juice—and nothing else. In more recent issues of the Las Vegas telephone directory, forty to fifty pages of entertainment ads reinforce the image that anything goes in Las Vegas.

A 1991 review of the names of the owners of these four types of sexually oriented businesses (those licensed by Las Vegas or Clark County authorities) indicates that Italian Americans have not dominated this area of Las Vegas entertainment. Indeed, the percentage of owners of sexually oriented businesses who are Italian Americans is just over the percentage of Italian Americans in the Las Vegas population. Ralph Petillo, a septuagenarian who over the past twenty-seven years owned and managed a series of publications that have provided visitors with information on hotel entertainment, sports betting, and sexually oriented businesses, confirmed this conclusion in a 1991 interview. He stressed that the owners and managers of sexually oriented businesses have been ethnically diverse. (He also mentioned that although his publication *After Dark* had the largest circulation of the available guides, many of his competitors were not of Italian background.)

Food and Beverage

Italian—a few hearing this term initially think of art or music, but almost everyone quickly associates the word with food. So it is no surprise that Italian Americans owned and operated a great many restaurants, including many of Las Vegas's most notable, during the corporate era. One of the best known has been the Bootlegger, which Lorraine Perri Hunt and her second husband, Blackie Hunt, opened in 1972. Their original goal was to open a small bar and restaurant to appeal primarily to entertainers seeking a comfortable place to relax after performances. Lorraine and Blackie were overwhelmed by the crowd on opening night; a long line of hungry people waited outside for the chance to enjoy good Italian food. Lorraine said she quickly engaged the services of her mother, Maria, and very soon the original goal was forgotten as more and more Italian specialties were added to the menu and the facilities were expanded.

Since the 1960s Italian restaurants have proliferated throughout the rapidly growing Las Vegas area. Of course, some have failed, and others are undistinguished. Yet so many Italian eating establishments are generally regarded as excellent that it is impossible to mention them all here. Interestingly, several of the most successful newcomers—Café Chiasso, Pasta Mia, Café Milano, Ferraro's, Cipriani, Vincenzo's, and the Sicilian Café—were owned and operated by Italian-born chefs in the early 1990s. In addition, three Italian-born chefs worked at the Italian American Club in the 1980s and early 1990s.

Certainly the dean of Italian-born chefs is Battista Locatelli. Born and raised in Bergamo, Italy, Locatelli came to California in 1949. During the next twenty years he worked as a farm laborer, miner, slaughterhouse butcher, waiter, and, finally as an oil truck driver before coming to Las Vegas in the hope of pursuing a singing career. Unable to find employment in any of the Las Vegas stage spectaculars or lounges, he opened a small restaurant, Battista's Hole in the Wall, on Flamingo Road about a hundred yards east of the Strip, at the same time that Las Vegas financier Kirk Kerkorian decided to build a huge resort, the MGM Grand Hotel, directly across Flamingo Road. Locatelli's restaurant quickly gained a reputation for tasty Italian dishes. The opening of the MGM Grand in 1973 ensured a steady stream of customers, so Locatelli added on to the restaurant and upgraded the decor. In a 1992 interview, Locatelli estimated that 75 to 80 percent of his large clientele (he sometimes serves nine hundred meals on a Saturday evening) are tourists.

In a 1991 interview Giovanni Vanchieri, owner of Cafés Milano and Chiasso, said that Italians are not immune to failure in the restaurant business, and several Italians with restaurant experience in Los Angeles had been unsuccessful in Las Vegas, because they moved too quickly and did not study their market thoroughly.

Other Italian-born entrepreneurs have recently opened Italian food establishments—Siena Deli, east of the Strip, and Avanti Deli to the west. They must compete with delicatessens owned by the Mauro and Montesano families. The Mauros migrated to Las Vegas from Canada and opened Teresa's Deli near the Strip in 1972; the Montesanos came from New York and opened their Italian food shop about four miles west of the Strip in 1992. Giovanni Parente, an Italian-born assistant maitre d' at the Dunes showroom since 1980, started Italcream to produce and distribute Italian ice cream, sherbet, and desserts. At first he found local buyers hesitant, but he educated them regarding the superior quality of his product, and by the early 1990s his business had grown to the point that many of his fellow Italians were ordering *gelato* and *sorbetto*.

Perhaps the best way for a Las Vegan to sample a variety of Italian food has been to attend the San Gennaro Feast, held in late August every year since 1984. This southern Italian festival (Gennaro is the patron saint of Naples) was established in Las Vegas by Vincent "Jimmy Dee" Palmisano, initially in cooperation with the Italian American Club. Several Las Vegas Italian restaurants, delicatessens, and pizza shops are represented at the Festival, which runs from late August through the second week of September each year. Locals and visitors can sample calzone, stromboli, sausage rolls, and a host of other Italian foods. The San Gennaro Feast and the annual Columbus Day Parade, begun in 1988, are the two celebrations Las Vegans associate with Italian Americans.

Palmisano recalled that several problems that existed when the first feast was held at the Club convinced him to hold subsequent feasts at various Strip hotels. Palmisano, who came to Las Vegas with a lot of experience running festivals in other parts of the country, expressed great pride in the success of his Las Vegas effort, particularly because the money the event brought in aided a local charity, the Help Them Walk Again Foundation. In a 1990 interview he said that the Feast drew many tourists, including groups of Italian Americans from southern California, Arizona, and the East, who plan their Las Vegas vacations to coincide with the event.

Palmisano has not escaped controversy. *Review-Journal* columnist John Smith reported in the summer of 1992 that Palmisano had a criminal record going back fifty years, including convictions for counterfeiting, attempted grand larceny, fraud, and extortion. Smith also reported that Palmisano is listed by the U.S. Senate Permanent Subcommittee on Investigations as a member of New York's Gambino crime family. Smith's investigation of Palmisano was prompted by charges from three Las Vegas charities, including the Help Them Walk Again Foundation, that Palmisano had overstated the charitable aspect of the festival and used the charities' nonprofit status to get a temporary liquor license. Officials of other local charities stated that no misrepresentation had occurred.[27]

Waste Disposal and Construction

Italian Americans were most active in the rapid physical development of Las Vegas during the corporate era. Several of the contractors mentioned in the preceding chapter, most notably the Isolas, the Tibertis, and John DeBiase, expanded their businesses, and in some cases their sons formed companies of their own. For instance, the Isolas built the nation's largest privately operated transfer station in North Las Vegas. The $8.5 million facility, constructed by Tiberti Construction Company, was financed by the sale of pollution bonds issued by the City of North Las Vegas. In recent years Tom Isola, the college-educated vice president of Silver State Disposal, has focused on the development of technologies and facilities to keep pace with increasing national concerns about both proper hazardous waste disposal and the recycling of paper, aluminum cans, and glass bottles. In 1989 Tom Isola developed Environmental Technologies of Nevada, Inc., to safely haul and dispose of liquid and solid hazardous waste, medical wastes, and asbestos. In 1991 the Isolas opened a recycling facility built by Mike Fauci and began collecting recyclable wastes throughout the county. In a 1990 interview Tom Isola was very enthusiastic about his company's capacity to simplify hazardous waste disposal and promote recycling in the areas of biotechnology and supercritical heating. He was optimistic that soon bacteria will be created to break down the hydrocarbons of petroleum products, and that a process will be developed to extract metal from water.

Anthony Marnell Jr.'s career provides a good example of both the generational continuity in Las Vegas–area Italian-American construction businesses and the substantial impact of these businesses on Las Vegas's development as a major city in the American Southwest. Anthony Marnell Sr. recounted that after his son earned a degree in architecture from the University of Southern California, he returned to Nevada and worked for several different companies, including Carrao Construction Company, which had built hotels in the Reno and Lake Tahoe areas. The younger Marnell and Lud Carrao eventually formed a partnership with the goal of becoming the gaming industry's foremost builder. Following the successful completion of their first major project, the Maxim, a medium-sized hotel on Flamingo Road less than a block from the Strip, they built Caesars in Atlantic City, New Jersey, and played leading roles in the construction of several Las Vegas properties, most notably Steve Wynn's Mirage. Marnell and Carrao also built and then operated the Rio, a suites-only hotel and casino on Flamingo Road, less than a mile west of the Strip, which opened in January of 1990. The recession of 1990–91 reduced the Rio's anticipated revenues and led Marnell and Carrao to postpone plans to build another off-Strip casino. When the economy picked up in 1993, Marnell and Carrao began a major expansion of the Rio.

Mike Fauci's career also illustrates the continuity of the family business. His Sicilian-born father, Charles Fauci, moved from New York to southern California in 1953, where he established a small construction company. In 1957, at age fifty, Charles came to Las Vegas, built some custom homes, and then retired.[28] Uncertain at first about whether he wanted to pursue a career in construction, his son Mike established a pool-cleaning service in the 1960s. Feeling more confident a few years later, he started a small commercial construction company that grew rapidly in the 1970s and 1980s.

Mike Fauci decided in 1988 to enter gaming because, like many others, he recognized the potential of rapidly growing northwest Las Vegas. He tried to buy land for a hotel/casino near Route 95, close to a new upscale residential subdivision (not far from where the Santa Fe Hotel was later built), but local residents and their elected representatives stopped him. Undaunted, he obtained an option to purchase land at the corner of Rancho Drive and Carey Avenue—still in the northwest but within the jurisdiction of the City of North Las Vegas. Nearby homeowners again protested his plans to build the Big Horn Hotel and Casino, but the North Las Vegas mayor and city council, anxious to see their city get its first hotel, approved the plan in 1989.[29] Fauci acknowledged that getting the purchase option for the land and approval for the Big Horn plans were the easy tasks; he was unable to borrow money from local lenders, so he had to give up the purchase option. Fauci was a few years too early with his plans—a hotel opened in late 1994 next to the area where Fauci had hoped to build the Big Horn.

Tony Tegano's change of careers illustrates, as does Sam Iacovetto's, the opportunities Las Vegas has provided for individuals with entrepreneurial spirit, some capital, modest expertise, and a willingness to take a chance. The gaming industry drew Iacovetto and Tegano to Las Vegas and then provided them with the capital to start new businesses. Tegano, raised in Brooklyn, New York, had several relatives who were prominent gamblers in Steubenville, Ohio. On moving to Las Vegas in 1959 he took a "break-in" job at the Nevada Club, a small Downtown casino located in the block now occupied by the Golden Nugget. He soon moved to the Canino brothers' Silver Slipper, and then to the Sans Souci (later renamed the Castaways), a Strip property that he claimed was owned by Italian Americans. When the San Souci failed, he continued to deal at the Mint and then went to the Dunes in late 1961. The Dunes, with its packed showrooms, eighteen-hole golf course, and nearly five hundred rooms was a moneymaker in the 1960s and 1970s.[30]

After dealing at the Dunes for five years, Tegano was promoted to pit boss, a position he held until he left in 1972. Tegano had made a good move by entering the swimming pool construction business a year earlier. Las Vegas was one of the fastest-growing metropolitan areas in the United States, and a pool was a virtual necessity for every homeowner who could afford one. In addition, it was rare that an apartment complex did not provide at least one pool for its tenants. So within a few years of starting the business, Tegano's company, Tango Pools, had become the leading commercial and residential pool construction company in Southern Nevada, employing more than sixty employees in 1991. Tango Pools works closely with R. V. Jones Company, the foremost developer of apartment complexes, and with most of the major developers of detached homes. Although most of the major hotels already had pools before 1971, in 1990 Tango Pools built the pool for the Stardust's new thirty-two-story tower, and the pools at the Edgewater in Laughlin and the Stagecoach in rural Beatty, Nevada.[31]

The remarkable population growth of the greater Las Vegas area has attracted scores of experienced contractors since the end of World War II, and Italian Americans have been well represented among them. Richard Rizzo, president of the Phoenix-based Mardian Construction Company (a subsidiary of the Perini Corporation), brought his company to Nevada in the late 1970s, building the America West Airlines terminal at McCarran International Airport as well as a dog racetrack in Henderson. Mardian quickly became the major competitor of Marcor Development Company (founded by Marnell and Corrao), vying for Las Vegas hotel construction. Mardian has built more than eight thousand hotel rooms since 1984; working on the Tropicana, Holiday Inn, and Flamingo expansions in Las Vegas as well as the Flamingo expansion in Laughlin and phase 2 of Harrah's Del Rio, also in Laughlin, are among its most important achievements.[32] In late April 1992 Mardian was awarded the construction contract for Circus Circus Enterprises' new Luxor resort, next to the Excalibur on the Strip.

Las Vegas's burgeoning population brought many types of developers and contractors—both large and small. Larry Canarelli, Perry DiLoreto, and the Catello brothers are good examples of Italian Americans who built large companies. In

1985 Canarelli left a top position with Metropolitan Development to found American West Development, which has since built more than 2,500 homes in the Las Vegas area. Perry DiLoreto, who grew up in the San Francisco Bay Area, started his home construction business there and then expanded into northern Nevada. Successful in residential and commercial construction in the Reno/Sparks area, in 1986 he brought DiLoreto Construction to Las Vegas and began building homes in the southeast and northwest sections of the city.[33]

Four brothers from the San Francisco Bay Area who learned the tile and marble trade from their father contributed to the development of Las Vegas. Chuck Catello came to Las Vegas in the late 1960s, a period when construction was stagnant. Although he obtained a license to do tile work, at first he concentrated on managing a bar he had bought. A younger brother, Joe, disgusted with the traffic and long commute characteristic of the Bay Area, moved to Las Vegas with his family in 1968 and began working for Pardee Construction, which was building tract homes east of the Strip. Soon Joe was anxious to start his own business, so he used Chuck's license and won contracts to work on apartment houses, custom homes, and tract home developments. He was shortly joined by Chuck, who then sold the bar, and another brother, Ben, who had been working in California.

In 1971, when Las Vegas gaming entrepreneur Kirk Kerkorian announced plans to build a first-class hotel (the MGM Grand) on the Strip, Chuck and Joe saw an opportunity to make the Catello name synonymous with quality. They called their brother Carmine for assistance and joined with another Las Vegas tile and marble company to bid for the extensive MGM Grand contract. Larger companies had bid for the project, so the Catellos were quite pleasantly surprised to win the $1.5 million job. Joe Catello said that they worked hard, established an excellent name for the Catello family, but because they had presented a low bid, they realized very little profit in their first contract with a Strip hotel. Their reputations established, Carmine and Joe (Chuck and Ben eventually left Las Vegas) were sought by Las Vegas builders—including Marcor, Mardian, Sierra, and Tiberti—for tile and marble work. Joe acknowledged that Italian Americans were prominent among the owners and executives of these four construction companies, but he stressed that ethnic affiliation played no role in the business relationships. The Catellos are particularly proud of the six hundred suite bathtubs they installed in the Fantasy Towers at Caesars Palace; they have also worked in most Downtown and Strip hotels. Among their numerous nongaming contracts have been the Greystone Building, Rose de Lima Hospital, and three Las Vegas shopping malls— Boulevard, Fashion Show, and Meadows—built in the late 1960s and 1970s.

The Catellos' excellent reputation has helped them get contracts outside Las Vegas. They did the original tile and marble work on Caesars at Lake Tahoe and the Phoenician Hotel in Scottsdale, Arizona, and most of the tile and marble work at several Atlantic City hotels. Joe Catello said in a 1991 interview that although Catello Tile and Marble reached a peak with more than four hundred employees in 1990, the Catellos still have as much work now as they could ever desire.

Angelo Cassaro and Gary Cavaretta are excellent examples of contractors who started small and expanded, albeit not as rapidly as did the Catellos. Both men grew up in an Italian neighborhood in Buffalo and have remained friends ever since. Like many other Italian Americans, they followed their fathers into the building trades. In the mid-1970s Buffalo's economy was stagnant, and both Angelo and Gary had heard from friends and relatives who had visited Las Vegas about the area's rapid expansion. Indeed, Cavaretta had cousins who were regular performers at Circus Circus, a Strip casino featuring daily circus acts. Gary and his brother Michael came to Las Vegas in 1977 and started Brothers Plumbing Company. The business grew during the next five years, slowed during the recession of 1982–83, and then picked up again. More recently Gary has formed a general contracting firm, Cavaretta Developing and Investments. In a 1990 interview he said of both companies, "I have more business than I can handle."

In 1979 Cassaro joined Cavaretta in Las Vegas, initially hoping to get work as a plumber. He quickly learned that there were no opportunities for someone with a "traveling" union card. Local union officials helped local men, not out-of-staters, get Las Vegas construction jobs. Determined to find a niche in Las Vegas's expanding economy, Cassaro started A A Cassaro Plumbing. He and his brother Joe, who has supervised the plumbing business in recent years, were successful. Indeed, in 1984 Angelo Cassaro joined with another Upstate New York "refugee," Nick Montana, and established Multi-Structure Development to build various residential projects, including duplexes and fourplexes in North Las Vegas, as well as apartments and condominiums throughout the Las Vegas Valley. Ten years after coming to Las Vegas, Cassaro was elected president of the Plumbers and Mechanical Contractors Association, a group of almost eighteen hundred non-union members from forty-five different companies.[34] Cassaro and Cavaretta have remained close friends, and Cavaretta was elected in 1991 to the executive board of the Plumbers and Mechanical Contractors Association.

Julio Lucchesi was impressed by both the openness of Las Vegas society and the opportunities for professional achievement. Like the Catellos, he was born and raised in the San Francisco Bay Area. After pursuing a career as an architect in the Los Angeles area, he and a partner came to Las Vegas in 1950 to design a building at the Desert Inn. Although their plans were not used, Julio liked Las Vegas and decided to continue his career "in a town where you could get to know everyone, and business deals were made often on the basis of a handshake." He and his partner split in the mid-1950s, but Lucchesi continued his work, sometimes with other architects and sometimes on his own. He worked mostly on small commercial projects or residences, taking on some casino remodeling or expansion jobs, most notably the Horseshoe Downtown and Thunderbird on the

Strip. In 1972, having seen Las Vegas grow rapidly in the 1950s and 1960s, Lucchesi decided to develop an architectural program at the University of Nevada, Las Vegas (UNLV). He and two other local architects began lobbying UNLV administrators, University of Nevada Board of Regents members, and state legislators. Lucchesi remembered that progress was agonizingly slow because UNLV, overshadowed at that time by the University of Nevada in Reno, had many higher priorities. By the late 1970s the administrators and most elected officials from the Las Vegas area felt that the development of an architecture program was timely.

Lucchesi's son Ray, who had earned a degree in architecture from Arizona State University, was a prime mover in the establishment of UNLV's architecture program. In 1981 he and two other local architects volunteered to teach some architecture courses the UNLV administrators cautiously billed as experimental. Registration for each lecture class exceeded a hundred students, and almost seventy attended the studio class. The overwhelming response shocked even optimists such as Ray. UNLV President Leonard Goodall soon authorized a half-time architecture courses coordinator, and Ray was appointed coordinator in the fall semester of 1982. "Everything was on a shoestring," Ray recalled in a 1991 interview. "The classrooms were crammed, students were doubled up on twenty-year-old drafting tables, and students were turned away from courses." Ray admitted that he cherished the experience. He wrote a four-year degree program, later approved by the University of Nevada Board of Regents, and then got a commitment in June 1984 from UNLV's recently appointed president, Robert Maxson, to support the establishment of an accredited architecture program. Progress was rapid. Full-time faculty were hired, and Hugh Burgess, formerly dean of Arizona State University's School of Architecture, was appointed head of UNLV's fledgling program. An assistant professor at the school in 1992, Ray spoke with great enthusiasm about the future of architecture at UNLV, predicting accreditation for a separate College of Architecture by 1994 and the creation of a doctoral program in urban planning by 1995. (The latter prediction was too optimistic.)

While Ray was helping to build an architecture program at UNLV, he was also trying to expand the influence and visibility of Lucchesi and Associates (he and Julio are partners). He was well aware that Las Vegas was not a typical city; indeed, gaming industry leaders had seldom expressed concerns about the development of aesthetically pleasing or harmonious buildings. "Put it up fast and start making your buck" was the way Ray described their attitude. Similarly, residential developments had been poorly planned until the 1980s. Nonetheless, confident that as Las Vegas matured consumers would demand better architecture, Ray decided to offer a level of design not common to Las Vegas and to focus on high-visibility public projects. He, Julio, and their small staff have done the architectural planning for the Veterans Cemetery in Boulder City, phase 2 of CCSN's Health Services Center in western Las Vegas, a women's prison near Nellis Air

Force Base, and the State of Nevada office building, which was constructed across from Cashman Field, not far from Downtown.

Understandably, Ray was particularly pleased at the time of the interview that his firm was on the shortlist of architects being considered for planning UNLV's architecture building. Lucchesi and Associates gained the much sought after contract in a bitterly contested 5–4 vote in early 1992, but Ray and Julio had little cause for joy. Scarcely a week passed that the *Las Vegas Review-Journal* reporters did not write about charges and countercharges alleging unethical behavior on the part of Lucchesi, Dean Hugh Burgess (who did not vote for the Lucchesi proposal), and the Nevada Public Works Board executive secretary, Robert Ferrari. Several of Lucchesi's UNLV faculty colleagues were also publicly critical of the contract award. In July 1992 the Nevada Ethics Commission ruled unanimously that Lucchesi and two other architects who were also UNLV faculty members should not have bid on the design contract. A Nevada court later sustained the ruling of the Ethics Commission.

The Lucchesis' dispute with the system reflects the growing pains that have been experienced in many areas of Nevada owing to the rapid growth in population and economic diversification. Many of the newcomers to Nevada came from states where policies about matters such as the awarding of state contracts were more formalized than in Nevada. Nevada had been a state where, until this decade, few questions were asked about conflicts of interest. Indeed, only in 1991 did the Nevada legislature empower the Ethics Commission to deal with issues such as faculty members bidding for a contract at the public institution where they were employed. Not until 1992 did the editorial staff of the *Las Vegas Review-Journal* raise questions about the propriety of schoolteachers and University and Community College System of Nevada professors serving in the legislature, which has substantial discretion over the budgets of the seventeen county school districts, the two universities, and the four community colleges.

Las Vegas's Italian-American contracting entrepreneurs over the last twenty-five years have had lives far different from those of the millions of Italian men who came to the United States between 1880 and 1920 seeking work as laborers in construction projects in the East or factories and mines from Pennsylvania to California. Many of the earlier settlers, almost 50 percent, returned to Italy after encountering hardship, unemployment, and discrimination. Others endured, hoping their children would do better, but few of the early immigrants prospered. Often their children continued as skilled tradesmen, the most able and energetic forming contracting companies and sometimes becoming leaders in their communities and beyond.[35] Las Vegas, for decades one of the fastest-growing metropolitan areas in North America, attracted many Italian-American contractors. They prospered, and Las Vegas is a bigger and better city because of their skill and determination.

Real Estate and Banking

As today's builder is tomorrow's developer, it is not surprising that, like William Peccole, many later Italian Americans began planning homes and commercial centers for the desert area known as Las Vegas. Frank Coniglio was foremost among them. He came to Las Vegas from Los Angeles in 1969 as a franchise director for a restaurant chain. When the chain failed, Coniglio, seeing the potential of the relatively barren Las Vegas area, took a job developing commercial property for Pardee-Phillips Company. In 1972 he started the Real Corporation. Irwin Molasky, a Jewish-American business associate of Moe Dalitz and a prominent Las Vegas commercial developer, was Coniglio's first client.[36] Coniglio handled Molasky's leasing of the Valley Bank Plaza in the Downtown area, the Park Sahara commercial complex east of the Strip, and several medical/professional complexes, as well as Molasky's retail center in La Costa, California. Coniglio's association with Molasky proved quite profitable, and Coniglio rapidly expanded his business. Real Corporation is now the largest Las Vegas–based real estate development company, managing more than two million square feet of retail space and developing another one million.

Bankers provide the lifeblood for architects, contractors, and real estate developers, and Italian Americans such as Reno Fruzza, Ernie Martinelli, Dan Rotunno, and Lewis Capurro are among Las Vegas's leading bankers of the past twenty-five years. Fruzza was a senior vice president with First National Bank of Nevada (FNBN) and continued in that position when FNBN became First Interstate Bank (FIB) in the late 1970s. Widely known and respected throughout Southern Nevada, he concentrated on developing new business. When he reached his mid-sixties Fruzza retired from FIB, and then in 1985 he took a vice presidency at Security Bank of Nevada. When Security Bank merged with Valley Bank in January 1987, Fruzza was appointed senior vice president for business development. He retired again in 1990, though he made it clear that he might again reenter banking.

Ernie Martinelli, Fruzza's boss at FNBN, FIB, and Security Bank, has been Nevada's most prominent Italian-American banker for the past twenty-five years. He served as president of the Bank of Nevada in Reno, and then as president of FNBN when that bank merged with the Bank of Nevada. When FNBN became FIB, Martinelli was made vice chairman of the board of directors. Soon thereafter, he moved to Las Vegas, where he enjoyed the same reputation for excellence that he had established in Reno. Upon retiring in 1983 because of policy disagreements with the FIB board of directors, he returned to Reno and almost immediately was appointed chairman of the board and chief executive officer of the newly established Security Bank of Nevada. In his talks with the author, Martinelli emphasized that over the four years that he was at Security Bank he spent a good deal of time at its Las Vegas branches. When that institution and Valley Bank merged in 1987, Martinelli became vice chairman of the board of directors and was chosen to run the northern Nevada operations. He retained this position when the new entity merged with the Bank of America in 1992.

Although he was a bit embarrassed by Fruzza's and Rotunno's praise of him, Martinelli agreed that he had contributed to Las Vegas's growth in his capacity as a banking executive and a member of the Nevada Development Authority, a primarily private organization committed to enlarging and diversifying the Southern Nevada economy. Stressing his team concept of management, Martinelli acknowledged that Joe Blasko, developer of the exclusive Spanish Trails homes and condominiums, had referred to him as the father of Spanish Trails because Martinelli had granted him an initial loan for the project. Martinelli also expressed, albeit with some reluctance, pride in the work he had done with the Nevada Development Authority. Martinelli served as vice chair of its executive committee, the group that actively recruited new business for the Las Vegas area. As chief executive officer of Security Bank, Nevada's largest lending institution until 1992, Martinelli was often the liaison with the chief executive officers of firms considering expansion or relocation in Southern Nevada. Once again, stressing that no single individual is ever responsible for an area's economic development, he did mention that he had been instrumental in persuading candy magnate Forrest Mars to build the Ethel M Chocolate factory in Henderson.

Dan Rotunno's career provides a good example of how talented Las Vegans could progress in the field of banking. Coming from Phoenix in 1967 to teach in the Clark County School District, he enjoyed his junior-high-school students but found a teacher's pay insufficient. His experience with a Phoenix lending institution helped him get a job with Valley Bank in the installment loan department. Valley Bank (formerly the Bank of Las Vegas) was growing, and Rotunno was soon promoted to manager of the Henderson office and then, in late 1973, the new Charleston Heights office. Rotunno expressed pride in his achievements, particularly at the Charleston Heights office, where bank assets increased from $12.5 million to $60 million during his seven-and-a-half-year tenure. In 1981 he left the Charleston Heights office to open a new West Sahara branch, and there he was promoted to senior vice president.

Rotunno explained that although he enjoyed everything about his job at Valley Bank, he could not reject the 25 percent salary increase offered by the directors of the newly formed Continental National Bank in October 1983. Expressing no regrets about this move, he asserted that his knowledge of the Las Vegas business community was crucial to Continental's growth. He remained at that institution for nearly four years before returning to Valley Bank.

The Las Vegas boom attracted several Italian-American banking professionals from the Reno area. Insurance executive Lewis Capurro was, like Ernie Martinelli, part of the large and well-established Italian-American community in the Reno area. Many Italian Americans, almost all of northern Italian ancestry, had entered banking in Reno, and by the 1960s a number of them owned or managed most of the area's banks.[37] In response to some consolidation in banking, several prominent Italian-American businessmen and professionals led by Lewis Capurro joined with Paul Laiolo, who had served for several years as executive vice president at Nevada Bank of Commerce, in establishing Pioneer Citizens Bank of Nevada (PCBN). They targeted Reno-area Italian Americans as both shareholders and service users. Operating conservatively, but successfully, the group opened a Las Vegas branch in 1972. Capurro, who has remained chairman of the board, tried to recruit Reno Fruzza to manage the Las Vegas branch, but he could not provide a compensation package attractive enough to lure Fruzza from FNBN.[38] PCBN had a nongaming orientation, so it did not lend to Las Vegas gamers, which might seem surprising given the number of Italian Americans involved in the gaming industry. However, while the overwhelming majority of Las Vegas–area Italian Americans were of southern Italian and Sicilian background, Capurro and his associates were of northern Italian ancestry. The former had considerable experience in gaming, while those few among the latter who did get involved in gaming, such as members of the Carano and Corrao families, had already established themselves in other businesses. Interestingly, the only gaming loans that Pioneer Bank made were to Italian Americans—the Caranos and Carraos, who needed to fund their Eldorado expansion in Reno. As one of Lewis Capurro's sons, Randy, observed, PCBN really contributed to Las Vegas, despite the bank's small reserves and its nongaming orientation. "It was an intermediate lender filling a need for small business and real estate projects," explained the younger Capurro. "We lent primarily to small businesses with solid track records. Our projects are dwarfed by the developments financed by Valley, FIB, and Security Pacific but are an important part of Las Vegas."

The Professionals

During the corporate era, more Italian Americans entered the professions in Las Vegas than in the earlier years. Among the substantial numbers of Italian Americans who have arrived in Las Vegas during the past twenty-five years have been numerous attorneys and physicians. By the 1980s Italian Americans were practicing in the Las Vegas area in all the legal and medical specialties. Dominic Gentile, a leader in the Las Vegas Italian-American community, was the best known attorney in the late 1980s. Born and raised in Chicago, Gentile came to Las Vegas from Houston in 1979 after spending more than a decade doing mostly criminal defense work and almost eighteen months serving as associate dean of the National College for Criminal Defense Lawyers and Public Defenders at the University of Houston's Bates College of Law.

Controversy often surrounds effective criminal defense attorneys, and Gentile proved no exception. Gentile recalled that upon his arrival there were rumors that "the Mafia leadership" had become dissatisfied with well-known Mob attorney Oscar Goodman and expected Gentile to take over the defense of Mafia representatives in Las Vegas. Gentile did not let these bizarre stories bother him. He quickly set about establishing a reputation as an excellent courtroom attorney. Gentile did not challenge Goodman's role; indeed, the two defense attorneys occasionally cooperated. One such endeavor placed Gentile in controversy once again. Tony Spilotro, widely reported to represent the Chicago Mob in Las Vegas, contacted Goodman when IRS agents searched his home one Sunday. Goodman, who was out of town defending an alleged organized crime figure, telephoned Gentile to ask him to advise Spilotro. Gentile said that in the course of his rather frank exchange of views with the IRS agents, he cast aspersions on the masculinity of one of them, suggesting that he was unable to father a child. Two days later *Review-Journal* staff writer Diane Russell wrote, "Las Vegas attorney Dominic Gentile threatened an IRS agent during a Sunday raid on the home of reputed mobster Anthony Spilotro, the agent claimed Monday." The writer implied that Gentile threatened the agent's children, though Russell did quote Gentile as saying, "I did not intimidate the man and I think he is out of line for making such an accusation."[39]

Even though Gentile seldom represented alleged Mafia figures, his successful defense of other notable people has kept him in the limelight.[40] Gentile has a penchant for publicity and is willing to fight for a principle, as he showed in the aftermath of receiving a private reprimand (the mildest form of punishment) from the Board of Governors of the Nevada Bar Association in 1991. Gentile came under fire because following a jury's decision that his client was not guilty, Gentile suggested publicly that he knew the undercover police officer who should have been prosecuted in the case. Gentile believed that the Board of Governors' decision had abridged his First Amendment rights. His costly and time-consuming court battle to void the punishment gained him (and his law firm, Gentile, Porter and Kelesis) much local, and eventually, national publicity. The U.S. Supreme Court agreed in a 5–4 vote that the Nevada Bar Association had violated Gentile's First Amendment rights because its written rules of conduct were too vague to support the issuing of such a reprimand (the reprimand, in effect, was made void); however, five justices also decided that state bar associations did have the general power to punish attorneys for violating rules of conduct.

Gentile also displayed a talent for leadership. Tom Pitaro, another prominent Italian-American criminal defense attorney, noted in a 1991 interview, "Dominic is just brilliant when it comes to bringing together people concerned about a particular issue." Pitaro explained that most often Gentile would briefly play a direct leadership role in a new organization, urging others to take the helm once the organization was firmly established. Pitaro credited Gentile with forming Nevada Attorneys for Criminal Justice, thereby providing a lobby for usually individualistic criminal defense lawyers. His leadership in this and two Italian-American organizations (to be discussed later) helped Gentile win election to the Board of Governors of the Nevada Bar Association in 1991.

Dr. Anthony Marlon, the most successful, at least financially, of the many physicians of Italian background who have come to Las Vegas in the past twenty-five years, is an interesting contrast to Gentile in many ways. Born Anthony Moschitta in New York City, he changed his name upon graduating from Holy Cross College, not because he had faced overt discrimination, but rather, as he explained in a late 1991 interview, because he believed that a neutral name might be more advantageous to his medical career. He added that he did not fear discrimination; instead he wanted to optimize his opportunities. After graduating from New York's Downstate Medical Center in 1967, he spent five years at Stanford University Hospital fulfilling internship and residency requirements in cardiology. He was appointed chief cardiologist at Southern Nevada Memorial Hospital (now University Medical Center) on July 1, 1972, and continued in that capacity until 1984, when he decided to devote his full attention to his rapidly expanding medical insurance business. During the next seven years Marlon expanded his company, Sierra Health Services, adding a health management organization, a life insurance company, a home health agency, a hospice, and a benefits administration company. Unlike Gentile, who enjoyed his courtroom appearances, Marlon asserted that he has been so busy that he never even thinks of medicine—his original profession. Also, in contrast to Gentile, Marlon expressed little interest in Italian-American issues or organizations, confessing that he joined the Augustus Society in mid-1991 largely at Gentile's urging.

Some of the Italian Americans who pursued careers as educators in Las Vegas have joined earlier arrivals as top administrators. Dr. Arthur Gentile (no relation to Dominic) served as vice president of academic affairs at the University of Nevada, Las Vegas during the late 1970s, and the author held the same position at the Community College of Southern Nevada (CCSN) several years later. These two institutions, as well as the Clark County School District, were growing rapidly, and Italian Americans constituted about 7 to 8 percent of the teaching staff. Certainly the university's most controversial recruit was Al Negratti, hired in December 1979 as athletic director. Negratti, who had been embroiled in conflict as athletic director at the University of California, Santa Barbara, decided to make UNLV's athletics program profitable within a year's time. Although Negratti did not cause problems with Jerry Tarkanian, UNLV's successful basketball coach, Negratti began to argue more and more with other staff members, some of whom had supporters among influential Las Vegans or members of the Board of Regents. Former UNLV President Leonard Goodall explained that he was forced to fire Negratti because he would not slow down.

Maurice Finocchiaro has been the most noteworthy of the Italian-American professors at UNLV. After completing his doctorate at the University of California, Berkeley, the Sicilian-born Finocchiaro was hired by the university in 1970. Soon he was receiving national recognition as a result of the articles and books he had written on logic and the history of science and the many awards he had received for his teaching and publications. Finocchiaro is one of only five faculty members to be named a Barrick Distinguished Professor and the only one to receive the annual Barrick Distinguished Scholar Award twice. His *The Galileo Affair: A Documentary History,* published in 1989, brought him international renown. It provided in a single volume the essential documents related to the trial and condemnation of Galileo in 1633. Chair of the Philosophy Department since 1987, Finocchiaro was arguably the most renowned scholar on the UNLV faculty. His presence at the university, like Frank Gagliardi's, lent credence to the claims of university president Robert Maxson (1984–94) that UNLV is a young, proud, and growing institution dedicated to academic excellence.

Don Digilio is the most controversial of the several Italian-American journalists who joined the staffs of Las Vegas's two major dailies in the 1970s and 1980s. Digilio began his Las Vegas career as an entertainment columnist for the *Sun* in the early 1950s and moved to the *Review-Journal* in 1960. He advanced in pay and status and was appointed editor in 1975. Digilio was invited to join the usual civic boards and was gaining prestige until he ran articles charging that a nurse at Sunrise Hospital was switching off the life-support systems of terminally ill patients. The nurse hired nationally known San Francisco attorney Melvin Belli, Sunrise Hospital administrators denied the charges, and Clark County law enforcement and health officials investigated. Soon it was evident that the charges had no basis in fact. Already on shaky ground at the *Review-Journal,* Digilio was attacked for close friendships with Clark County Sheriff Ralph Lamb and casino developer Jay Sarno. In each case his adversaries charged that those friendships led to business deals that hindered Digilio's ability to cover the news accurately and fairly. Digilio left the *Review-Journal* in July 1980, shortly after it was revealed that he was involved with Jay Sarno in shady stock sales. Digilio then worked as a publicist for various hotels for several years, returning to journalism in 1986 as a *Sun* columnist.[41] That he could still get a job at the *Sun* is another example of Las Vegans' capacity to forgive and forget past, even recently past, transgressions.

Public Service

Jim Santini was the most widely known of the several Italian Americans who sought elective office from 1970 to the present. He was elected justice of the peace by an overwhelming margin in 1970. When the Nevada legislature increased the number of district court judges in Clark County from eight to ten, Santini was appointed to one of the new positions by Governor Mike O'Callaghan in 1972. Elected later that year to the position, he served until March 1974, when he campaigned for and won Nevada's one seat in the U.S. House of Representatives (Nevada gained another seat after the 1980 Census). In the spring of 1982 Santini launched a campaign to defeat fellow Democrat Howard Cannon, who had served as one of Nevada's U.S. senators for the previous twenty-four years.[42] Santini lost a costly and bitter struggle to Cannon. Several interviewees recalled that Santini often visited the Italian American Club and joined the Sons of Italy when he was active in local politics, but that his interest quickly waned following his election as congressman.

Two other Las Vegas Italian Americans have been elected to the district court. Joseph Bonaventure, like Santini, began as a justice of the peace. In 1986, after eight years in that capacity, he was elected district court judge. The next year Gerald Bongiovanni, who had worked as a Las Vegas attorney for fifteen years, defeated longtime incumbent John Mendoza and joined Bonaventure on the sixteen-member district court. Not all Italian-American candidates for judicial office were as successful. Three aspirants for justice of the peace positions in the small towns of Goodsprings, Overton, and the growing riverside gambling center of Laughlin were defeated in 1978 and 1988 contests. Joseph Bonaventure's brother, Frank Bonaventura (he retained the Italian spelling of the family name), served two four-year terms as Las Vegas constable.[43]

Italian-American candidates for local government positions also achieved mixed results. Hal Morelli, a local businessman who served on the Las Vegas City Commission (reconstituted as the City Council in 1983) from 1971 to 1975, was the last Italian American to seek one of the four slots. Jack Petitti was the most recent Italian American to serve on the North Las Vegas City Council, although two others, Tony Gravanti and Guido Ravelo, unsuccessfully battled Theron Goynes and Gary Bingham, respectively, for seats in 1981. Petitti and Dick Ronzone held county commission seats from 1972 through 1984. Both left public life under difficult circumstances.

Petitti was one of several Southern Nevada politicians who spent time in federal prison after been netted in an FBI sting operation. In March 1984 he was convicted of accepting a $5,000 bribe from an FBI undercover agent in return for supporting changes in zoning regulations. Ronzone, president of the Las Vegas Valley Water District Board since 1978, came under criticism in 1983 when it came

Left to right: Leo Massero, Phil Carlino, and Tony Silvestri at the Sixth Annual International Food Festival, 1981. (Courtesy Phil Carlino)

to light that the district's general manager often used his company credit card to purchase meals and other items for Ronzone and himself. Ralph Mosa, a businessman who had come to Las Vegas from Wyoming after World War II, lost a close election to Tom Wiesner for a commission seat in 1974. Robert Ferraro has served thirteen years on the five-member Boulder City Council and was elected mayor by that body in 1974, 1983, and 1985.[44]

Italian Americans have also sought to represent Clark County in the state legislature between 1970 and 1992. Only one major party candidate, John Ingrassia, sought a senate seat, and he was soundly defeated by longtime legislator Jack Vergiels in 1988. Eight Italian-American men and two Italian-American women sought state assembly seats. (There are twice as many state assembly seats allocated to Clark County as state senate seats.) Five candidates were successful in their bids to join the assembly: Ronzone in 1970 and Jim Spinello in 1986 and 1988, Chris Giunchigliani in 1990 and 1992, and John Bonaventura and Kathy Alfano Augustine in 1992.[45] Bonaventura, the nephew of Judge Bonaventure and the son of former Constable Frank Bonaventura, agreed with Italian Americans who had sought elective office in the 1960s that Italian ancestry neither gained nor lost a candidate any significant number of votes. Overall, Italian Americans have gained elective office in numbers roughly proportional to the percentage of Italian Americans in the Southern Nevada population, another sign of the extent of their assimilation in Las Vegas.[46]

Phil Carlino's career gives further testimony to the notion that ambitious Ital-

Nevada Assemblywoman Chris Giunchigliani.
(Courtesy Chris Giunchigliani)

ian Americans could rise to civic leadership positions in Las Vegas with relative
ease. Carlino had been very impressed with both the climate and the growth
potential of the city when he coordinated a coin show at the Royal Nevada on the
Strip in 1960, so he left Upstate New York for Las Vegas three years later. In addition to pursuing his coin and precious metal business, he immediately became
active in the social concerns committee of the Methodist Church and the Sons of
Italy (his paternal grandfather had been one of the founders of the national organization) and then chaired the constitution and bylaws committee for the county
and state Democratic Party. Elected chairman of Nevada's Democratic Party in
1970, he served for four years until he lost an election for secretary of state. Remaining quite active in politics, he established Carlino and Carlino Advertising
Ltd. in 1974, primarily to handle political campaign accounts.[47] His daughter
Beverly Carlino was also active in politics. She was unsuccessful in her 1978 bid
for a state assembly seat but was selected by fellow Democrats to be a national
committeewoman in 1989. In the spring of 1992 she launched a strong but unsuccessful effort to gain the chair of the Nevada Democratic Party.

   A look at the careers of Didi Carson (née Fugazi) and Chris Giunchigliani offers evidence that Las Vegas also provided Italian-American women with unique opportunities to achieve prestige and power. Like Carlino, Didi Carson became active in the Democratic Party early on in her career. She, too, rose rapidly in its hierarchy, serving four years as vice chair of the statewide party organization before being elected chair in 1974. In 1978 she was selected as national committeewoman, a position she held until 1982. Subsequently she was hired by Valley Bank, where she worked as a business development officer.[48] Dan Rotunno reported that her many activities in Nevada politics have helped her effectively secure the campaign accounts of leading Nevada Democrats for Valley Bank.

Chris Giunchigliani's rise to prominence was exceptionally rapid, even by Las Vegas standards. Born in northern Italy and raised in Chicago, Giunchigliani was working as a schoolteacher in Kansas City, Kansas, when she visited Las Vegas and decided to stay. In 1979 she enrolled in a master's degree program in education at the University of Nevada, Las Vegas. Giunchigliani worked as a bartender at Jubilation, a nightclub near the Strip, the owners of which were rumored to be associates of the Chicago Mob. She recalled that the Stardust casino manager, Frank "Lefty" Rosenthal, Teamsters Central States Pension Fund executive Allen Dorfman, and Tony "the Ant" Spilotro—all Chicago natives—were some of the more shady individuals who frequented Jubilation. The following year she began full-time teaching in the Clark County School District. She joined the Clark County Classroom Teachers Association (CCTA), the collective bargaining agent for Clark County teachers and a component of the Nevada State Education Association (NSEA), and volunteered to serve on the Instruction and Professional Development Committee. In 1981 she chaired that committee and also coordinated CCTA assistance to Karen Hayes, a candidate for county commissioner at the time. Giunchigliani found that she enjoyed politics, so she went on to coordinate all CCTA assistance to candidates for elective office in 1982 and also served on the NSEA board of directors. In 1983 Giunchigliani, not yet thirty, was elected president of CCTA, which had more than three thousand dues-paying members. She established a reputation as a tough negotiator committed to higher pay and professional recognition for teachers. She was reelected CCTA president in 1985, and with the strong support of CCTA members, she won the NSEA presidency in 1987 and again in 1989.

Carlino, Carson, and Giunchigliani were able to rise to prominence in Las Vegas in less than a decade, and they faced little discrimination as recent migrants or as Italian Americans. Carson and Giunchigliani faced some resentment from males in the Democratic Party and CCTA respectively, but no more than they would have encountered in other American cities. They agreed that the rapidly growing Sunbelt city with its tradition of quickly accepting newcomers into leadership roles offered them unique opportunities for economic advancement, prestige, and power.

Phil Carlino, a leader in both the Sons of Italy and the Italian American Club.
(Courtesy Phil Carlino)

The most powerful Italian American in Southern Nevada politics has been a Catholic priest, Caesar Caviglia, who was born and raised in White Pine County, not far from the Idaho border. Caviglia's initial assignments as a cleric included a stint in Carson City, where he renewed his friendship with Paul Laxalt, who later served as governor of Nevada and then U.S. senator. In 1962 Caviglia returned to Las Vegas to serve as an assistant pastor at St. Anne's Parish. During his four and a half years at St. Anne's, the energetic Caviglia also served as superintendent for Catholic schools in Southern Nevada, assistant director to the Catholic community welfare agency, and chaplain to the Newman Club at Nevada Southern University (the predecessor to the University of Nevada, Las Vegas). Caviglia left Las Vegas in 1967 to pursue a master's degree in education at the University of San Francisco. Subsequently he edited the *Nevada Register,* a Catholic weekly newspaper. He later returned to the University of San Francisco as a member of the research faculty. In 1972 Caviglia, by this time widely known in Nevada political circles, was appointed pastor of St. Peter's in Henderson, the industrial community adjacent to Las Vegas.

Caviglia was determined to enhance the economic condition of Henderson residents, and he immediately became involved in local civic affairs. He explained in a 1992 telephone conversation that his modus operandi was to take the lead on an issue, to contact influential Nevadans to gain support, and then to teach others how to start up and manage an organization to ensure continued progress on an issue. He readily admitted disliking bureaucratic procedures. Caviglia was particularly active, and successful, in three areas: expanding access to postsecondary education, providing economic diversification, and improving Henderson's image.

To expand postsecondary educational opportunities for Henderson residents, Caviglia and Betty Scott, a former nun, began by offering adult education courses at St. Peter's in September of 1972. Understanding the need to affiliate with an accredited college or university, they approached UNLV officials. Rebuffed, they then contacted the dean of instruction at the community college (now Community College of Southern Nevada [CCSN]) that had just been created by the Nevada legislature. Over time the number and variety of courses offered in Henderson increased, and Betty Scott was appointed the college's coordinator for the Henderson and Boulder City areas. Dr. Herman Van Betten, CCSN's dean of the Henderson campus from 1984 to 1995 and a former UNLV professor and member of the Clark County School Board, identified Caviglia as, at the least, first among equals in lobbying for construction of a college campus in Henderson. Their success was not assured because other areas of the Las Vegas Valley were also vying for a campus. Caviglia, Scott, and their many allies, including State Senator and Mormon leader Jim Gibson, fought hard and smart, and the Henderson campus opened in June 1981.

No one involved in politics wins all battles. Caviglia was chair of CCSN's advi-

sory committee from 1978 through 1981, yet he failed in his efforts to have Betty
Scott appointed campus chief executive. Judith Eaton, a strong-willed woman
who was appointed college president in July 1979, perceived that Caviglia wanted
the Henderson campus to become a separate college, so she removed Scott as
campus coordinator and replaced her with a loyal administrator. Caviglia was
outraged, Henderson leaders were dismayed, but Eaton won that battle.

In a sense, though, Caviglia won the war. He remained on the college's advisory committee and continued to promote the development of the Henderson
campus. After Eaton left in July 1983 to become president of a large community
college in Philadelphia, the new president, Paul Meacham, valued Caviglia's political clout and sought his assistance in lobbying state and local officials on behalf of the college. Caviglia remained an active member of CCSN's advisory committee through 1994 and was awarded an honorary associate degree at the May
1992 graduation ceremonies. Betty Scott was appointed to a cabinet-level ad-
ministrative position at CCSN in 1989.

Caviglia has remained committed to expanding Henderson's economic base.
Unafraid of controversy, he advocated that the city build a convention center when
many influential Southern Nevadans, including some Henderson leaders, regarded
such a project as a white elephant. Working diligently to overcome the resistance,
Caviglia received a million-dollar grant from the Las Vegas Convention and Visitors Authority. Caviglia felt great satisfaction in June 1982 when the Henderson
Convention Center opened with a champagne reception that was attended by a
host of city, county, and state elected officials. Serving as chairman of the Henderson
Convention Center board through January 1985, he later resigned in protest over
personnel and policy decisions made by Henderson's mayor and city council.[49]
Caviglia takes pride in the fact that the convention center has been financially
successful; it certainly is not the white elephant some suggested it would be.

Caviglia has been equally committed to improving Henderson's image. In 1983
he and Henderson Chamber of Commerce officials began studying ways to beautify
the city's main thoroughfare, Boulder Highway. They planned a greenbelt along a
section of the highway that would make use of irrigation water runoff from a
nearby golf course and park. The greenbelt was to include a two-mile-long walk-
ing and jogging path with exercise stations and barbecue pits. Caviglia's longtime
friendship with Senator Paul Laxalt helped the chamber of commerce obtain a
$4,800,000 federal grant for the project. More recently, Caviglia, a member of the
Nevada Highway Commission, has given interstate highway travelers four opportunities to exit in Henderson, including an off-ramp leading directly to the
expanding Henderson campus of CCSN, even though the next off-ramp is only
half a mile away. Caviglia has long believed that any increase in the college's
visibility enhances the city's image.[50]

Summary

Men and women of Italian heritage have been involved in every sphere of business, the professions, and government in Las Vegas for the past twenty-five years. In the corporate era, no doors were closed to them. Indeed, Italian Americans were more likely to be at the helm of Las Vegas's major hotels in the 1980s than they had been in the 1950s, when so many Italian Americans skilled in managing gambling enterprises were migrating to Las Vegas. In recent years Italian Americans have served as chief executives of Hilton Nevada Corporation, the Ramada Gaming Group, Desert Inn and Country Club, the Riviera, and Caesars World.[51] In addition, Italian Americans have recently held second rank (vice president or the equivalent) at most Strip and Downtown hotels and at hotels owned or managed by Italian Americans: Palace Station, Rio, Showboat, and Golden Gate. Italian names appear regularly in the society page of the *Las Vegas Review-Journal*, on lists of major donors to UNLV, and on the roster of companies constituting the Nevada Development Authority.

Italian Americans were accepted as part of the civic elite, while at the same time the newspapers were carrying stories about the Mob. Such stories, always good copy, were often based on a mixture of rumors, deliberate leaks by law enforcement agencies, and some facts. Of course, The Boys were still in town—or, at the least, they visited Las Vegas frequently.[52] After all, in the 1970s and 1980s and earlier Italian Americans and Jewish Americans were noticeably overrepresented among the alleged and the convicted perpetrators of major casino skimming. Names such as Blitzstein, Dorfman, Glick, and Rosenthal appeared in newspaper stories and court depositions along with Agosto, Civella, Danolfo, Ponti, and Spilotro. Agosto, the producer of the famed Folies Bergeres show at the Tropicana, and Tony Spilotro, whose many endeavors included a jewelry store at Circus Circus, clearly led the field of names receiving newspaper publicity. From 1975, when the Sicilian-born Agosto was arrested and charged with being an illegal alien, until he was convicted and sentenced for coordinating the mammoth Tropicana skimming operation, more than 110 stories about him appeared in Las Vegas dailies. But he was not as newsworthy as Spilotro, who generated more than 130 stories between his arrival in 1977 and his murder in 1986. Inescapably, Las Vegas newspaper readers closely associated Italian Americans with organized crime.

Italian names also dominated the Black Book—the list of individuals with reputations so nefarious that they are prohibited from even entering Nevada gaming establishments. As mentioned previously, since the Black Book was instituted in 1960, the majority of names listed there have been Italian American. Of course, each new entry in the Black Book merited at least several stories in the local press.

The often-sensational newspaper stories about Mob leaders, the irrefutable fact that Italian Americans were overrepresented among those coordinating the casino skims, and the dominance of Italian Americans in the Black Book made it difficult for longtime Italian American gamers to shed the Mafia image. This extraordinary situation is at least partly attributable to the near absence of effective Italian American civil rights organizations during the past four decades.

Frank Fertitta demonstrated that Italian Americans who started their careers when The Boys were in town could overcome the Mafia stereotype. Gaming regulators no doubt took note that Fertitta had worked at three hotels where substantial skimming had taken place—the Stardust, the Tropicana, and the Fremont—but Fertitta did not come under direct investigation until 1985, when a witness at the Stardust skimming trial, a casino security guard, testified that a man named Frank had been involved in skimming at the Fremont.[53] (Both the Stardust and the Fremont were owned by Argent Corporation, which received millions of dollars from the Teamsters Pension Fund and was closely associated with organized crime.) Since Frank Fertitta was general manager of the Fremont during the period of time addressed by the witness, the Gaming Control Board launched an investigation.

Fertitta responded by refusing to comment on the charges, continuing at the same time the quite remarkable expansion of Palace Station and making large charitable gifts to popular Las Vegas institutions and causes. In 1988 he contributed $300,000 to the UNLV Foundation, the next year $1 million for a UNLV tennis complex, and later $70,000 for the medical expenses of Leslie Randolph, a young African-American Las Vegas mother of young children who needed a heart transplant operation. His generosity certainly did not go unnoticed by prominent Las Vegans and probably influenced Sherman Frederick, editor of the *Review-Journal,* to write on September 29, 1989: "For four long years, the Gaming Control Board has been probing skimming allegations against Palace Station owner Frank Fertitta. It is high time the Control Board resolve this matter. It is unconscionable to keep Fertitta twisting slowly in the wind for so long, whether or not he's guilty of any wrongdoing. The Control Board should make a determination in this case or drop it." When the Control Board decided to drop the case in early November, citing lack of evidence, Frederick expressed his support, describing Fertitta as "a generous benefactor of UNLV."[54]

At the same time, Fertitta displayed great political acumen by recruiting two very powerful Nevadans—Richard Bunker, the interim president of the Nevada Resort Association, and Jim Joyce, for decades the premier political campaign consultant and gaming lobbyist—to convince the Clark County Commission to let him build a casino near a residential neighborhood several miles east of the Strip. Their task was a challenging one because there had already been recent public outcry against proposed casinos (one of which was Mike Fauci's) in that

area, miles away from Downtown or the Strip. As usual, Bunker and Joyce succeeded, and Fertitta received permission to build.[55] Wishing no enemies in the
White House, in January 1992 Fertitta contributed $1,000 to George Bush's re-
election campaign; his wife, Victoria, donated equally to Democratic front-runner
Bill Clinton. Also concerned about maintaining good relations with law enforcement agencies, in April 1992 Fertitta hired John Schreiber, former special agent in
charge of the Las Vegas FBI office, as vice president of governmental affairs at
Palace Station. Schreiber, who had served as deputy assistant director of the FBI's
criminal investigative division in Washington, D.C., after his Las Vegas service,
was also quite knowledgeable about Nevada's gaming industry, having served as
director of the Nevada Resort Association from 1987 to 1989, and, more recently,
as vice president of Caesars World.[56] Clearly Fertitta had learned what Moe Dalitz,
the early gaming entrepreneur knew well—giving generously to local charities
and associating with powerful political figures greatly diminishes suspicions about
one's past and facilitates winning favors from public officials that are not neces-
sarily in the public interest.

Fertitta continued to seek new opportunities for investment. In a March 1992
interview with *Las Vegas Sun* gaming columnist Phil Hevener, Fertitta's son, also
named Frank, said plans for construction of Boulder Station, a hotel and casino
east of the Strip, were delayed for long-range financial planning. The son hinted
that like their counterparts at such Strip properties as Circus Circus, the Hilton,
and the Mirage, the Fertittas were considering out-of-state investments in Colorado and several midwestern states. At the same time the senior Fertitta joined
with fellow Italian American Tito Tiberti (J. A. Tiberti's son) and with Don Laughlin,
Riverside Hotel owner and the founder of Laughlin, Nevada, to announce a cooperative 10,000-acre development in Bullhead City, Arizona, across the Colorado River from Nevada. Initially the group planned to develop 2,000 acres, but
they will eventually build more than 5,000 homes, apartments, and condominiums, commercial and industrial facilities, and a golf course. Fertitta and Tiberti
also bought more than 80 acres on Laughlin's Casino Row. (Since 1984 seven
resorts and two casinos have opened there, and eight more resorts are planned.)[57]
Boulder Station opened in August 1994. Eleven months later, the senior Fertitta
opened Texas, a large casino, movie theater complex, and small hotel about five
miles northwest of Downtown.

The quincentenary of Columbus's voyage to the New World found Italian Americans working and prospering in every major field in Las Vegas. No doors are closed;
indeed, even the many Italian-American interviewees who stressed that their
achievements were based on energy, diligence, and intellect admitted that Italian
ancestry might have been somewhat advantageous in the fields of entertainment
and restaurant management. The openness and fluidity of Las Vegas society made
assimilation easy for Italian Americans. Those with an entrepreneurial spirit could

find financial success in Las Vegas; money then opened the doors to power and prestige. The Las Vegas elite had been infused with new blood both when The Boys were in town and during the corporate era.

Considering that the millions of mostly impoverished peasants who came to America from southern Italy and Sicily between 1880 and 1914 had limited opportunities and skills for moving up in the world, it is not surprising that Italian Americans are still overrepresented in gaming, construction, and related businesses, and in the ownership and management of Italian restaurants. Perhaps reflecting both the adjustment of a few immigrants to the difficult conditions of the urban ghettoes and the American fascination with the Mafia, large numbers of Italian Americans continue to be listed in the Black Book and featured in newspaper stories about organized crime in Las Vegas. In the corporate era, as previously, the Italian-American casino executives and dealers, builders and developers, restaurateurs, professionals—and, yes, even Tony Spilotro and wiseguys of lesser status—all contributed to both the substance and the myth of Las Vegas.

Chapter Four

Italian American Organizations:

Preserving Ethnic Heritage

in a Time of Assimilation

Early Organization

Italian Americans are now fading into the twilight of ethnicity. Few among the almost 15 million people who identified themselves as fully or partly of Italian descent in the 1990 U.S. Census have not acquired the language, dress, manners, and values of American society, and the great majority no longer prefer their co-ethnics as neighbors, friends, or even spouses. Indeed, it is rare to meet an Italian American under thirty who is not partly of some other ancestry. Despite their nearly complete assimilation, Las Vegas Italian Americans in good numbers are still joining organizations dedicated at least in part to preserving their ethnic heritage. Included among these groups are some that were formed more than thirty years ago and have adapted to the rapid assimilation of Las Vegas Italian Americans, as well as organizations formed within the past ten years by successful professionals and business persons.

The Italian American Club (known as the Club) is the oldest Italian-American organization in Las Vegas. It grew rapidly at a time when many of Las Vegas's Italian Americans preferred to associate with their co-ethnics, declined during an extended period of factionalism and oligarchy, and then revitalized and adapted to the growing assimilation of Italian Americans.

In the early 1950s several Italian-American men, recent arrivals as well as pre–World War II immigrants, began meeting in a couple of the many Italian-American-owned restaurants in Las Vegas to develop an organization to preserve their heritage.[1] When the Club was officially formed, the leadership included men with ancestry in the major regions of Italy, long-term residents of Las Vegas as well as recent arrivals. Providing representation of areas as diverse as Piedmont and Sicily or Alto Adige and Calabria was important within the Club, even almost forty years after the last major wave of Italian immigration. While nation-

Left to right: Italian American Club leaders Vic Silvagni, son of P. O. Silvagni, Pete Bommarito, and Bernard Provenzano. (Courtesy Al Bossi)

ally the Italian regional and provincial rivalries diminished somewhat over time, particularly when the new arrivals realized that they were all just "dagos" and "wops" to many prospective employers, at the same time in the East, many local Italian-American social organizations continued to restrict membership on the basis of local, provincial, or regional ancestry. That the Club's first president, Al Bossi, was of northern Italian background and his successor, Pete Bommarito, was of Sicilian ancestry helped to ensure that all Italian Americans felt welcome. The Club grew rapidly to almost three hundred members by 1962. Many members were recruited by personal friends or coworkers, especially in the gaming industry; a few learned of the Club through newspaper articles.

Reflecting the customs of the time, the men who established the Club and their wives also formed a Ladies Auxiliary. The Auxiliary also attracted a large membership, in part because spouses of non-Italian background not only were made to feel welcome but were encouraged to seek leadership positions. In addition to the primary goal of raising funds for a permanent headquarters, the Club contributed to charities, including providing food and clothing to the Native Americans of Moapa Valley.[2] Al Bossi recalled that he and some other Club members discussed working to increase Italian-American representation among local and

Honorary Italian American Club member Frank Sinatra receives an honorary life membership from Al Bossi, the club's first president, in 1963. (Courtesy Al Bossi)

state elected officials, but that nothing came of it.

The presence of a large number of Italian-American Strip entertainers greatly aided the Club's fund-raising efforts. Frank Sinatra, Dean Martin, Tony Bennett, and numerous other Strip performers became honorary or regular members of the Club. In May 1961 more than 2,500 people attended the Club's Italian Carnival of Stars at the Riviera Hotel, which starred such nationally known Italian-American entertainers as Vic Damone, Jimmy Durante, Phil Harris, and Frankie Laine, as well as such local favorites as Sonny King, the Happy Jesters, and the Characters.[3] The event was a great financial success for the Club. Al Bossi recalled that the 1962 Carnival held at the Flamingo Hotel was also well attended. "What an experience!— First Sinatra, then Dean Martin, then another star, then a group, and another— everyone wanted to assist," he recounted. These fund-raisers were so successful that the organization managed to raise the money to purchase land for a clubhouse near the intersection of Eastern and Sahara, about three and a half miles east of the Strip. Several Italian-American contractors, most notably Dominic Bianchi and Tony Marnell, helped with the construction by contributing building materials, time, and expertise. The 12,000-square-foot building was completed in 1966.[4]

In American cities with large Italian-American populations, there were numer-

Entertainer Phil Harris (far left) with Sons of Italy Lodge leaders at the 1967
Scholarship Benefit. Left to right: Victor Silvagni, Frank Lisa, Peter DeSantis, and
Angelo Manzi. (Courtesy Phil Carlino)

ous organizations ranging from such branch groups as the Dante Society and the
Order of the Sons of Italy in America (henceforth referred to as Sons of Italy) to
storefront social clubs that required that members be from a particular province
or region of Italy. Their goals were often dissimilar and sometimes conflicting.[5]
The Club was the only Italian-American organization in Las Vegas for six years.
Then in 1965 several Italian Americans, led by Nevada Test Site employee Leonard
Arcadipane, established the Las Vegas lodge of the Sons of Italy, a branch of the
well-established national organization with tens of thousands of members in
lodges throughout the United States.

The Sons of Italy lodge grew rapidly, flourished, and then entered a long period
of decline as the membership aged and the leadership lacked the ability to revi-
talize it. The national organization stressed the preservation of Italian culture,
but, like the Club, it also provided an environment for Italian-American men and
women (while most members were male, women were permitted to join as equals)
to interact, raise funds for local and national charities, and enhance the image of
Italian Americans. The lodge's officers and members included newcomers and
longtime residents as well as men and women whose parents or grandparents
came from a variety of regions of Italy—another similarity to the Club.

In 1965 and 1966 a significant number of Italian Americans joined both the
Club and the Sons of Italy lodge. During that time the two organizations cooper-

The Supreme Lodge, Order Sons of Italy of America, presented a charter to the Las Vegas Lodge on January 10, 1965. Phil LaLoggia, organizer of the Las Vegas group (right), receives the charter. (Courtesy Phil Carlino)

The installation of the Las Vegas Lodge, Sons of Italy. Left to right: James Russo, Al DePaulis, Leonard Arcadipane, and Elaine Pileggi. (Courtesy Phil Carlino)

Italian American Club leader Nick Kelly (left) with Nevada Governor Grant Sawyer.
(Courtesy Al Bossi)

ated in several undertakings, most notably the First Annual Columbus Day Dinner. That Governor Grant Sawyer was the featured speaker and U.S. Senators
Alan Bible and Howard Cannon, Congressman Walter Baring, Washoe County
District Attorney William Raggio, Dean Martin, and Frank Sinatra were guests
demonstrates the initial success of both organizations.[6]

Understandably, even now few Italian Americans feel comfortable discussing
the causes of the conflict that arose between the two organizations in 1967. The
best evidence points to a clash of personalities involving Leonard Arcadipane,
venerable (the Sons of Italy's term for lodge chief executive) of the Las Vegas
lodge for eight years (1969–73 and 1975–79), and Nick "Kelly" Fiore, president of
the Club in the late 1960s and its guiding force for many years thereafter. One
Italian American who has been active in civic affairs for a long time and was a
member of both groups in the early 1990s recalled that at one point Arcadipane
and others suggested that the Club become part of the Sons of Italy and hand
over its clubhouse and property to the national headquarters of the Sons of Italy.
Nick Kelly and his supporters at the Club became incensed that an out-of-state
organization might gain control, especially since establishing the clubhouse had

Left to right: Gus Giuffre, Pat Bove, Nick Kelly, and Pop Mirabelli at the Italian American Club in the mid-1960s. Pat Bove was the first vice-president of the Club. (Courtesy Al Bossi)

been the group's major achievement. The resulting ill will precluded any cooperation between the two groups for the next twenty-two years, and fewer than half a dozen Italian Americans remained as members of both organizations.[7]

Despite a lack of cooperation, the two organizations followed broadly similar paths during this period. Their objectives were similar, and each appealed to Las Vegas newcomers seeking both social and employment opportunities. Finally, each assisted a variety of local and national charities, thereby giving the increasingly assimilated members a sense of contributing to their community. Yearly activities for both groups were virtually the same, including celebrations of such traditional Italian holidays as St. Joseph's Day, dinners or balls on Columbus Day, two or three quite successful fund-raisers for local or national charities, scholarships for deserving Italian Americans, and banquets featuring man of the year awards.[8] The Sons of Italy and the Club continued to attract new members in the late 1960s through the mid-1970s, as large numbers of Italian Americans streamed into Las Vegas. The Club's membership peaked at just under four hundred, and the Sons of Italy lodge's top enrollment was a little over three hundred.

It is worth noting that no more than 5 percent of Italian-American adults in Southern Nevada have ever belonged to either of these organizations. This is not an unusual rate of participation. In his in-depth study of ethnic groups in the Albany-Schenectady-Troy metropolitan area of New York State, sociologist Richard Alba found that Italian Americans, like people of other European backgrounds,

Left to right: Active Italian American Club leaders at the annual children's Christmas party. Dr. Leonard Carpi, Las Vegas optometrist, Pete Bommarito, and Nick Kelly. (Courtesy Al Bossi)

generally do not feel an intense identification with their heritage. His results indicated that people of Italian ancestry were somewhat more likely than people of Dutch, English, French-Canadian, German, Polish, or Scottish ancestry both to have long-standing friendships with co-ethnics and to join ethnic organizations. Participation in such clubs was more typical for those who still resided in ethnic enclaves—which have never existed in Las Vegas.[9]

The Club was more successful than the Sons of Italy in gaining and retaining members because it provided a pleasant social environment. Its clubhouse is large and houses not only a restaurant and bar, but also a variety of rooms catering to activities ranging from card playing to banquets and wedding receptions. Behind the building is a Mediterranean courtyard leading to a bocce court. In designing the building and grounds the Club's planners maintained a bit of southern Europe in the urban center of Southern Nevada. While the Club was open most evenings, the members of the Sons of Italy had an opportunity to socialize "officially" at organized monthly meetings.

During the 1970s the Club's leadership base narrowed. The strong personalities of two Club presidents, Nick Kelly and Mike Pisanello, a Culinary Union official, attracted new members but also led to many resignations. Although most of the people interviewed by the author spoke highly of Kelly's leadership and commitment, asserting that it was a rare Italian American who refused his invitation to join the Club, several others interviewed, most notably golf pro Frank Catania, sports-book manager George Ligouri, and casino host Joe Spinuzzi, did resist Kelly's entreaties. Indeed, Al Bossi and Charles Cocuzza, a small-business owner, said that by the late 1970s Kelly had become too possessive about the Club and too dictatorial with Club members who questioned his opinions or those of his good friend Mike Pisanello. Cocuzza served as president for only seven months rather than the two-year term because Nick Kelly constantly undermined his efforts to manage the Club professionally. Kelly spoke so often of "my Club" that Bossi had to confront Kelly with legal documents showing that he did not own the Club building and property. By this time Kelly, a bachelor, had retired from his maitre d' position and was spending almost every waking hour at the Club. Since he virtually served as an unpaid manager and Pisanello often served as an unpaid chef, they effectively ran the Club.

A typical example of Kelly's modus operandi occurred one evening when the San Gennaro Feast was held at the Club. With patrons almost six-deep at the bar, Kelly, who always sat on a "throne" next to the bar, decided at about 10:30 P.M. to go home. Much to the amazement of the crowd, he imperiously announced, "Last call," and a few minutes later ordered the bar closed. No Club member dared challenge Kelly's decision. This style of management struck many younger, upwardly mobile Italian Americans as old-fashioned, so not surprisingly recruitment, once Kelly's strong suit, tapered off by the early 1980s.[10]

Several middle-aged Italian-American interviewees, as well as this author, visited the Club soon after settling in Las Vegas in the late 1970s and early 1980s and rather quickly got the distinct impression that the leadership sought out only new members who were friends of longtime members. In more recent years, any Italian American inquiring about membership is treated cordially by Club leaders. But the Club had already lost scores of potential new and younger members because of this narrow approach to recruitment.

The Sons of Italy also experienced serious problems with recruitment. Tony DiIorio, president from 1973 through 1975 while he worked as a casino executive at the MGM Grand Hotel, almost equaled Kelly in his ability to recruit Italian Americans from the gaming industry. But he, too, tended to neglect to recruit younger men and women. DiIorio, as well as Leonard Arcadipane, businessman Phil Carlino, and a handful of others made the Sons of Italy viable into the early 1980s. But since the organization recruited few new members, it lost its vitality as older leaders died, became incapacitated, or, as was the case with DiIorio, joined new, more dynamic Italian-American groups. By 1990 the Sons of Italy meetings were dominated by seniors who often spent their time

Bocce at the Italian American Club. (Courtesy Tony Allotta)

Bocce at the Italian American Club. (Courtesy Tony Allotta)

Phil Mirabelli (left) receives the Italian American Club Presidential gavel from outgoing President Pete Bommarito (center). Back, left to right: Nick Kelly, Bill Raggio, Al Bossi. (Courtesy Al Bossi)

Italian American Club leaders (left to right) Paul Rinaldi, Nick Kelly, and Al Bossi greet Nevada Lt. Gov. Rex Bell (second from right). (Courtesy Al Bossi)

together exchanging stories of aches and pains. Such an atmosphere was not conducive to either the retention of middle-aged members or the recruitment of younger Italian Americans.

Religious Organizations

Since almost all the Italians who came to the United States were at least nominally affiliated with the Roman Catholic Church, it is not surprising that Las Vegas Italian-American religious organizations have been associated only with that faith. Before the substantial influx of East and West Coast Italian Americans in the decades following World War II, there were so few Italian-American Catholics in Las Vegas that forming a distinctly Italian-American Catholic organization would not have been feasible. In 1973 several Italian Americans, mostly parishioners from St. Viator Church, worked with Father Zanoni of the San Francisco–based Italian Catholic Federation (ICF) to establish a local chapter. The ICF, with many chapters in California and a few in northern Nevada and Illinois, provided Italian-American Catholics with an opportunity to reaffirm their faith and their culture.

Like the Club and the Sons of Italy lodges, the ICF chapters (others were later formed in the area) engaged in philanthropy and provided opportunities for members to socialize with one another. The chapters also held monthly meetings, commemorated traditional Italian saints' days, and offered scholarships for Italian-American youth. In addition, members aided needy Italian-American families and elderly and, of course, their own parishes.[11] Like the Club and the Sons of Italy, the ICF chapters brought together those who valued the traditions of their parents. Of course, the ICF chapters were more specialized, appealing only to those for whom worshipping in the Roman Catholic faith was intertwined with a desire to preserve their Italian ancestry.

The issue of national control versus local autonomy, which had been a major factor in the split between the Club and the Sons of Italy, also led to a split within the St. Viator ICF. Izzy Marion, a controversial Italian American who has owned beauty parlors, hosted a local television program, served as a casino executive, and was one of the ICF chapter founders, played a part in the dispute. He took the lead in protesting new member payments to the ICF Central Council in San Francisco. Marion asserted in a 1991 interview that since the Central Council was adamant about the payments, he and most of the other members formed a separate group, the Association of Italian Catholics (AIC), with the full support of the St. Viator clergy. The AIC has remained at St. Viator. Other people who remained with the ICF took a different view of the events surrounding the schism, emphasizing that the majority of the ICF members chose to move the chapter from St.

Viator to the Holy Family Parish in 1977. The ICF chapter remained at Holy Family Parish for eleven years and then moved to St. Anne's Parish because of irreconcilable differences between the organization and Holy Family's Italian-American pastor, Rev. Benjamin Franzinelli.

Marion, whose personality is as strong as the late Nick Kelly's was, has remained the unchallenged leader of the AIC. In May 1992 he asserted that the AIC had more than ninety members, including many non-Italians and even some non-Catholics. With great enthusiasm, Marion described such recent AIC activities as annual pasta and memorial dinners, a July picnic, and fund-raising events for both St. Viator Parish and the Southern Nevada Children's Home. He probably substantially overstated the membership. Nonetheless, that the AIC has continued to exist for almost two decades is a tribute to Marion's strong personality. As no other AIC leaders have emerged, the organization will probably not outlive Izzy Marion.

The ICF expanded its Las Vegas membership. The St. Anne's chapter, headed by Angelo Nicassio, a former Californian, remained vital through the early 1990s, and two other chapters have been formed. One, at St. Francis de Sales Parish, has experienced some disruption as a result of differences among past leaders, but it continued to provide about thirty to forty mostly older Italian-American Catholics and their spouses with opportunities to meet and do philanthropic and spiritual work. Another chapter of the ICF was started at Our Lady of Las Vegas Parish in the summer of 1991. Angelo Nicassio and Dr. Emil Cava, a retired physician, helped an ICF field director with the organizing efforts. Cava said in a 1992 interview that he enjoyed serving as the chapter's first president. Most of the nearly fifty members were older, and Cava estimated that about one third were men and women who, while not of Italian ancestry, had previously lived in Italian neighborhoods in California or the East and enjoyed the company of Italian Americans.

Non-Catholic Italian Americans were not difficult to find in Las Vegas. Those who came from homes where allegiance to Catholicism was nominal often have no affiliation with any religion. Some have married non-Catholics and adopted their spouse's religion. A few are descendants of Italian Protestants, particularly the Waldensians, a religious group whose origins preceded Martin Luther by more than three hundred years. Others have become disaffected with aspects of Catholic theology or tradition and joined Pentecostal churches. Several are the descendants of Italians who migrated to Utah and converted to the Mormon faith.

The Italian Americans associated with mainline Protestant, Pentecostal, or Mormon churches were too few to have formed any religious organizations that might reaffirm their Italian heritage. Although conversions of Italian Americans to Pentecostalism and Mormonism have increased in the past decade, the emergence of an Italian-American religious organization remains unlikely. Both Rev. Paul Messineo, appointed in 1987 as pastor of First Presbyterian Church, the largest church of that denomination in Nevada, and Dr. Andrea Fontana, an Italian-born professor of sociology at UNLV and an elder at First Presbyterian, suggested that mainline Protestant denominations' emphases on reason, a direct relationship with the Almighty, and the equality of all communicants conflict with the traditional Italian practice of Roman Catholicism, which stresses dogma, veneration of saints, and deference to priestly authority. Similarly, the total devotion characteristic of members of Pentecostal sects and the Mormon Church (Church of Jesus Christ of Latter-day Saints) usually separates Italian Americans from their cultural roots. Adherents of both groups invest much of their time and energy in church activities, so they have little contact with other Italian Americans and are not likely to preserve any family traditions that are not consistent with their religious practices. Phil Carlino, an active Methodist whose mother's family had been Waldensians for many generations, was proof that one does not have to be Catholic to preserve an Italian heritage. Yet he has been the exception.

Comparisons and Contrasts

During the early 1980s Southern Nevada's Italian-American organizations shared many positive traits. Their regular meetings gave Italian Americans opportunities both to socialize and to reemphasize their cultural heritage; their fund-raisers provided members with a sense of giving back to the community; and the recounting of some members' trips to Italy as well as the very occasional visits of Italian officials or airmen (who came to the area to participate in NATO exercises at nearby Nellis Air Force Base) affirmed the members' tenuous connection with the land of their ancestors.

The organizations also had some negative attributes in common. Their numbers were gradually declining, and the average age of members was increasing. None of the organizations had developed programs to appeal to Italian Americans twenty to forty years old. In addition, no leader had made an effort to enlist the support of other organizations in causes that might have gained broad support from the Italian-American community. Unfortunately there continued to be ill will between the leadership of the Club and the Sons of Italy. An active member of the Sons of Italy, who wished to remain anonymous, vividly recalled that in the mid-1970s Nick Kelly not only refused to help organize a Columbus Day parade; he also informed influential Las Vegans that if they cooperated with the Sons of Italy, their businesses would be boycotted by Italian Americans. In April 1973 when Leonard Arcadipane, Peter Anthony, and three other Sons of Italy leaders traveled to Carson City to testify in favor of Senate Bill 339, a proposal to make Columbus Day a legal holiday in Nevada, they did not seek assistance from spokesmen of other Italian-American organizations.[12]

Cooperation was also lacking in antidiscrimination efforts. Longtime Club member Tony Allotta recalled that while he and some other active Club members contributed cash in the late 1960s to representatives of the Italian American Civil Rights League (led by reputed Mafioso Joseph Colombo) who traveled to Las Vegas regularly, none of the Southern Nevada Italian-American organizations worked with the national Italian-American antidiscrimination associations that had formed in the late 1960s.[13] This is not to say that there were no efforts to counter ethnic stereotyping, for occasionally Club members countered offensive comments. Tony Neno, manager of the Club from 1982 through 1987, and Tony Allotta recalled that the Club aggressively protested defamatory comments made about Italian Americans by a local sportscaster, a comedian, and a *Las Vegas Sun* columnist. Joe Minetti, editor of the Club's monthly newsletter, wrote official protest letters, and other Club members contacted both the offenders and their employers. Yet none of the Italian Americans the author interviewed recalled any effort to challenge the presence of so many Italian Americans in Nevada's Black Book.

The graying of the membership of Italian-American organizations, the lack of an appropriate social milieu for well-assimilated and successful middle-aged and younger Italian Americans, and the need to promote positive attitudes toward Italian Americans set the stage for both the development of new Italian-American groups and the revitalization of the Club in the mid-1980s. The promotion of positive attitudes toward Italian Americans was particularly important at the time because the Las Vegas newspapers were filled with stories about Tony Spilotro, the alleged representative of the Chicago Mob, and Italian-American organized crime families.

Recent Organizations

The Augustus Society was formed in 1983 by a small group of successful Italian-American men and women, including attorneys Carmine Colucci, Dominic Gentile, and Al Massi, businesswoman Roseanne Gargano, and banker Dan Rotunno. Though memories fade, evidence indicates that Dominic Gentile was the single most important participant. Soon after forming, the group recruited Ruth Catalano and Dino Sorrentino, small-business owners, and Dr. Franco Erculei, a physician and a friend of Rotunno.[14] The Augustus Society's stated goals were improving the image of Italian Americans, furthering the educational attainments of Italian-American high-school graduates, and assisting needy Italian Americans, particularly seniors.

After much discussion the annual membership fee was set at $1,000, primarily to ensure that only the most successful Italian Americans would seek membership. In the first five years, enrollment increased from the original six founders in

*Dominic Gentile, founder and first president
of the Nevada Society of Italian-American
Lawyers and a founder of the Augustus
Society. (Courtesy Augustus Society)*

1983 to more than sixty. Roseanne Gargano DePalma recalled that progress was slow but steady. The Society recruited Palace Station owner Frank Fertitta and Showboat chief executive Frank Modica. Modica declined, citing his extensive responsibilities in both New Jersey and Nevada. Former Sons of Italy venerable Tony DiIorio joined and was elected president. He was almost as effective recruiting members for the Society as he had been for the Sons of Italy. All the members tried to recruit an Italian-American friend or business associate. Total membership rose each year, although some people did not renew their memberships. Some left because the annual dues proved too expensive, others because job advancement made attendance at Society meetings difficult. One resigned because he felt that the Society had become too much like a Rotary Club; conversely, another member quit because he perceived that the Society was becoming too political. No effort was made to recruit the several Italian-born or Italian-American professors at CCSN and UNLV; of course, the high annual dues probably would have shocked the academics. Eventually, however, a CCSN criminal justice professor, a UNLV architecture lecturer, and a UNLV professor of educational psychology, all business owners, joined the Society.

An annual highlight of the Augustus Society's activities was the spring scholarship dinner featuring Dr. Robert Maxson, the UNLV president. In 1992 Maxson's popularity plummeted among Las Vegas's many basketball fanatics when Jerry Tarkanian and his supporters charged that the UNLV president had led a con-spiracy to oust the revered basketball coach. The sports-conscious leaders of the Augustus Society were split over whether or not to invite Maxson for the scholar-ship dinner that year. Finally, they voted to do so. Maxson declined, explaining that he had a previous commitment. Rollie Massimino, the Italian American ap-pointed by Maxson to replace Tarkanian, attended the 1992 scholarship dinner instead. Augustus Society members are proud that for each of the past five years more than fifteen deserving Italian-American students have been awarded $1,000 scholarships at the scholarship dinners. Unlike most other national or local eth-nic organizations, the Society has had no difficulty raising funds.

The Society's leadership also remains committed to assisting seniors. But according to former presidents Mike Fauci and Dino Sorrentino, needy Italian-American seniors in Southern Nevada have been difficult to locate. One Christmas Mike Fauci asked several of the laborers employed by his construction company to deliver Society food baskets to older Italian Americans who had been identi-fied as needy by Society members. Many of the recipients expressed their disdain for the effort. (The laborers told Fauci that most of the dwellings they visited were far from humble.) As Italian Americans had the third highest income of all the ethnic groups surveyed in Clark County according to the 1980 U.S. Census, it is not surprising that this charitable endeavor was not welcomed. Undaunted, Society leaders searched for better ways to identify and serve Italian-American seniors.

Enhancing the image of Italian Americans has also been an important goal of the Society. In 1990 its board of directors allocated $8,000 for an advertising cam-paign to inform Las Vegas of the achievements of Italians and Italian Americans.[15] In December 1992 the Society joined with the Club, the Sons of Italy, and the Nevada Society of Italian American Lawyers to underwrite the costs of three public television programs about the achievements of Italians—two about Christopher Columbus and one featuring Luciano Pavarotti.

The positive image campaign was developed with the full cooperation of the Nevada Society of Italian American Lawyers (NSIAL), an organization formed in 1987 by Dominic Gentile to enhance the image of Italian Americans. As several of the most active members of NSIAL were also active in the Augustus Society, the antidefamation and image enhancement efforts were coordinated between the two groups. Dominic Gentile served as chair of the Society's cultural affairs com-mittee; he and NSIAL member Jerry DePalma served as chairs of the Society's board of directors; and Nikolos Mastrangelo took office as Society president in October 1992. NSIAL's presidents following Dominic Gentile—Carl Piazza, Nikolas Mastrangelo, and most recently Vince Consul—have actively protested the negative stereotyping of Italian Americans by some gaming regulators and journalists. They and the NSIAL's membership (numbering 40–50 and including District Court Judges Bonaventure and Bongiovanni) generally have taken a low-key but effective approach to assisting Italian Americans who believe that their gaming careers have been limited by employer or gaming regulator prejudice. The Society has also assisted Italian immigrants who are having difficulties with the U.S. Immigration and Naturalization Service.[16]

Of course, since NSIAL is composed of well-assimilated attorneys, it has also worked to promote the image of all lawyers, primarily by sponsoring a Red Mass. Rev. Francis Vivona, trained in the Canon law at the Pontifical College in Rome and serving as judicial vicar of the Catholic diocese of Reno–Las Vegas, approached NSIAL leaders in the winter of 1991 about supporting a Red Mass, the traditional Catholic ceremony to honor the role of lawyers in society. The first Red Mass held at Our Lady of Las Vegas Church in September 1991 was a success. Many donations were made to the diocese, attendance was good, and leaders of other religious groups came to the Mass. Vivona attended the April 1992 NSIAL meeting and explained that owing to the success of the initial effort, Nevada's Bishop, Daniel Walsh, had offered the group use of the Guardian Angel Cathedral, located just off the Strip, for the second Las Vegas Red Mass.

In addition to these events, NSIAL has provided members with opportunities to socialize and to exchange information about the legal profession. The members' ages have ranged from the mid-twenties to the sixties, and meetings have been characterized by convivial and frank exchanges of political and professional ideas. Italian food has been served at all meetings, but the group has had only one member who is fluent in Italian. Very few in this group of well-assimilated Italian Americans had spouses of Italian ancestry.

Regardless of who holds the presidency, Dominic Gentile clearly has been the leader of NSIAL. When Gentile speaks, the other roughly fifteen attorneys attending monthly meetings listen. His ideas about which activities the NSIAL should support set the agenda. Careful not to appear to dominate, Gentile welcomes opposing points of view, yet as often occurs in the courtroom, Gentile's logic prevails.

Another recently formed organization is the Las Vegas Chapter of the National Italian American Sports Hall of Fame (NIASHF). The Illinois-based parent organization, founded by a group of Italian-American businessmen in 1978, has as goals providing proper recognition of Italian-American sports greats and awarding scholarships to deserving student athletes without regard to race, creed, or color. The local chapter was started in 1986 by Andy Jerry. Fewer than a dozen Italian Americans had joined the organization until John Tassone, a golf tournament organizer, was elected president in 1990. Under his leadership the membership had reached sixty by late 1991, a local scholarship program had been established, and a man of the year award banquet had been initiated. Tassone and other chapter officers presented the first award to William Peccole. This was a wise choice, since Peccole's business associates, particularly contractors working on the huge Peccole Ranch development, with hundreds of homes and apartment houses, bought almost three hundred tickets for the banquet.[17] It is still too early to determine whether the chapter will continue to attract new members. A development with positive ramifications for the group's future viability occurred in November 1991 when the membership decisively rejected a proposal to separate from the parent organization.

Overall, Italian-American organizations are faring well considering that third- and fourth-generation Italian Americans are so thoroughly assimilated. Italian Americans are indistinguishable by their behavior from the general population. Their speech, dress, and mannerisms no longer set them apart from the majority of Americans. Italian Americans have served as cabinet secretaries, governors, U.S. senators, and chief executive officers of Fortune 500 companies. The most convincing example of their assimilation is their contemporary rate of intermarriage, which is now over 80 percent for fourth-generation Italian Americans.[18] Few are those who perceive an Italian-American organization as the only relaxing setting for social relations. Many other social, philanthropic, and business organizations beckon.

The future is brighter for some Italian-American organizations than for others. The Augustus Society and the NSIAL appeal to fourth-generation Italian Americans who are both proud of their heritage (which may include other ethnic backgrounds) and desirous of expanding their social and business contacts. Members may have a considerable advantage, as several researchers on ethnicity have suggested, since financial success and integration in American society may be correlated with maintaining ethnic identity, at least a symbolic ethnicity that is confined to a few ethnic symbols and does not interfere with individuals' otherwise assimilated daily life.[19]

Yet the Club, the Sons of Italy, the ICF chapters, and the AIC must all address the serious problem of aging memberships. This issue has been most compelling for the Sons of Italy, which is grappling with aging and declining memberships in chapters throughout the United States. In recent years the Las Vegas lodge's monthly meetings have attracted mostly seniors and very few younger members. Perhaps the best evidence of the difficult future of this organization was an early 1991 exchange between Venerable Ann Little and a member of more than two decades. "Joe, you should come to meetings more often. We need young people like you." He responded, "Young, I'm fifty now, Ann!" The Sons of Italy lodge will remain viable as long as Phil Carlino remains active. His energy and enthusiasm, as of this writing, ensure the immediate future of the Sons of Italy, but there are no potential leaders waiting in the wings. Indeed, when Ann Little resigned at the end of 1991, Carlino's wife, Florence, a longtime active member of the Sons of

Italy, though not Italian American, was appointed Venerable. The Sons of Italy, the ICF chapters, and the AIC will remain active organizations into the twenty-first century only if they can attract younger men and women, including those with leadership abilities. As of this writing they had not yet done so.

The Club has had some limited success in developing a mixture of both traditional gatherings for older members and innovative programs to attract new and younger members. Angelo Cassaro, the youngest president in more than twenty years, led the Club to expand its array of events. Amateur boxing, opera performances, and an Italian music hour each Sunday on a local radio station were initiated in 1991. In addition, Cassaro and the chair of CCSN's foreign languages department arranged for a three-semester series of conversational Italian courses at the Club in 1989–90. This undertaking was a success, bringing together Club members of diverse ages.

Cassaro, Vice President Tony Allotta, and other Club officers, all senior to Cassaro, were careful not to neglect older Club members. They continued to sponsor the dances, traditional Italian celebrations, and bocce tournaments that appealed to those over fifty years of age—the great bulk of the membership. Most important for many long-standing members, the Club provided a place to relax, drink, and play cards. Using the card room for the conversational Italian class, which ended before 9:00 P.M. was acceptable; however, several members complained that their leisure activities were disrupted when the card room was used for late-night restaurant overflow.

Cassaro and other officials were well aware that the Club was the only Italian-American organization in Nevada with a separate auxiliary membership for women. Cassaro repeatedly informed this author between 1988 and 1992 of his commitment to merge the two organizations eventually. He recognized the need for caution in making this transition because several Club and Ladies Auxiliary leaders felt the present system worked well. Elsie Formica, the Ladies Auxiliary president in 1992, felt that most members (only about 15 percent of the 120 members were younger than forty years old) liked the separation. Previous presidents Alice Allotta and Mary Baldassore agreed with her. Many members felt that the separation afforded women a greater opportunity to relax, make their own decisions, and assume leadership positions. Formica and several other past and present leaders of the Ladies Auxiliary reluctantly agreed that this separation discouraged younger women from becoming involved in the largest and oldest Italian-American organization in Southern Nevada.

Positive developments for Southern Nevada's Italian-American organizations are overlapping memberships and growing cooperation between groups. Several Augustus Society members, including three past presidents of the Nevada Society of Italian American Lawyers, have joined the Club, as has Phil Carlino of the Sons of Italy. The Augustus Society occasionally meets at the Club, and for sev-

Bocce team captain Carmen Annillo in a 1987 competition.
(James Kenney, Las Vegas Sun)

Las Vegas Bocce team players in June 1987. Left to right: Lucio Zanin, Rosario Cristina, and Gino Bartoletti. (James Kenney, Las Vegas Sun)

eral years it held its annual Christmas party there.

The best example of cooperative spirit was the establishment of the Columbus Day Parade Association. For the great majority of Clark County's more than 55,000 Italian Americans, Columbus Day has been one of the few connections they have with the land of some of their ancestors. The celebration of Columbus Day is an excellent example of the practice of symbolic ethnicity that many sociologists, most notably Richard Alba, Herbert Gans, and Stephen Steinberg, contend has become increasingly common for well-assimilated Americans of European background.[20] It has been a token acknowledgment of one's particular European ancestry. It does not require any sacrifice, does not interfere with the need to intermix socially, and reaffirms just how American men and women of that heritage are.

The leaders of the Augustus Society, the Club, two ICF chapters, NIASHF, NSIAL, and the Sons of Italy attended a "summit meeting" on January 26, 1989, to plan the Columbus Day Parade.[21] All of the organizations were committed to carrying out the first annual parade. Dino Sorrentino and Charles Cocuzza, members of both the Augustus Society and the Club, were chosen as chair and cochair of the Columbus Day Parade Association. The parade was a success: politicians, entertainers, journalists, and business leaders of various ethnic backgrounds served on an advisory board, two Downtown hotels sponsored the event, and a Strip hotel hosted a Queen Isabella Pageant. The two ICF chapters and the NIASHF, with limited memberships and funds, did not contribute as much as the larger and newer organizations and did not participate in subsequent years. Association members Phil Carlino, Angelo Cassaro, Charles Cocuzza, Doug Ferrari, Carl Piazza (like Graziadei, Gentile, and DePalma, a former Chicago lawyer), Dino Sorrentino, and Charles Russo, all successful business owners except Ferrari (who was the slots manager at the Tropicana), developed an excellent working relationship.

Subsequent parades, like the first one, provided examples of just how assimilated Las Vegas Italian Americans are. Politicians of the Democratic, Libertarian, and Republican parties walked and waved to crowds lining Fremont Street in downtown Las Vegas; several marching bands played, gymnasts performed, members of the Sons of Erin relaxed and drank beer on the back of a flatbed truck, and men and women of Scottish heritage (presumably) played the bagpipes. The only distinctly Italian aspect of the parade was the food served at a block party that followed. Everyone associated with the parade, especially the people who were celebrating the quincentennial of Columbus's voyage, felt a sense of pride; none apparently stopped to consider how little of anything distinctly Italian was celebrated. The parade has been an excellent example of the pervasiveness of symbolic ethnicity.

The Columbus Day Ball provided another example of both cooperation and symbolic ethnicity. The ball generated at least as much enthusiasm for the Augustus Society as the annual scholarship dinner each spring. This black-tie affair, attended by three hundred to four hundred men and women, was held in a Strip hotel ballroom, and an award was given to the outstanding Italian American. As is the case with the Columbus Day Parade, all profits went toward a scholarship fund. Three hotel chief executives, John Chiero (the Tropicana), John Giovenco (the Hilton), and Frank Modica (the Showboat), as well as Nevada Secretary of State (and now Attorney General) Frankie Sue Del Papa and businesswoman Lorraine Perri Hunt have been recipients. Thanks largely to Dominic Gentile, the NSIAL began cosponsoring the Columbus Day Ball in 1991. Longtime Las Vegas attorney George Graziadei was chosen to receive the first Justinian Award (named in honor of the Byzantine emperor who codified Roman laws and legal opinions in the sixth century), presented at the ball. Not surprisingly, in April 1992 the NSIAL membership selected Dominic Gentile as the second Justinian Award recipient.

Finally, the Club, NSIAL, the Augustus Society, and the Sons of Italy agreed in 1992 to underwrite the cost of television programs dealing with Columbus's voyage and opera. They appeared on KLVX, the Public Broadcasting Service station in Las Vegas. The prime mover in this project was Phil Carlino, whose ethnic identification was far from only symbolic. The four organizations were given credit for their contributions in the monthly bulletin sent to all Southern Nevadans who contributed to KLVX and on television immediately preceding and following airing of the two programs.

During the last forty years the Italian-American organizations of Southern Nevada have served the social and philanthropic needs of the relatively small minority of Italian Americans who both value their ethnic heritage and enjoy socializing with other Italian Americans. These groups have provided a sense of continuity with the past, particularly for those Italian Americans who have come to Las Vegas from ethnic enclaves in the East. Those organizations that offer innovative programs of particular interest to younger, more assimilated Italian Americans and that are willing to cooperate with other Italian-American groups will survive into the twenty-first century.

Chapter Five

Conclusion:

The Immigrant Upraised

Andrew Rolle wrote in the concluding chapter of his study of Italian immigrants in the West that for Italian immigrants "life was not a disappointment but, rather, a challenge, even an adventure. . . . They generally escaped ethnic crowding, slums, ghettoes, and a large measure of prejudice, partly because of the western outlook. Western attitudes were often generous and easy going, especially in small communities. . . . Despite their initial sufferings, the immigrants found freedom in America's West rather than rigidity, openness rather than closed privilege."[1] This is a good, though incomplete, summary of the experience of Italian immigrants, their children and grandchildren in Las Vegas specifically. Las Vegans were generous and easygoing, not only when Las Vegas was a dusty railroad stop, but also during its rapid growth into a major metropolitan area.

Las Vegas has provided the Italian born and Italian Americans unequaled opportunities. The Champos, Graglias, Matteucis, Pecettos, and Silvagnis, all hardworking and intelligent people, better realized their potentials in the open atmosphere of a growing desert town than they would have in the urban ghettoes of Eastern cities. Even Tony Cornero, whose Italian ancestry and a rum-running conviction brought him great scrutiny, eventually had an opportunity to begin construction on the Stardust. More recent immigrants from the East and California, men and women with such diverse interests and backgrounds as Al Isola, Frank Sala, Tony Tegano, Angelo Cassaro, Peter Anthony, Dominic Gentile, and Chris Giunchigliani took advantage of the opportunities provided by an open and rapidly growing city in the Sunbelt and contributed to Las Vegas's development. In return, Las Vegans recognized them as leaders in business and the professions and welcomed their involvement in civic activities. Lorraine Perri Hunt's easy transition from Strip entertainer to restaurant owner and then to membership on the board of directors of Continental National Bank and in 1994 the Clark County Commission affirms the exceptional opportunities for economic and social mobility that have been available in Las Vegas.

The impact of Italian-American bankers, builders, and developers is seen everywhere in Las Vegas. Whether driving on the Strip or traveling through one of

131

Civic and business leader Lorraine Perri Hunt, Nevada Italian American Leader of the Year in 1991. (Courtesy Clark County Commissioner Lorraine Perri Hunt)

Las Vegas's many residential areas, one sees the results of substantial Italian-American involvement in the financing, planning, construction, and sales of hotels, commercial developments, apartment houses, and homes. Every construction boom since 1930 has brought more Italian-American builders and developers to Las Vegas, the boom of the late 1980s and early 1990s being no exception. Some of these businesspeople made long-term contributions to the development of Las Vegas; a few left without making an impact on the city. Most achieved financial success and gained social status.

The steady influx of Italian-born chefs and restaurateurs ensures the continuation of the tradition of culinary excellence established by Louis Coniglio, Battista Locatelli, and the Perri and Ruvo families.[2] Tourists and locals have enjoyed choosing from among many fine Italian restaurants Downtown, along the Strip, and, more recently, in the suburbs. The presence of these establishments has contributed to Las Vegas's appeal as a resort city.

The extent of Italian-American assimilation in Las Vegas is reflected by the fact that no Italian-American elected official has ever been dependent on "the Italian vote." No ethnic neighborhoods have ever existed, and only a small minority of Italian Americans participate in ethnic organizations. Italian Americans have represented Las Vegans in the Nevada legislature and on the Board of Regents; they have served as city commissioners, county commissioners, district court judges, and constables. Their Italian ancestry has not been an issue in any campaign. Unlike Italian Americans in such cities as New York, Boston, Philadelphia, and Chicago, and, indeed, unlike Cuban Americans in Miami and Mexican Americans in cities of the Southwest, Las Vegas Italian Americans were well assimilated and have had no need to develop the politics of ethnic accommodation.

Italian Americans have been active participants in every aspect of Las Vegas's hotel business since Nevada re-legalized gambling in 1931. On the casino floor as dealers, pit bosses, and shift bosses, in the executive offices as hosts, entertainment directors, vice presidents, and, more recently, as chief executive officers, in the showrooms or lounges as performers, men, and less often women, of Italian background have been present in numbers far exceeding their representation in the national or Las Vegas population. Similarly, Italian Americans were well represented behind the scenes in the 1950s and 1960s, arranging for the injections of capital from Meyer Lansky and Frank Costello or the Teamsters Central States Pension Fund that were so vital to the development of Las Vegas. More than any other American city, Las Vegas gave migrants a second chance. Past transgressions were usually forgotten, and for those who accumulated wealth, social prestige and political power were also attainable. Americans of other European ancestries also benefited from the tolerant attitude in Las Vegas, but as Italian Americans and Jewish Americans had already developed so many of the illegal but profitable gambling enterprises in the East, they were the greatest beneficiaries.

Yet the pervasive myth of the Mafia as an all-powerful worldwide crime network centered in Sicily has made life more difficult for some of the more ambitious Italian Americans with gambling experience who settled in Las Vegas in the 1950s and 1960s.[3] If they chose to advance into management, they were often the object of extra scrutiny and sometimes discrimination by Nevada gaming regulators.

A recent example of such extra scrutiny involved the restoration of the work card of the Mirage executive casino host Charlie Meyerson by the Clark County Business Licensing Department. The story was analyzed in an April 1992 *Review-Journal* staff editorial. Meyerson, a Jewish American, had been a New York City bookie and longtime friend of Mirage owner Steve Wynn's father. In late 1991 the Las Vegas Metropolitan Police had, with maximum publicity, revoked Meyerson's work card because he had provided free rooms and other privileges (termed "comps" in Las Vegas) to three alleged Italian-American Mafiosi from New York. Meyerson denied knowing that the three had ties to organized crime.

Basically sympathetic to Meyerson, the *Review-Journal* editorial suggested that since the three were not in Nevada's Black Book, no one was obligated to deny them the usual high-roller comps, much less access to a casino. The editorial continued: "Are Nevada casinos obliged to run background checks on all guests, even those not listed in the Black Book? Obviously, that would verge on the logistically impossible. As a shortcut, should they check only the backgrounds of guests who have Italian American surnames and live in the northeastern United States? Who must 'OK' them? And does that mean gangsters, drug dealers and bunko artists from Colombia and Japan are all right, that by definition their presence cannot 'embarrass Las Vegas'?"[4]

The *Review-Journal* captured the feelings of many Italian-American interviewees who question why criminals of backgrounds other than Italian are admitted to the casinos, while Italian Americans receive greater scrutiny and are disproportionately featured in the Black Book. Is this treatment a result of the myth of the Mafia as an all-powerful international enterprise with tentacles reaching from Sicily to every corner of the globe? This question has never been answered to their satisfaction.

Yet more important, neither the Black Book nor the negative publicity about alleged or convicted Mafiosi has significantly affected most Italian Americans in Las Vegas. Entertainers, restaurant owners, builders, professionals, and public officials have not been extensively scrutinized when they chose to expand their businesses or advance in their professions. These well-assimilated Italian Americans have been able to relax more than their gaming industry counterparts could, enjoy success, and form high-profile Italian-American organizations to publicize their philanthropy and enhance the Italian-American image.

Summary

Las Vegas and its Italian Americans have had a mutually beneficial relationship. Once a convenient place to relax on the railroad journey between Los Angeles and Salt Lake City and now a world-renowned resort city, Las Vegas has been a land of opportunity for Italian Americans with intelligence and ambition. It would be an overstatement to assert that Italian Americans made Las Vegas. Jewish-American gaming entrepreneurs, Mormon bankers and politicians, as well as builders and developers of a dozen different ethnic backgrounds can all claim some credit for building Las Vegas. Nonetheless, Las Vegas is a bigger, brighter, and more exciting city thanks to Italian Americans.

List of Interviewees

Mark Alden
Jacqueline Oliva Allen
Alice Allotta
Tony Allotta
Russ Anderson
Al Aniello
Carmen Annillo
Peter Anthony
Rose Antonello
Mary Baldassore
Pete Barbuti
Catherine Barcal
Mary Jean Barozzi
Ed Becker
Dominic Bianchi
Joan Bommarito
Ted Bommarito
John Bonaventura
Anthony Borelli
Silvio Borla
Al Bossi
Frank Brusa
William Bunker
Kevin Burr
Tony Calabro
Ted Canino
Randy Capurro
Phil Carlino
Didi Carson
Al Casarotto
Angelo Cassaro
Don Cassella
Ruth Catalano
Frank Catania
Joe Catello

Emil Cava
Gary Cavaretta
Caesar Caviglia
John Chiero
Harry Claiborne
Charles Cocuzza
Carmine Colucci
Julius Conigliaro
Frank Coniglio
Vince Consul
John DeBiase
Syl DeGregorio
Joe Delaney
Ralph Denton
Jerry DePalma
Roseanne Gargano
   DePalma
Roland DiIorio
Phil Dioguardi
Chuck DiRocco
Tony DiVecchio
Joe Domina
Ray Eade
Joe Farina
Mike Fauci
Christina Fenton
Doug Ferrari
Frank Fertitta
Jerry Filipelli
Maurice Finocchiaro
Harry Fletcher
Joseph Foley
Thomas Foley
Andrea Fontana
Willie Fopiano

Elsie Formica
Joe Formica
Benjamin Franzinelli
Reno Fruzza
Frank Gagliardi
Dominic Gentile
Chuck Giampa
Chris Giunchigliani
Leonard Goodall
George Graziadei
Italo Guelfi
Rudy Guerrero
Jean Harris
Tracey Heberling
Rose Hill
Lorraine Perri Hunt
Stella Champo Iaconis
Sam Iacovetto
Al Isola
Linda DeLuca Isola
Tom Isola
Andy Jerry
Toni Tucci Lamb
Battista Locatelli
Joseph La Mancusa
Lou La Porta
Joe Lendini
Wilbur Leypoldt
George Ligouri
John Ligouri
Ann Little
Battista Locatelli
Al Lodati
Dante Lorenzi
Julio Lucchesi

Ray Lucchesi
Jeanne Maini
Jim Mancuso
David Manzi
John Manzonie
Izzy Marion
Anthony Marlon
Tony Marnell
Ernie Martinelli
Mark Massagli
Nikolas Mastrangelo
Victor Matera
Gene Matteuci
Tony Mazzucca
John McVeigh
Anthony Messina
Paul Messineo
Phil Mirabelli
Frank Modica
Olga Silvagni Moe
Mario Monaco
Frank Musso
Tony Neno
Angelo Nicassio
Ed Nigro
Ray Paglia

Marie Palmieri
Vincent Palmisano
William Papagna
Giovanni Parente
Rodney Pass
William Peccole
Ralph Petillo
Jack Petitti
Judy Pisanello
Tom Pitaro
John Pollostro
Tony Ponticello
Tony Ricci
Sharon Richardson
Jeanne DeLucchi Roberts
Anthony Robone
Donald Romeo
Dick Ronzone
Nick Rossi
Dan Rotunno
Larry Ruvo
Richard Saber
Frank Sala
Vic Salerno
Pamela Salvucci

Sandy Sandquist
Blake Sartini
Steve Savoldelli
Frank Silvaggio
Janie Silvaggio
Charles Silvestri
Dino Sorrentino
Joe Spinuzzi
Vito Stolfa
Vic Taucer
Tony Tegano
Mike Terlizzi
Guido Testolin
J. H. Tiberti
Joe Todaro
Verdun Trione
Herman Van Betten
Pat Van Betten
Giovanni Vanchieri
Tom Vannozzi
Don Vincent
Francis Vivona
Vern Willis
Rudy Yacenda
Peter Zavattaro

Notes

1. The terms *Mafia, Mob,* and *organized crime* are used by most journalists, authors, and academics interchangeably. I have used the word *Mob* in cases where these various terms appeared interchangeably in the original source(s). I refer to Las Vegans widely reputed to have a direct or indirect connection with organized crime as *The Boys.* This term has several advantages. First, it does not imply that organized crime is more ethnically monolithic than it really is; the terms *Mob* and *Mafia* do. Second, it is a less negative term than *Mob associate* or *Mafia associate,* reflecting the fact that the line between legitimate and illegitimate business is often vague. Third, it is not offensive to members of any ethnic group. When one writes about the Jewish Mafia, the Irish Mafia, or the Nigerian Mafia, one may offend Italians and Italian Americans by implying that the highest form of criminal enterprise had its origins in Italy and can only be imitated by non-Italians. Perhaps members of other ethnic groups should also feel offended. Finally, *The Boys* is a term used by many Las Vegans who lived and worked in Las Vegas in the 1950s and 1960s.

2. Sociologist Daniel Bell argued persuasively forty years ago, in "Crime as an American Way of Life," *Antioch Review* 13 (1953): 115–36, that Italian Americans and Jewish Americans were relative newcomers to leadership positions in organized crime. Joseph Albini also made this argument in "The Genesis and Development of Criminal Syndicates in the United States," a chapter in his *The American Mafia: Genesis of a Legend* (New York: Appleton-Century-Crofts, 1971). Alan Block details the relationships among Italian-American and Jewish-American mobsters in his well-documented *East Side–West Side: Organizing Crime in New York 1930–1950* (New Brunswick: Transaction Books, 1983).

CHAPTER ONE. THE EARLY YEARS:
FROM LABORERS TO SUCCESSFUL ENTREPRENEURS

1. Wilbur S. Shepperson, *Restless Strangers: Nevada's Immigrants and Their Interpreters* (Reno: University of Nevada Press, 1970), p. 14; and Thirteenth Census of the United States, 1910 Abstract with a Supplement for Nevada (Washington, D.C., 1913), p. 209.

2. Like others who have written about Italian Americans in the Western United

States, I have included individuals who emigrated from Switzerland's Italian-speaking cantons. The same approach is taken by Albin J. Cofone, "Reno's Little Italy: Italian Entrepreneurship and Culture in Northern Nevada," *Nevada Historical Society Quarterly* 26 (Summer 1983): 97–110; and "Themes in the Italian Settlement of Nevada," *Nevada Historical Society Quarterly* 25 (Summer 1982): 116–32. Cofone's article "Italian Images in Northern Nevada Writing," *Nevada Historical Society Quarterly* 27 (Winter 1984): 260–67; and articles by Phillip Earl and Wilbur Shepperson in the Summer 1969 *Nevada Historical Society Quarterly* comprehensively present the important role of the Italian born and Italian Americans in Nevada's history.

3. Herbert J. Gans, *The Urban Villagers: Group and Class in the Life of Italian-Americans* (New York: Free Press, 1962), is probably the foremost of several sociological studies of Italian-American communities on the East Coast showing the initially slow movement of first- and second-generation Italian Americans to acculturation and middle-class status. In *Italians in Chicago, 1880–1930: A Study in Ethnic Mobility* (New York: Oxford University Press, 1970), Humbert Nelli perceived more mobility than did Gans.

4. Andrew F. Rolle, *The Immigrant Upraised: Italian Adventurers and Colonists in an Expanding America* (Norman: University of Oklahoma Press, 1968), p. 11.

5. Ibid., p. 7; see also Micaela di Leonardo's *The Varieties of Ethnic Experience: Kinship, Class, and Gender among California Italian-Americans* (Ithaca and London: Cornell University Press, 1984). He argues that the diversity of the California economy allowed Italian immigrants a greater opportunity for financial advancement than did the economies of Eastern and Midwest states.

6. Payroll and Labor Distribution files of San Pedro, Los Angeles, and Salt Lake Railroad Company. Special Collections of University of Nevada, Las Vegas.

7. U.S. Department of Commerce, Bureau of the Census, Thirteenth U.S. Census, 1910 Abstract, pp. 43, 582.

8. Thirteenth U.S. Census, 1910 Manuscript Census.

9. *Las Vegas Age,* May 11, 1907, p. 8.

10. Thirteenth U.S. Census, 1910 Manuscript Census.

11. *Las Vegas Age,* August 8, 1905, p. 4.

12. Ibid., September 23, 1905, p. 4.

13. Ibid., July 31, 1915, p. 2.

14. Ibid., January 6, 1917, p. 1.

15. Ibid., June 10, 1905, p. 1.

16. Ibid., April 1, 1911, p. 1.

17. Ibid., June 10, 1905; and April 1, 1911.

18. Elizabeth Patrick, "The Champos: An Italian Family Rose to Prosperity in 1920's Las Vegas," *The Nevadan,* March 27, 1982, pp. 6–7.

19. Interview with Stella Champo Iaconis.

20. *Las Vegas Age,* August 15, 1912, p. 2.

21. Stephen Thernstrom's *A History of the American People,* Vol. 2 (San Diego: Harcourt Brace Jovanovich, 1984), pp. 554–60, is one of many sources of information on these subjects.

22. *Las Vegas Age,* October 7, 1916, p. 1; October 6, 1917, p. 2; September 29, 1917, p. 2.

23. Roy Chesson, "The Man Who Settled the Dust with Wine," *The Nevadan,* June 8, 1967, pp. 26–27. See also *Las Vegas Age,* December 30, 1922, p. 1.

24. D. G. Lorenzi's daughter, Mrs. Louise Fountain, informed me that her father came from an area of France close to the Italian border and did not consider himself Italian, stressing rather that his family members were cousins of the Grimaldis, Monaco's ruling family. Since Mr. Lorenzi was rather widely considered to be of Italian background, I have included him in this study.

25. *Las Vegas Age,* January 10, 1914, p. 3.

26. Interviews with Dick Ronzone and Jack Petitti.

27. *The Nevadan,* June 18, 1967, pp. 26–27. See also *Las Vegas Age,* December 30, 1922, p. 1.

28. *Las Vegas Age,* November 6, 1920, p. 1.

29. Ibid., January 15, 1916, p. 1.

30. Ibid., April 21, 1923, p. 1; August 16, 1924, p. 1; August 27, 1931, p. 6; and July 22, 1938, p. 1.

31. Russell R. Elliott, *History of Nevada* (Lincoln and London: University of Nebraska Press, 1973), pp. 277–78.

32. *Las Vegas Age,* February 21, 1929, p. 1; and March 16, 1934, p. 1.

33. Ibid., March 23, 1934, p. 1.

34. Ibid., January 19, 1929, p. 1; and February 24, 1944, p. 5. Additional information on John Vinassa is available in the *Las Vegas Age,* April 5, 1932, p. 6; and February 7, 1939, p. 2.

35. Interview with Dick Ronzone, January 10, 1989.

36. *Las Vegas Review-Journal,* February 20, 1951, p. 1; and interview with Dick Ronzone.

37. *Las Vegas Evening Review-Journal and Boulder City Journal,* February 10, 1948, p. 2.

38. *Las Vegas Age,* May 3, 1931, ten-page section devoted to the Meadows casino.

39. Ibid., July 1, 1931, p. 1.

40. Ibid., February 28, 1932, p. 4; *Las Vegas Review-Journal,* January 5, 1932, p. 2; and February 29, 1932, p. 1. No additional information on Marchetti was available from either newspapers or interviewees.

41. *Las Vegas Evening Review-Journal and Boulder City Journal,* February 10, 1948, p. 2. Information on Tony Cornero's California activities is found in the *Las Vegas Evening Review-Journal,* July 22, 1938, p. 4; and September 8, 1938, p. 1. Frank Cornero died a few years later in an automobile accident on Mt. Charleston Road in Las Vegas. Louis Cornero became a successful vintner in California's Napa Valley.

42. Eugene P. Moehring, *Resort City in the Sunbelt: Las Vegas, 1930–1970* (Reno and Las Vegas: University of Nevada Press, 1989), pp. 42–43.

43. Interviews with Phil Mirabelli and Olga Silvagni Moe. See also Helen Z. Papanikolas, ed., *The Peoples of Utah* (Salt Lake City: Utah State Historical Society, 1976), p. 311, for information about the Italian community in Carbon County.

44. Interview with Olga Silvagni Moe.

45. *Las Vegas Evening Review-Journal,* March 8, 1932, p. 1; and March 18, 1932, p. 1.

46. *Las Vegas Age,* September 9, 1933; interviews with Olga Silvagni Moe and Guido

Testolin.

47. Interviews with Phil Mirabelli, Olga Silvagni Moe, and Guido Testolin; *Las Vegas Sun,* January 10, 1980, p. 4.

48. The voter lists were published in the *Las Vegas Age* of November 4, 1924, pp. 12–15; and October 30, 1936, 14 pp. All interviewees who lived in Las Vegas in the 1930s recalled only a small number of Italian Americans.

49. Telephone directories for 1926, 1931–36; Directory of Las Vegas and Vicinity, 1943–44, Special Collections, UNLV; *Seventy-five Years of Catholic Life in Nevada (1860–1935),* courtesy of Dr. Kevin Rafferty, Community College of Southern Nevada.

50. Interview with Mary Jean Barozzi; *Las Vegas Sun,* January 30, 1989 (obituary of Aldo Barozzi). See *Las Vegas Evening Review-Journal,* October 18, 1931, p. 3, for Roma Café advertisement.

51. Interviews with Mary Jean Barozzi, Stella Champo Iaconis, Joe Lendini, Phil Mirabelli, Jeanne DeLucchi Roberts, and Guido Testolin. See also *Las Vegas Evening Review-Journal and Boulder City Journal,* February 22, 1946, p. 12; and March 20, 1946, p. 8 for more specific information on Pete Peccole's real estate holdings.

52. Interview with Jack Petitti.

53. *County Political Directory for Nevada, Clark County,* Nevada Historical Society, Reno, Nevada.

54. Interview with Linda Isola (née DeLuca). See also *Las Vegas Evening Review-Journal and Boulder City Journal,* July 11, 1944, p. 2; and October 25, 1945, p. 6 for more specific information on business transactions.

55. Interview with Linda DeLuca Isola.

56. *Las Vegas Evening Review-Journal and Boulder City Journal,* December 7, 1944, p. 1.

57. Ibid., December 8, 1944, p. 3.

58. Ibid., December 22, 1944, p. 3.

59. Ibid., June 30, 1945, p. 1.

60. Ibid., February 7, 1946, p. 1.

61. Ibid., May 2, 1946, p. 12.

62. Ed Reid and Ovid Demaris, *The Green Felt Jungle* (New York: Trident Press, 1963), pp. 12–13.

63. *Las Vegas Evening Review-Journal and Boulder City Journal,* August 5, 1946, p. 1.

64. Ibid., May 3, 1946, p. 1.

65. Nate Mack's early casino investments and his role in management of Eldorado Club and the Flamingo Hotel are mentioned in the *Las Vegas Evening Review-Journal and Boulder City Journal,* December 30, 1947, p. 3; and May 17, 1948, p. 5; *Las Vegas Review-Journal,* July 14, 1949, p. 2; and January 13, 1950, p. 10.

66. Craig Swallow, "The Ku Klux Klan in Nevada During the 1920's" (M.A. thesis, 1978, UNLV), p. 98.

67. Interviews with Stella Champo Iaconis, Phil Mirabelli, Olga Silvagni Moe, and Guido Testolin.

68. The confining nature of life in Italian neighborhoods is discussed thoroughly in Gans, *The Urban Villagers,* and Richard Gambino, *Blood of My Blood: The Dilemma of*

the Italian Americans (Garden City, N.Y.: Doubleday, 1974). The Dante Society's efforts are discussed by Albin J. Cofone, "Reno's Little Italy," pp. 108–109.

CHAPTER TWO. THE RAPID GROWTH YEARS: ITALIAN AMERICANS COME TO LAS VEGAS

1. John W. Findlay, *People of Chance: Gambling in American Society from Jamestown to Las Vegas* (New York: Oxford University Press, 1986), p. 173, discusses the population growth. "Boomtown in the Desert," a chapter in Eugene P. Moehring's *Resort City in the Sunbelt: Las Vegas, 1930–1970* (Reno and Las Vegas: University of Nevada Press, 1989), presents a comprehensive picture of the rapid development of Las Vegas.

2. The extent of the U.S. population of Italian heritage was, and remains today, a subject of dispute, with estimates ranging from 4 to 8 percent. The best estimate is 6 percent. See Joseph Velikonja's "Demographic and Cultural Aspects of Italian Americans" in Graziano Battistella, ed., *Italian Americans in the 80's: A Sociodemographic Profile* (New York: Center for Migration Studies, 1989) for information about Italian Americans gained in the 1980 U.S. Census. Velikonja noted in the January 1993 *Newsletter of the American Italian Historical Association* that the recently released 1990 U.S. Census reported that 14,714,939 of 248,709,873 people in the United States declared Italian ancestry: 5.93 percent of the 1990 population. The figure represents an absolute and relative increase from 1980, when 12,183,693 people or 5.39 percent of the total population identified their Italian ancestry. The absolute increase of 2,531,247 in ten years implies greater awareness of ethnic ancestry rather than an increase owing to birth or immigration. This author's estimate of the Las Vegas population was premised on defining an Italian American as someone with an Italian name. Resources for the estimates included voter registration lists published in the *Las Vegas Age*, October 30, 1936; and the *Las Vegas Review-Journal*, April 26, 1957; and telephone directories for the years under review, available in UNLV Special Collections.

3. The family-based value system of Italian Americans, particularly of those of southern Italian origin, has been discussed in many works, most notably Richard D. Alba's *Italian-Americans: Into the Twilight of Ethnicity* (Englewood Cliffs, N.J.: Prentice-Hall, 1985), and Richard Gambino's *Blood of My Blood: The Dilemma of the Italian Americans* (Garden City, N.Y.: Doubleday and Company, 1974). Chapter 4 of William Foote Whyte's *Street Corner Society: The Social Structure of an Italian Slum* (Chicago: University of Chicago Press, 1981) provides information about the nature and extent of illegal gambling in Italian-American neighborhoods.

4. The nature and extent of the illegal enterprises operated by Las Vegas's founding fathers is an often-told tale. Chapters 1–5 in Ed Reid and Ovid Demaris's *The Green Felt Jungle* (New York: Trident Press, 1963) provide a thorough though somewhat sensational review of this matter. See also George Stamos, "The Great Resorts of Las Vegas: How They Began," *Las Vegas Sun Magazine*, a series that ran from April 1979 to December 1979. In these works, as well as in the proceedings of Senator Kefauver's committee, Italian and Jewish names figured prominently.

5. Interviews with Rev. Caesar Caviglia, Rev. Benjamin Franzinelli, and Rev. John McVeigh.

6. Alan Balboni, "Tony's Carpet Joint," pp. 12S–13S. See also John F. Cahlan, Reminiscences of a Reno and Las Vegas Newspaperman, University Regent, and Public-Spirited Citizen, pp. 115–18. University of Nevada Oral History Project, 1969, UNLV Special Collections. Based on interviews with acquaintances of Cornero, Dennis Boyles, the author of *Mr. Lucky* (expected publication in 1996 by Houghton Mifflin), suggests that Cornero's apparent fatal heart attack resulted from a poison injection received from a mobster working for Moe Dalitz and Italian-American associates from Chicago. They regarded the former rumrunner as a loose cannon who was taking control of the Stardust.

7. Interview with Jacqueline Oliva Allen, a relative of Sam Baker.

8. *Las Vegas Review-Journal*, March 26, 1948, p. 1.

9. Jane Ann Morrison, "Spotlight on Searchlight," *The Nevadan*, October 9, 1977, pp. 3–4.

10. Interviews with Rose Hill and Sandy Sandquist; see *Las Vegas Review-Journal*, December 3, 1946, p. 7; September 1, 1949, p. 5; and February 1, 1950, p. 10, for information on some of the business activities of Willie Martello and one of his brothers. See *Las Vegas Sun*, May 20, 1990, p. 1AA for information on the investments of two other brothers.

11. U.S. Congress, Senate Special Committee to Investigate Organized Crime in Interstate Commerce. Part 10 (Nevada-California), 1951. Washington, D.C.: Government Printing Office, pp. 540–41 and 638–39.

12. Ibid., p. 636.

13. Lester Ben "Benny" Binion, Some Recollections of a Texas and Las Vegas Gaming Operator, p. 35. University of Nevada Oral History Project, 1976, UNLV Special Collections.

14. *Las Vegas Review-Journal*, November 16, 1950, p. 1; November 22, 1950, p. 1; and May 17, 1951, p. 1. Georgetti was convicted in federal court in San Francisco of income tax evasion and fined $200,000 in 1953.

15. Interviews with Syl DeGregorio, William Peccole, Guido Testolin, and another Italian American who wished to remain anonymous.

16. Reid and Demaris, *The Green Felt Jungle*, Appendix; interviews with Thomas Foley, George Ligouri, William Papagna, and Frank Sala; *Las Vegas Review-Journal*, December 31, 1991, p. 2B.

17. Several interviewees vaguely remembered Ricky Filigenzi as a major investor in the Sans Souci (later renamed the Castaways), a rather small Strip gaming property. Information on Filigenzi is not available since his widow refused requests for an interview.

18. Reid and Demaris, *The Green Felt Jungle*, pp. 208–209; interview with Ted Canino.

19. Stamos, "The Great Resorts of Las Vegas," June 3, 1979, pp. 6–7; interview with Charles Silvestri.

20. Interviews with Al Casarotto and Frank Modica.

21. Moehring, *Resort City in the Sunbelt*, p. 79.

22. The Italian-American businessman wished to remain anonymous. Fratianno's conversation with Ovid Demaris is recounted on pages 129–30 of Ovid Demaris's *The Last Mafioso* (New York: Bantam, 1980). Ed Becker offered his opinion in a conversation with this author in August 1991. Information on the respect shown alleged Mafia leaders is found in *The Last Mafioso,* Rappleye and Becker's works, *The Green Felt Jungle,* and Antoinette Giancana and Thomas C. Renner's *Mafia Princess: Growing Up in Sam Giancana's Family* (New York: Avon Books, 1985), *passim.* Ronald Farrell and Carole Case, UNLV criminal justice professors, make the argument that the myth of the Mafia as a structured organization controlling organized crime made it very difficult for Italian Americans with shady pasts to buy legitimacy in Nevada. See *The Black Book and the Mob* (Madison: University of Wisconsin Press, 1995), pp. 37–38 and 227–29.

23. Interviews with Al Bossi, Judy Pisanello, and Joe Todaro.

24. Interviews with Al Bossi, Rev. Caesar Caviglia, Rudy Guerrero (maitre d' at the Sands), Frank Musso, Giovanni Parente (assistant maitre d' at the Dunes), and others.

25. Charles Rappleye and Ed Becker, *All American Mafioso: The Johnny Rosselli Story* (New York: Doubleday, 1991), pp. 294, 367. See *Las Vegas Review-Journal,* February 4, 1993, p. 2F for additional information on Frank Sennes.

26. *Luskey's City Directories,* 1954–69, Special Collections, UNLV.

27. Interviews with Lou La Porta, Wilbur "Butch" Leypoldt (Clark County Sheriff, 1954–60), Rev. John McVeigh, and others, including Elliot Krane.

28. "Retired Las Vegas Restaurateur Dies," *Las Vegas Sun,* January 13, 1990, p. 13. Comments in Coniglio's obituary substantiated the memories of interviewees.

29. Jacqueline Oliva Allen, George Graziadei, Rudy Guerrero, and Toni Tucci Lamb provided information only about the quality of the restaurants. Tom Vannozzi substantiated Peter Zavattaro's memories of Cioppino's. John Smith, *Las Vegas Review-Journal* columnist, wrote about the Villa d'Este and the Mob on March 12, 1992, p. 1B; and February 10, 1993, p. 1B.

30. *Luskey's,* 1954–67; interviews with Professor Russell Anderson, Reno Fruzza, and Rev. John McVeigh substantiated Lorraine Hunt's recollections.

31. Interviews with Julius Conigliaro, Frank Musso, Tony Tegano (pit boss at the Dunes in the mid- and late 1960s and presently the owner of Tango Pool Company), Don Vincent, and an Italian American who wished to remain anonymous. See also *Las Vegas Review-Journal,* October 6, 1954, pp. 17, 23 for information on Mike's Market.

32. Interviews with Al Bossi, Reno Fruzza, Al Isola, and Tom Isola. See "Largest Private Transfer Station Open for Business," *World Wastes* (March 1983): 14–15 for information on the Isolas' commitment to state-of-the-art technology in waste disposal.

33. Interviews with Al Isola and Tom Isola.

34. Las Vegas Chamber of Commerce, *Business-Professional Directory,* 1954, UNLV Special Collections; *Luskey's,* 1954–69; and Nevada State Contractors Board, *Directory of Licensed Contractors,* 1967.

35. *Las Vegas Review-Journal,* December 30, 1944, p. 2; February 22, 1946, p. 5; February 4, 1951, p. 3; and interview with attorney John Manzonie.

36. Interviews with Al Bossi, attorney John Manzonie, Tony Ricci (an officer of the Italian American Club in the 1960s and 1970s); *Luskey's,* 1968–69.

37. Interviews with Tony Allotta (a subcontractor in the 1960s), Domenic Bianchi, Mike Fauci (son of Charles Fauci, a small contractor in the 1950s and 1960s; Mike is now president of M. G. Fauci Construction Company), and Tony Marnell; *Luskey's,* 1956–69.

38. *Luskey's,* 1957–69; interviews with Domenic Bianchi, Lou La Porta, and Ray Paglia Jr. See also Moehring, *Resort City in the Sunbelt,* p. 25, regarding the extensive home building of the Miranti brothers. The details of Gus Rapone's and Sierra Construction Company's rapid rise to success are not widely known. My many efforts to contact Gus Rapone by both telephone and letter were repeatedly thwarted by Kitty Rodman, one of the company's three founding partners.

39. *Las Vegas Review-Journal,* November 7, 1947, p. 2; interview with J. A. Tiberti.

40. Interviews with Tony Allotta, Julius Conigliaro, Rev. John McVeigh, and J. A. Tiberti. See *Las Vegas Review-Journal,* February 3, 1950, p. 1 for information on Indian Springs Air Force Base construction; and May 27, 1960, p. 1 for information on the awarding by Clark County School District to Tiberti Company of the $2,220,000 contract to build Western High School. (Actually, J. A. Tiberti did recall building three homes during the 1947–70 period.)

41. Interviews with Harry Fletcher (his father was an FNBN official and friend of Manente), attorney Joseph Foley, Reno Fruzza, Frank Modica, William Peccole, and Frank Sala. See also Moehring, *Resort City in the Sunbelt,* p. 231 for information about just one of Manente's many civic contributions.

42. Interviews with Harry Fletcher, Joseph Foley, and Reno Fruzza.

43. Interview with Guido Testolin. See also *Las Vegas Evening Review-Journal,* November 5, 1937, p. 4; April 5, 1940, p. 7 for additional information on Berto Testolin's business interests.

44. Nevada Superintendent of Banks, "Biennial Report of Superintendent of Banks," *Appendix to Journals of Senate and Assembly.* 1959 (Vol. 2); 1961 (Vol. 2); 1963 (Vol. 3); and 1969 (Vol. 2); interviews with William Peccole and Guido Testolin.

45. *Luskey's,* 1954–69; interviews with Al Aniello, Harry Claiborne, Lou La Porta, David Manzi, Phil Mirabelli, William Peccole, and Frank Sala. See *Las Vegas Evening Review-Journal and Boulder City Journal,* February 22, 1946, p. 12 for information on the real estate holdings of Peter Peccole, William's father.

46. *Luskey's,* 1957–69; interviews with Reno Fruzza, Dan Rotunno, and Frank Sala; *Las Vegas Review-Journal,* February 7, 1993, p. 1B.

47. *Luskey's,* 1954–69.

48. Gambino, *Blood of My Blood,* pp. 78–80 discusses the high levels of illiteracy of southern Italian immigrants and the limited education of most second-generation Italian Americans. Dr. Gambino, speaking at the Italian American Club in Las Vegas on November 17, 1989, said that Italian Americans differed from many other ethnic groups because their educational attainments followed rather than preceded their

economic advancements.

49. Interviews with Al Bossi, Harry Claiborne, John Manzonie, and Gene Matteuci; Waller H. Reed, comp., *A Political Directory for the Incorporated Communities of Nevada*, Nevada Historical Society, Reno, Nevada, 1982; *Luskey's*, 1961–69.

50. Interview with Gene Matteuci; Reed, *A Political Directory; Luskey's*, 1961–69. (Harry Claiborne served as attorney for Boulder City for only three weeks.)

51. *Luskey's*, 1957–69.

52. *Luskey's*, 1954–69; *History of Clark County Schools* by Harvey Dondero, compiled and edited by Billie F. Shank (Clark County School District, 1986); interviews with Frank Brusa, Rev. Caesar Caviglia, Mario Monaco, and Charles Silvestri.

53. Robbins Cahill, Recollections of Work in State Politics, Government, Taxation, Gaming Control, Clark County Administration, and the Nevada Resort Association, University of Nevada Oral History Project, 1973, Vol. 6, pp. 1295–99 and 1316–19, UNLV Special Collections.

54. "Former Water District Exec Dies," *Las Vegas Sun*, January 30, 1989, obituary page; *Luskey's*, 1951–69. Florence Lee Jones and John Cahlan, *Water: A History of Las Vegas. History of the Las Vegas Land and Water Company*, Vol. 2. (Las Vegas Water District, 1976) substantiates Mary Jean Barozzi's recollections on pp. 53, 70, and 154. See Moehring, *Resort City in the Sunbelt*, pp. 15–16 for general information on the development of water resources in the early 1950s.

55. *Las Vegas Sun*, April 24, 1982, p. 15.

56. See *Las Vegas Review-Journal*, November 19, 1990, p. 1 for an evaluation of Pisciotta's performance as director; and November 9, 1989, p. 1, for a review of the charges leading to Sartini's resignation.

57. Moehring, *Resort City in the Sunbelt*, pp. 56–58.

58. Reed, *A Political Directory;* Moehring, *Resort City in the Sunbelt*, pp. 71–72, 100–101; Binion, Texas and Las Vegas Gaming Operator, p. 69.

59. Reed, *A Political Directory;* Peccole stressed in the interview that he did nothing to bring about the defeat of Sharp, whom he regarded as a friend.

60. Ibid.; interviews with Jack Pettiti and Dick Ronzone. See *Las Vegas Evening Review-Journal*, December 17, 1937, p. 11; December 15, 1939, p. 10; June 17, 1946, p. 6; and February 4, 1949 for information of Pettiti's athletic achievements. See November 6, 1950, p. 1 for information on Ronzone's first bid for elective office.

61. *A Political History of Nevada*, Office of the Secretary of State, 1986; Reed, *A Political Directory.*

62. Both Pettiti and Ronzone became more interested in their Italian heritage after retiring from politics. Pettiti visited the area of northern Italy from which his father's parents had emigrated. Ronzone, whose grandfather had also come from northern Italy, had been studying his Ronzone family history, with a map of Italy at his side, when this author interviewed him shortly before his death. He expressed regret that he had not been more involved in Italian-American matters.

63. Candace Kant discussed the cinematic image of Las Vegas as a place where dreams come true in "City of Dreams: Las Vegas in the Cinema, 1980–1989," *Nevada Magazine* 50 (January/February 1990): 11–14 and 54–56.

64. See Humbert S. Nelli, *The Business of Crime: Italians and Syndicate Crime in the United States* (New York: Oxford University Press, 1976); and Stephen Fox, *Blood and Power: Organized Crime in Twentieth-Century America* (New York: William Morrow, 1989) for a most balanced presentation of the complex and emotionally charged issue of the role of some ethnic groups in organized crime. See also Demaris, *The Last Mafioso*, for an insider's perspective on the involvement of both Italian Americans and Jewish Americans in organized crime.

CHAPTER THREE. THE CORPORATE ERA: ITALIAN AMERICANS PROSPER

1. See Charles Rappleye and Ed Becker, *All American Mafioso: The Johnny Rosselli Story* (New York: Doubleday, 1991), pp. 282–84; and Peter Wiley and Robert Gottlieb, *Empires in the Sun: The Rise of the New American West* (New York: G. P. Putnam's Sons, 1982), pp. 201–203, for a quite credible account of the roles of Greenspun, Dalitz, and Rosselli.

2. Eugene P. Moehring, *Resort City in the Sunbelt: Las Vegas, 1930–1970* (Reno and Las Vegas: University of Nevada Press, 1989), p. 51.

3. Rappleye and Becker, *All American Mafioso.*

4. Ibid., p. 285.

5. Interviews with Al Casarotto, Frank Modica, and Tony Ponticello (a commercial real estate broker).

6. Only stockholders with at least a 5 percent interest had to undergo the extensive background investigations required of casino owners. See the discussion in Russell R. Elliott, *History of Nevada* (Lincoln and London: University of Nebraska Press, 1973), pp. 336–37.

7. *Mob on the Run*, 1987, UNLV Special Collections—a series of investigations appearing on KLAS-TV and coordinated by Ned Day, also an investigative reporter for the *Review-Journal*—provides the most comprehensive review of organized crime activities in the 1970s and 1980s. Additional information on the Parvin-Dohrmann Company and its intimate connections with organized crime is found in Ovid Demaris's *The Last Mafioso* (New York: Bantam, 1980), pp. 247, 256–57, 310, and 526. See also Sergio Lalli's "The Saga of the Stardust Skim," an unusually detailed article in the *Las Vegas Review-Journal*, January 26, 1986, p. 1.

8. Rappleye and Becker, *All American Mafioso*, p. 289.

9. Interviews with Al Casarotto, Phil Dioguardi, Reno Fruzza, Frank Modica, and Dan Rotunno.

10. Rappleye and Becker, *All American Mafioso*, p. 285.

11. *Las Vegas Review-Journal*, December 1, 1976, p. 3.

12. Ibid., October 14, 1977, p. 12A.

13. Ibid., October 11, 1977, p. 1.

14. *Mob on the Run* videotape.

15. See *Las Vegas Review-Journal*, March 9, 1991, p. 9C for information on the legal

complexities that followed the looting of the Tropicana.

16. See *Las Vegas Sun,* May 22, 1980, p. 1; and June 13, 1980, p. 13 for more information on Casarotto's post-Tropicana career.

17. See *Las Vegas Review-Journal,* August 10, 1978, p. 3A; *Las Vegas Sun,* August 11, 1978, p. 8; and August 18, 1978, p. 6; and *Las Vegas Review-Journal,* November 17, 1978, p. 1B for more detailed information on the charges and Marino's responses.

18. *Las Vegas Sun,* December 11, 1980, p. 3.

19. *Las Vegas Review-Journal,* January 22, 1981, p. 1B; and January 23, 1981, p. 1B.

20. Information provided by Dorothy Von Der Bruck, Henderson City Clerk.

21. *Las Vegas Sun,* February 23, 1978, p. 3; *Las Vegas Review-Journal,* March 3, 1978, p. 6A; and March 4, 1978, p. 3A.

22. *Las Vegas Sun,* December 9, 1982, p. 15.

23. *Las Vegas Review-Journal,* August 10, 1991, p. 90.

24. *Las Vegas Review-Journal/Sun,* October 20, 1990, p. 4B; and September 22, 1991, p. 1B.

25. Feist was identified as one of the three most prominent Las Vegans, along with fellow Italian American Vic Salerno as well as Roxey Roxborough, in the rapidly growing sports betting business by Stephen Nover, a *Las Vegas Review-Journal* sports columnist who coauthored a four-part series entitled "Parlaying Success: The Growth of Sports Gaming." The articles ran January 17–20, 1993, in the sports section.

26. Selected entertainment sections of *Las Vegas Review-Journal* and *Las Vegas Sun,* 1970–87.

27. *Las Vegas Review-Journal,* September 27, 1992, p. 1B.

28. Interviews with Tracey Heberling (a neighbor of Charles Fauci) and Mike Fauci.

29. Interview with Mike Fauci; *Las Vegas Sun,* April 11, 1990, p. 1B.

30. Moehring, *Resort City in the Sunbelt,* p. 80.

31. Interviews with Tony Tegano and Rodney Pass (Tango Pools employee); *Las Vegas Review-Journal,* September 21, 1989, p. 15E.

32. *Las Vegas Review-Journal,* March 12, 1989, p. 1BB.

33. Ibid., July 23, 1989, p. 1DD; and December 17, 1989, p. 1; and *Nevada Business Journal* (August 1990): 20.

34. Interviews with Angelo Cassaro and Gary Cavaretta; *Las Vegas Review-Journal,* August 26, 1990, p. 1M.

35. See Michael La Sorte's *La Merica: Images of the Italian Greenhorn Experience* (Philadelphia: Temple University Press, 1985) for a compilation of firsthand accounts of the difficulties of Italian immigrants.

36. Moehring, *Resort City in the Sunbelt,* pp. 238–44, provides information about Molasky's business and evaluates his contribution to Las Vegas.

37. Cofone, "Reno's Little Italy: Italian Entrepreneurship and Culture in Northern Nevada." *Nevada Historical Society Quarterly* 26 (Summer 1983): 97–110.

38. Interview with Randy Capurro.

39. *Las Vegas Review-Journal,* December 2, 1980, p. 14B.

40. Several local and federal law enforcement officers have told this author that although they often hold his clients in contempt, Gentile is an always effective, and

sometimes masterful, communicator and trial strategist.

41. See *Las Vegas Review-Journal,* March 13, 1980, p. 1; March 18, 1980, pp. 1 and 7A; and *Las Vegas Sun,* March 24, 1980, pp. 1 and 6 for material relating to charges of mercy killing. Additional information on Digilio's rise and fall are found in the *Las Vegas Review-Journal,* November 4, 1975, p. 38; March 9, 1975, p. 19; January 11, 1976, p. 30; April 25, 1976, p. 4; September 30, 1978, p. 1; and July 25, 1980, p. 3E. Mr. Digilio refused my several requests for an interview, explaining once that he was an American, not an Italian American.

42. Waller H. Reed, comp., *A Political Directory for the Incorporated Communities of Nevada,* Nevada Historical Society, Reno, 1982; and *A Political History of Nevada.*

43. Reed, *A Political Directory.*

44. Ibid. See *Las Vegas Review-Journal,* March 14, 1984, pp. 1A and 2A; and April 26, 1984, p. 1A for reports on Petitti's conviction and sentence. See December 19, 1984, p. B5 for information on the scandal that ended Ronzone's political career.

45. Reed, *A Political Directory.*

46. In evaluating the role of Italian Americans in southern Nevada politics, it is necessary to remember that Jack Petitti was a Mormon, and Jim Santini was married to a Mormon woman. The Mormon community in southern Nevada, though never more than 20 percent of the Las Vegas–area population in the years under discussion, was well organized and politically active. Mormons were always well overrepresented among elective office holders.

47. Interviews with Phil Carlino and Dr. Herman Van Betten (an active participant in the Clark County Democratic Party for many years).

48. Interviews with Didi Carson and Dr. Herman Van Betten.

49. *Las Vegas Review-Journal,* January 30, 1985, p. 6.

50. Interview with Dr. Herman Van Betten; *Las Vegas Review-Journal,* April 24, 1988, p. N3.

51. *Las Vegas Review-Journal,* May 28, 1989, p. 4A.

52. *Mob on the Run* videotape.

53. *Las Vegas Review-Journal,* June 13, 1989, p. 6A.

54. Ibid., November 3, 1989, editorial.

55. *Las Vegas Sun,* October 20, 1989, p. 12.

56. *Las Vegas Review-Journal/Sun,* March 8, 1992, p. 4C; and *Las Vegas Review-Journal,* April 29, 1992, p. 5E.

57. Ibid., p. 6C; and March 1, 1992, p. 1E.

CHAPTER FOUR. ITALIAN AMERICAN ORGANIZATIONS:
PRESERVING ETHNIC HERITAGE IN A TIME OF ASSIMILATION

1. In the four decades before the Strip became an internationally recognized gambling center, Italian-born individuals and their children were so few that organizing was not a possibility.

2. *John DeLuca Italian American Club, 1959–1962,* Italian American Club, Las Vegas,

contains newspaper accounts and photographs of Club activities. John DeLuca's daughter, Linda Isola, informed the author that his children requested in the mid-1960s that his name no longer be used because they believed some Club members were associated with organized crime.

3. *John DeLuca Italian American Club, 1959–1962.*

4. Interviews with Al Bossi, Dominic Bianchi, Reno Fruzza (first treasurer of the Club), and Tony Marnell.

5. See Humbert Nelli, *Italians in Chicago, 1880–1930: A Study in Ethnic Mobility* (New York: Oxford University Press, 1970), pp. 176–78 for a discussion of this.

6. Scrapbooks and boxed materials of the Las Vegas Lodge of the Sons of Italy, containing newspaper accounts, photographs, and mementos, 1965–72, Moose Lodge, Las Vegas #1763.

7. Interviews with Tony Allotta, Al Bossi, Phil Carlino, and an Italian American who wishes to remain anonymous.

8. Scrapbooks and boxed materials of the Las Vegas Lodge of the Sons of Italy, 1965–83, Moose Lodge, Las Vegas #1763; interviews with numerous members of both groups.

9. Richard D. Alba, *Ethnic Identity: The Transformation of White America* (New Haven and London: Yale University Press, 1990), pp. 137–39, 250–52, and 308–10.

10. Interviewees included present and former Club officers Tony Allotta, Al Bossi, Phil Dioguardi, Phil Mirabelli, and Tony Ricci.

11. Italian Catholic Federation, a pamphlet of the ICF's Central Council, n.d.; interviews with past and present chapter leaders Catherine Barcal, Angelo Nicassio, Vito Stolfa, and Izzy Marion.

12. Interview with Peter Anthony; scrapbook of the Las Vegas Lodge of the Sons of Italy, 1973–83. Moose Lodge, Las Vegas #1763.

13. See Nicholas Gage, *The Mafia Is Not an Equal Opportunity Employer* (New York: McGraw-Hill, 1971), pp. 68–89, for information on this organization, which was run by reputed Mafia leader Joseph Colombo until his 1971 assassination at a Columbus Day rally in New York City.

14. Interviews with Ruth Catalano, Carmine Colucci, Roseanne Gargano DePalma, and Dan Rotunno.

15. Interview with Jerry DePalma; *Augustus Society Centurion,* 1987–91.

16. Interviews with Vince Consul, Jerry DePalma, and Dominic Gentile.

17. Brochure of National Italian American Sports Hall of Fame; 1991 newsletters of the Las Vegas Chapter; interviews with chapter officers Tony Allotta and Phil Dioguardi.

18. Richard D. Alba, *Italian Americans: Into the Twilight of Ethnicity* (Englewood Cliffs, N.J.: Prentice-Hall, 1985), pp. 89–90.

19. Alba, *Ethnic Identity,* pp. 28–30 and 77. The fullest treatment of symbolic ethnicity is presented by Herbert Gans in "Symbolic Ethnicity: The Future of Ethnic Groups and Cultures in America," *Ethnic and Racial Studies* 2, No. 1 (January 1979): 1–20.

20. Ibid.; Stephen Steinberg, *The Ethnic Myth: Race, Ethnicity, and Class in America* (Boston: Beacon Press, 1981), parts 1 and 2.

21. Izzy Marion explained in a 1991 interview that his noncooperation in the plan-

ning of the Columbus Day Parade was based on the other participants' rejection of his plan to establish a permanent coordinating council of Italian-American organizations.

CHAPTER FIVE. CONCLUSION: THE IMMIGRANT UPRAISED

1. Andrew F. Rolle, *The Immigrant Upraised: Italian Adventurers and Colonists in an Expanding America* (Norman: University of Oklahoma Press, 1968), pp. 335–36.

2. The Italian born, only a small proportion of the Italian Americans in the Las Vegas area, have increased in recent decades. A review of U.S. Census figures indicated 32 Italian born in 1910, 44 in 1920, 49 in 1930, 60 in 1940, 91 in 1950, 2,168 in 1960, 1,663 in 1970, and 1,004 in 1980. The 1950s was a decade of substantial Italian-American migration from the East to Las Vegas. It appears that hundreds of older, Italian-born men and women accompanied their children to Las Vegas.

3. Robert J. Kelly's *Organized Crime: A Global Perspective* (New York: Rowman and Littlefield Publishers, 1986) provides a balanced view of the role of the American Mafia and the Sicilian Mafia in organized crime. Two examples of the diverse and quickly changing nature of organized crime are provided by Alison Mitchell's "Russian Emigres Importing Thugs to Commit Contract Crimes in U.S.," *New York Times,* April 11, 1992; and Paul Barrett's "Nigerians Smuggling Heroin in Their Stomachs Pose Fast-Growing Problem for Federal Agents," *Wall Street Journal,* November 16, 1990, p. A16.

4. *Las Vegas Review-Journal,* April 29, 1992, p. 8B.

Selected Bibliography

BOOKS

Alba, Richard D. *Italian Americans: Into the Twilight of Ethnicity.* Englewood Cliffs: Prentice-Hall, 1985.

——. *Ethnic Identity: The Transformation of White America.* New Haven and London: Yale University Press, 1990.

Albini, Joseph L. *The American Mafia: Genesis of a Legend.* New York: Appleton Century-Crofts, 1971.

Anderson, Annelise Graebner. *The Business of Organized Crime.* Stanford: Hoover Institution Press, 1979.

Balsamo, William, and George Corpozi. *Under the Clock: The Inside Story of the Mafia's First 100 Years.* Far Hills: New Horizon Press, 1988.

Barlett, Donald L., and James B. Steele. *Empire: The Life, Legend, and Madness of Howard Hughes.* New York: W. W. Norton, 1979.

Battistella, Graziano, ed. *Italian Americans in the 80's: A Sociodemographic Profile.* New York: Center for Migration Studies, 1989.

Berman, Susan. *Easy Street.* New York: The Dial Press, 1981.

Block, Alan. *East Side–West Side: Organizing Crime in New York 1930–1950.* New Brunswick: Transaction Books, 1983.

——. *The Business of Crime: A Documentary Study of Organized Crime in the American Economy.* San Francisco: Westview Press, 1991.

Brill, Steven. *The Teamsters.* New York: Simon & Schuster, 1978.

Cinel, Dino. *From Italy to San Francisco: The Immigrant Experience.* Stanford: Stanford University Press, 1982.

Crispino, James. *The Assimilation of Ethnic Groups: The Italian Case.* New York: Center for Migration Studies, 1980.

DeConde, Alexander. *Half Bitter, Half Sweet: An Excursion into Italian-American History.* New York: Charles Scribner's Sons, 1971.

Demaris, Ovid. *The Last Mafioso.* New York: Bantam, 1980.

di Leonardo, Micaela. *The Varieties of Ethnic Experience: Kinship, Class, and Gender among California Italian-Americans.* Ithaca and London: Cornell University Press, 1984.

Edwards, Jerome E. *Pat McCarran: Political Boss of Nevada.* Reno: University of Nevada Press, 1982.

Eisenberg, Dennis, Uriel Dan, and Eli Landau. *Meyer Lansky: Mogul of the Mob.* New York: Paddington Press, 1978.

Elliott, Russell R. *History of Nevada.* Lincoln and London: University of Nebraska Press, 1973.

Farrell, Ronald, and Carole Case. *The Black Book and the Mob.* Madison: University of Wisconsin Press, 1995.

Findlay, John W. *People of Chance: Gambling in American Society from Jamestown to Las Vegas.* New York: Oxford University Press, 1986.

Fopiano, Willie. *The Godson: A True-Life Account of 20 Years Inside the Mob.* New York: St. Martin's Press, 1993.

Fox, Stephen. *Blood and Power: Organized Crime in Twentieth-Century America.* New York: William Morrow, 1989.

Gage, Nicholas. *The Mafia Is Not an Equal Opportunity Employer.* New York: McGraw-Hill, 1971.

Gambino, Richard. *Blood of My Blood: The Dilemma of the Italian Americans.* Garden City, N.Y.: Doubleday and Company, 1974.

Gans, Herbert J. *The Urban Villagers: Group and Class in the Life of Italian-Americans.* New York: The Free Press, 1962.

Giancana, Antoinette, and Thomas C. Renner. *Mafia Princess: Growing Up in Sam Giancana's Family.* New York: Avon Books, 1985.

Glanz, Rudolf. *Jew and Italian: Historic Group Relations and the New Immigration (1881–1924).* New York: NP, 1971.

Glass, Mary Ellen. *Nevada's Turbulent 50s: Decade of Political and Economic Change.* Reno: University of Nevada Press, 1981.

Gordon, Milton M. *Assimilation in American Life: The Role of Race, Religion and National Origins.* New York: Oxford University Press, 1964.

Gumina, Deanna Paoli. *The Italians of San Francisco 1850–1930.* New York: Center for Migration Studies, 1985.

Hammer, Richard. *The Illustrated History of Organized Crime.* Philadelphia: Running Press, 1973.

Hulse, James W. *The Silver State: Nevada's Heritage Reinterpreted.* Reno and Las Vegas: University of Nevada Press, 1991.

Ianni, Francis A. J. *A Family Business: Kinship and Social Control in Organized Crime.* New York: Russell Sage Foundation, 1972.

Iorizzo, Luciano J., and Salvatore Mondello. *The Italian-Americans.* Revised edition. Boston: Twayne Publishers, 1990.

Isaacs, Stephen D. *Jews and American Politics.* Garden City, N.Y.: Doubleday, 1974.

Jones, Florence Lee, and John Cahlan. *Water: A History of Las Vegas. History of the Las Vegas Land and Water Company.* 2 vols. Las Vegas: Las Vegas Valley Water District, 1975.

Kelly, Kitty. *His Way: The Unauthorized Biography of Frank Sinatra.* New York: Bantam Books, 1986.

Kelly, Robert J. *Organized Crime: A Global Perspective.* New York: Rowman and Littlefield Publishers, 1986.

Kessner, Thomas. *The Golden Door: Italian and Jewish Mobility in New York City 1880–1915*. New York: Oxford University Press, 1977.

Lacey, Robert. *Little Man: Meyer Lansky and the Gangster Life*. Boston: Little, Brown, 1991.

La Sorte, Michael. *La Merica: Images of Italian Greenhorn Experience*. Philadelphia: Temple University Press, 1985.

Lewis, Oscar. *Sagebrush Casinos: The Story of Legal Gambling in Nevada*. Garden City, N.Y.: Doubleday, 1953.

Lopreato, Joseph. *Italian Americans*. New York: Random House, 1970.

Maggio, Frank. *Las Vegas Calling*. Las Vegas: TAD Publishing Company, 1972.

Maheu, Robert, and Richard Hack. *Next to Hughes*. New York: HarperCollins Publishers, 1992.

Mangione, Jerre, and Ben Morreale. *La Storia: Five Centuries of the Italian American Experience*. New York: HarperCollins, 1992.

Martinelli, Phyllis Cancilla. *Ethnicity in the Sunbelt: Italian American Migrants in Scottsdale, Arizona*. New York: AMS Press, 1989.

Maselli, Joseph, ed. *Year 2000: Where Will Italian-American Organizations Be in the Year 2000?* Washington, D.C.: The National Italian American Foundation, 1990.

Messick, Hank. *The Beauties and the Beasts: The Mob in Show Business*. New York: McKay, 1973.

———. *Lansky*. New York: Berkley Publishing, 1971.

———. *John Edgar Hoover*. New York: David McKay Company, 1972.

Moehring, Eugene P. *Resort City in the Sunbelt: Las Vegas, 1930–1970*. Reno and Las Vegas: University of Nevada Press, 1989.

Mohl, Raymond A., ed. *Searching for the Sunbelt: Historical Perspectives on a Region*. Knoxville: University of Tennessee Press, 1990.

Moldea, Dan. *Interference: How Organized Crime Influences Professional Football*. New York: William Morrow, 1989.

Murray, George. *The Legacy of Al Capone: Portraits and Annals of Chicago's Public Enemies*. New York: G. P. Putnam's Sons, 1975.

Nash, Gerald. *The American West Transformed: The Impact of the Second World War*. Bloomington: Indiana University Press, 1985.

Nelli, Humbert S. *Italians in Chicago, 1880–1930: A Study in Ethnic Mobility*. New York: Oxford University Press, 1970.

———. *The Business of Crime: Italians and Syndicate Crime in the United States*. New York: Oxford University Press, 1976.

Novak, Michael. *The Rise of the Unmeltable Ethnics*. New York: Macmillan, 1971.

Papanikolas, Helen Z., ed. *The Peoples of Utah*. Salt Lake City: Utah State Historical Society, 1976.

Rappleye, Charles, and Ed Becker. *All American Mafioso: The Johnny Rosselli Story*. New York: Doubleday, 1991.

Reid, Ed, and Ovid Demaris. *Las Vegas: City Without Clocks*. Englewood Cliffs, N.J.: Prentice Hall, 1961.

———. *The Green Felt Jungle*. New York: Trident Press, 1963.

Roemer, William F. *Man Against the Mob.* New York: Ivy Books, 1991.

Rolle, Andrew F. *The Immigrant Upraised: Italian Adventurers and Colonists in an Expanding America.* Norman: University of Oklahoma Press, 1968.

———. *The Italian Americans: Troubled Roots.* Norman: University of Oklahoma Press, 1980.

Roske, Ralph. *Las Vegas: A Desert Paradise.* Tulsa: Continental Heritage Press, 1986.

Scarpaci, Jean, ed. *The Interaction of Italians and Jews in America.* New York: The American Italian Historical Association, 1975.

Shepperson, Wilbur S. *Restless Strangers: Nevada's Immigrants and Their Interpreters.* Reno: University of Nevada Press, 1970.

Skolnick, Jerome. *House of Cards: Legalization and Control of Casino Gambling.* Boston: Little, Brown, 1978.

Steinberg, Stephen. *The Ethnic Myth: Race, Ethnicity, and Class in America.* Boston: Beacon Press, 1981.

Thernstrom, Stephen. *A History of the American People.* Vol. 2. San Diego: Harcourt Brace Jovanovich, 1984.

Titus, A. Costandina. *Bombs in the Backyard: Atomic Testing and American Politics.* Reno and Las Vegas: University of Nevada Press, 1986.

Tosches, Nick. *Dino.* New York: Doubleday, 1992.

Turner, Wallace. *Gambler's Money: A New Force in American Life.* Boston: Riverside Press, 1965.

Wang, Peter H. *Legislating Normalcy: The Immigration Act of 1924.* San Francisco: R and E Research Association, 1975.

Whyte, William Foote. *Street Corner Society: The Social Structure of an Italian Slum.* 3d ed. Chicago: University of Chicago Press, 1981.

Wiley, Peter, and Robert Gottlieb. *Empires in the Sun: The Rise of the New American West.* New York: G. P. Putnam's Sons, 1982.

Wolfe, Tom. *The kandy-kolored tangerine-flake streamline baby.* New York: Farrar, Straus & Giroux, 1965.

ARTICLES

Balboni, Alan. "Tony's Carpet Joint." *Nevadan* (January 28, 1990): 12S–3S.

———. "From Laborer to Entrepreneur: The Italian-American in Southern Nevada." *Nevada Historical Society Quarterly* (1991): 257–72.

———. "From America's Little Italys to the Boomtown in the Desert: Italian Americans in Las Vegas, 1947–1970." *Nevada Historical Society Quarterly* (1991): 379–99.

Bell, Daniel. "Crime as an American Way of Life." *Antioch Review* 13 (1963): 115–36.

"Casino Man of the Year: L. Stephen Savoldelli." *Rouge et Noir News* (January–February 1977): 1–9.

Chesson, Roy. "The Man Who Settled the Dust with Wine." *The Nevadan* (June 8, 1967): 25–28.

Cofone, Albin J. "Themes in the Italian Settlement of Nevada." *Nevada Historical*

Society Quarterly 25 (Summer 1982): 116–32.

——. "Reno's Little Italy: Italian Entrepreneurship and Culture in Northern Nevada. "*Nevada Historical Society Quarterly* 26 (Summer 1983): 97–110.

——. "Italian Images in Northern Nevada Writing."*Nevada Historical Society Quarterly* 27 (Winter 1984): 260–67.

Earl, Phillip. "Nevada's Italian War."*Nevada Historical Society Quarterly* (Summer 1969): 48–87.

Edwards, Jerome E. "Nevada Gambling and the Federal–State Relationship." *Halcyon* (1989): 238–54.

Gans, Herbert J. "Symbolic Ethnicity: The Future of Ethnic Groups and Cultures in America."*Ethnic and Racial Studies* 2, no. 1 (January 1979): 1–20.

Kant, Candace. "City of Dreams: Las Vegas in the Cinema, 1980–1989."*Nevada Historical Society Quarterly* (1990): 1–12.

"Largest Private Transfer Station Open for Business. "*World Wastes* (March 1983): 14–15.

Moehring, Eugene P. "Suburban Resorts and the Triumph of Las Vegas."*Halcyon* (1988): 201–214.

Morrison, Jane Ann. "Spotlight on Searchlight."*The Nevadan* (October 9, 1977): 3–4.

Patrick, Elizabeth. "The Champos: An Italian Family Rose to Prosperity in 1920's Las Vegas." *The Nevadan* (March 27, 1982): 6–8.

Stamos, George. "The Great Resorts of Las Vegas: How They Began." *Las Vegas Sun Magazine.* A series from April 1979 through December 1979.

Vecoli, Rudolph J. "Contandini in Chicago: A Critique of the Uprooted."*The Journal of American History* (1964): 404–417.

Velikonja, Joseph. "The 1990 Census Data on Italian Ancestry."*Newsletter of the American Italian Historical Association.* (January 1993): 19.

NEWSPAPERS

Las Vegas Age
Las Vegas (Evening) Review-Journal (and Boulder City Journal)
Las Vegas Sun
New York Times
North Las Vegas Valley Times
Wall Street Journal

GOVERNMENT DOCUMENTS AND REPORTS

City of Las Vegas, Department of Business Activity. *Business Licenses–Sexually Oriented.* June 1991.

Commission on the Review of the National Policy Toward Gambling. *Appendix 1: Staff and Consultant Papers, Model Statutes, Bibliography, Correspondence.* Washington, D.C., 1976.

Nevada Commerce Department, Consumer Affairs Division. *Licensed Company Report–Sports Information Services.* July 1992.

Nevada Gaming Commission. Agenda, June 21, 1990 Meeting.

Nevada Gaming Commission. *List of Excluded Persons.* Carson City, 1990.

Nevada, Office of the Secretary of State. *A Political History of Nevada.* Carson City, 1986.

Nevada State Contractors Board. *Directory of Licensed Contractors.* Reno, 1967.

Nevada Superintendent of Banks. "Biennial Report: Appendix to Journals of Senate and Assembly." 1959 (Vol. 2); 1961 (Vol. 2); 1963 (Vol. 3); and 1969 (Vol. 2).

U.S. Attorney General's Commission on Pornography. Final Report, Part 2. 1986.

U.S. Congress, Senate Special Committee to Investigate Organized Crime in Interstate Commerce, Part 10 (Nevada–California). Washington, D.C., 1951.

U.S. Department of Commerce, Bureau of the Census. 1910 Manuscript Census. Washington, D.C., 1913.

———. 1920, 1930, 1940, 1950, 1960, 1970, and 1980 Abstract Census.

UNPUBLISHED MATERIALS

Augustus Society Centurion. 1987–1992.

Leonard T. Blood and Family. Files of the Superintendent of the Las Vegas office of the U.S. Employment Service During Boulder Dam Construction. Special Collections, UNLV.

Clark County, County Political Directory for Nevada. Nevada Historical Society, Reno.

John DeLuca Italian American Club, 1959–62. President's Office, Italian American Club, Las Vegas.

Dinnerstein, Leonard. "From Oasis in the Desert to the Desert Caucus, the Evolution of the Jewish Community in Tucson, Arizona." Paper, no date.

Directory of Las Vegas and Vicinity, 1943–1944. Telephone numbers and addresses. Special Collections, UNLV.

Dondero, Harvey, and Billie F. Shank. *History of Clark County Schools.* Clark County School District, 1986.

Italian American Club. Souvenir Program of the Italian American Fund Ball and Dinner, 1967.

Italian Catholic Federation pamphlets, no date.

Las Vegas Chamber of Commerce. *Business-Professional Directory,* 1954. Special Collections, UNLV.

Las Vegas Chamber of Commerce. *VIP Directory,* 1992.

Las Vegas Lodge of the Sons of Italy. Scrapbooks and Boxed Materials. Moose Lodge Las Vegas, #1763, #1963.

Las Vegas Telephone Directories for 1926, 1931–36, and 1950–62. Special Collections, UNLV.

Luskey's City Directories 1956–69. Special Collections, UNLV.

National Italian American Sports Hall of Fame. Newsletters. Las Vegas Chapter.

Nevada Development Authority. *Membership Directory,* 1991.

Palmieri, Marie. "Nevada's Italians Before 1900." Paper, no date.

Reed, Waller H., comp. *A Political Directory for the Incorporated Communities of Nevada.* Nevada Historical Society, Reno, 1982.

San Pedro, Los Angeles, and Salt Lake Railroad Company. Payroll and Labor Distribution Files. Special Collections, UNLV.

Stamos, George. "A Class Act—The Desert Inn." *Nevada Day 1864–1989.* Las Vegas, University Medical Center Foundation, 1989.

Swallow, Craig. "The Ku Klux Klan in Nevada During the 1920's." Master's thesis, UNLV 1978.

ORAL HISTORY

Binion, Lester Ben "Benny." Some Recollections of a Texas and Las Vegas Gaming Operator. University of Nevada Oral History Project, 1976. Special Collections, UNLV.

Cahill, Robbins. Recollections of Work in State Politics, Government, Taxation, Gaming Control, Clark County Administration and the Nevada Resort Association. University of Nevada Oral History Project, 1973. Special Collections, UNLV.

Cahlan, John. Reminiscences of a Reno and Las Vegas, Nevada, Newspaperman, University Regent, and Public-Spirited Citizen. University of Nevada Oral History Project, 1970. Special Collections, UNLV.

Petricciani, Silvio. The Evolution of Gaming in Nevada: The Twenties to the Eighties. University of Nevada Oral History Project, 1982. Special Collections, UNLV.

Russell, Charles. Reminiscences of a Nevada Congressman, Governor and Legislator. University of Nevada Oral History Project, 1967. Special Collections, UNLV.

VIDEOTAPES

Day, Ned. *Mob on the Run.* Videotape. 1987. Special Collections, UNLV.

Knapp, George. *Organized Crime in Las Vegas.* No date. KLAS-TV.

Index

Numbers in italics refer to photos.

159

Wilbur S. Shepperson Series in History and Humanities